The Shopaholic's Guide to
Buying for Mother and Child Online

Free Subscription Offer

www.thesiteguide.com

www.thesiteguide.com, described by Condé Nast's Glamour.com as 'the web's best shopping directory', is the web version of *The Shopaholic's Guide to Buying for Mother and Child Online*, where you'll find direct links through to all the website reviews, plus regular online shopping features and updates and news of the latest site launches.

We're delighted to offer you a year's free subscription (normally £9.99) to www.thesiteguide.com to thank you for purchasing this book. To take up this offer you need to click on to the site and subscribe. When you're prompted for a media code just use the password you'll find at the end of the introduction to Chapter 12: Baby Showers, and you'll be able to use the guide online.

If you would like to receive up-to-date information on other Shopaholics Guides to buying online, just sign up on the website to receive regular newsletters.

'Thesiteguide.com is the most comprehensive shopping directory I've found on the web, and is also the first to report on fabulous new sites.'

Condé Nast

'A comprehensive guide to all the best shopping destinations on the web.'

Vogue mail

'This is a good shortcut to smart shopping'

The *Evening Standard*

'thesiteguide.com ... provides a discerning and easy-to-use guide to the best retail sites on the web.'

The *Times*

The Shopaholic's Guide to

Buying for Mother and Child Online

Patricia Davidson

CAPSTONE

BICENTENNIAL
1807
WILEY
2007
BICENTENNIAL

Library of Congress Cataloging-in-Publication Data
Davidson, Patricia.
  The shopaholic's guide to buying for mother and child online / Patricia Davidson.
      p. cm.
  Includes index.
  ISBN 978-1-84112-780-4 (pbk. : alk. paper)
  1. Infants' clothing--Purchasing--Great Britain--Guidebooks. 2. Maternity clothes--
Purchasing--Great Britain--Guidebooks. 3. Teleshopping--Great Britain--Guidebooks. I.
Title.
  TT637.D38 2007
  381'.142--dc22

                                                                        2007011332

ISBN   978-184112-780-4

Anniversary Logo Design: Richard J. Pacifico

Set in Lucida Bright by Sparks (www.sparks.co.uk)
Printed and bound in Great Britain by TJ International Ltd, Padstow, Cornwall

Contents

Acknowledgements

First and foremost I'd like to thank my family, Andrew, Sholto, Calum and Kirstie, and reassure them that all the baby magazines left lying around were simply for my research for this book (just joking, I know you knew that). My thanks to the team at John Wiley and Capstone - Sally, Emma, Julia, Iain, Kate and Grace - working with you all is a new and marvellous experience. Thanks also to Kate Hordern, my agent - the devil is definitely in the details.

Finally, I'd just like to mention Emily, Victoria and Harrison: little did I know when I started writing this that for most of the time I would actually have under my roof six children (instead of the usual three), ranging in ages from four to nineteen. I have to admit it's been a joy - thanks for all the fun.

This book is really for Bridgette (mother of the extra three).
We love you babe.

About the Author

*A*fter twelve years in international designer fashion mail order, Patricia Davidson started www.thesiteguide.com, an online upmarket fashion, beauty and lifestyle website directory. Her first book, *The Shopaholic's Guide to Buying Online*, was published by Capstone in October 2006, followed by *The Shopaholic's Guide to Buying Fashion and Beauty Online* in May 2007. Patricia is a regular contributor to Condé Nast's easylivingmagazine.com and has also been published on online shopping in other women's titles and the national press. She lives in Buckinghamshire with her husband, three children and two dogs.

Introduction

Firstly I'd like to offer my credentials here: I am a mother of three children. Anyone who knows me will tell you that I'm a fraud as they're now nineteen, eighteen and sixteen (work that one out), but having had three within three and a quarter years at a time when there was no online shopping and very little mail-order shopping, I can tell you for certain that your timing, unlike mine, is perfect.

I'm sure you know you don't have to go out and buy nappies and baby food, and that they can be delivered with your weekly shop from Tesco or Ocado. Did you know also that there are marvellous places to find glam maternity clothes online, whether you're going to be relaxing at home or going to power lunches every other day and black-tie dinners as well? A bump doesn't mean you have to look any less chic and modern than at any other time – you just need to know where to shop.

There's a wealth of information to be found online on pregnancy, birth and everything afterwards, so that unlike when I was having mine, you don't have to go out and choose from half a dozen 'recommended' baby bibles – you can read everything online, then choose to buy a book if and when you want to, which (obviously) you can also order online.

Then with your new baby you can have great fun without having to trundle round the shops. Grab the moments (hours hopefully) when your new delight is fast asleep and browse the enchanting baby clothes you'll find here. Choose your new buggy, go on one of the price-comparison

xi

websites to make sure you're getting it for less, then just sit back and wait for it to arrive.

'Hold on,' do I hear you say? 'Are you telling me that I'm going to be stuck at home once I've had my baby, with no excuses to go out any more?' Far from it. What I am saying is that you no longer *have* to go out and buy everything. You can choose what you want to buy online and use the time that frees up (and believe me, it'll be more than you could imagine) to meet friends for coffee, buy special gifts and treat yourself to that post-baby dress you've been dreaming of for months.

Basically the web gives you the choice. You can opt to buy nothing from it, you can buy everything or you can go for something in between. I can assure you, for mother and baby basics there's simply no better place, and now you've bought this book you'll know exactly where to shop without having to search either. What more could you possibly want?

Why Shop for Mother and Child Online?

I'm sure you realise by now that having children is a tiring business. Whether you're working full time or not, and no matter how much help you have – from husbands, grandparents, au pairs and nannies – at the end of the day it all comes down to you. You're the one in charge and if you haven't yet lashed out at one of the above helpers for remarking complacently, 'Well of course, at the end of the day I know I can hand him back', I'm sure you soon will.

So, back to the question – it's obvious, isn't it? You can forget the reasons that I keep going on about for shopping online for everything else – convenience/time saving/choice/price (although they do come into it hugely). From what I can see, from expecting your first, second or third baby to caring for any number of babies, toddlers and almost-teens, being able to shop online is the answer to a prayer.

How many times have you been into a supermarket and heard a toddler screaming its head off? How many times have you seen a mother battle with said toddler *and* a baby in a buggy through a set of doors that no one helps with (until you come along, of course)?

When I started to write this book I'll agree that I was a (slightly) smug mother of three kids who have reached the independent ages of sixteen, eighteen and nineteen. My main problems were that a) they *still* argue *all the time*, b) *they always want money*, and c) *what does it take to get them to help* (with anything, *anything*)? But since then my home has been happily (for me) invaded with a family of five having work done on their house. Suddenly I've been plunged back into reading *Winnie the Pooh* to Harrison (four) in the bath and trying to concentrate while Emily (eleven) and Victoria (nine) are in fits of giggles in the background. And it's really taken me back.

So, all you who complain of being tired/having too much to do/having no time to yourself/having to go out food shopping with the kids - think. Plan ahead just a little and, yes, you can buy it all online. It will transform your life and while it might not give you your life back totally, believe me, you'll recover more of it than you expect because:

- You can shop when the children are asleep.
- You can have all your food delivered (organic or otherwise) and won't need to go out to the supermarket with the kids.
- You can use the free time you gain by doing some things for yourself.
- You can treat yourself when you need to - very important, that.
- When you do go out to shop it'll be for something you enjoy shopping for rather than for something you need.

Going back to what I said originally, I'd like to talk about choice and price. Choice is one of the main reasons for shopping online - for anything - and unless you know exactly what you're looking for, in which case you're not interested in the kind of choice I'm talking about, it would simply not be possible to go round and find in the shops the kind of comprehensive selection you can see almost instantly online. Even if you had a month, which most of us don't.

You can look at as many or as few products as you want, from travel systems and car seats to towelling robes and children's clothes, and see the full details and specification for each and every one.

Price and online shopping mean different things depending on what type of items you're talking about. For equipment such as buggies and prams, car seats and baby carriers, where you've chosen a specific type and brand, you need to go to price-comparison websites such as www. kelkoo.co.uk or www.uk.shopping.com and see who's offering the best deal. You just type the name and model number into the search box and you'll see what's on offer. Bear in mind that you won't view every single retailer on every price-comparison website; it depends on which retailers have signed up to each, so there will inevitably be some you don't find. If you use a retailer you don't know, first read through the tips on shopping safely online at the back of this book.

For other items there's a huge range of prices – different designers, different qualities, different styles and different fabrics. If you want something that's going to last a while you can spend a bit more, but bearing in mind how quickly kids grow, that divine, pale yellow cashmere sweater may not only totally impractical and expensive but, worst of all, redundant after two or three months.

Those are just my feelings – it's now over to you.

Using this Book

All the websites included in the guide have been looked at carefully not only for the service and products they offer but also for how easy the retailers make it for you to shop.

For almost every website you'll find something like the following:

Site Usability: ★★★★★	Based: UK
Product Range: ★★★★★	Express Delivery Option? (UK) Yes
Price Range: Medium	Gift Wrapping Option? Yes
Delivery Area: Worldwide	Returns Procedure: Down to you

In all cases the stars range from ★★★★★ to ★★★ – I'll explain as follows.

Site Usability

How quick and easy is it for you to click round the website and get to the products you're looking for? How quickly can you get to information on delivery, returns, whether or not gift wrapping is offered and how to contact the retailer? Are the pictures clear and attractive? Is there adequate information about every product offered?

Product Range

How much choice is there on the website? Fewer stars here do not mean a lower-quality product, just a smaller range.

Price Range

This is just a guide so you know what to expect.

Delivery Area

Does the retailer deliver to the UK, EU countries or worldwide?

Based

This tells you where the retailer is based, so you'll know straight away if you're going to be in for duty or extra shipping costs.

Express Delivery Option

Can you have your order tomorrow? Some websites are very quick anyway, but this is specifically for where next-day or express service is offered, usually within the country where the retailer is based.

Gift Wrapping Option

Do they or don't they?

Returns Procedure

'Down to you' means you pack it up and pay to send it back (unless your goods are faulty, in which case the retailer should pay for postage both ways). 'Free' means just that and they may even collect it from you. 'Complicated' means that they want you to call them and tell them you're sending your order back. This normally applies only where the product you've ordered is particularly valuable.

For more information on returns, turn to Chapter 39 in Section 4.

Section 1
Mothers Only

Yes, this section is for you. What I've tried to do is cover as many of the areas of buying online for expecting mothers as I can. Inevitably at the start you may well think you'd prefer to go round the stores and see what's there. The trouble is that (for most people) when you feel like doing that you probably won't have grown very much (bumpwise, I mean) and it may seem silly to buy maternity clothes for the size you'll almost certainly become.

Luckily for you it doesn't matter. In my day (don't I sound old?), if you left it until you couldn't wear your clothes any more you usually ended up going somewhere - anywhere - convenient and quick just to find something to fit. Now you can find everything online and most retailers offer next-day delivery, so whether you're looking for business suits, little black dresses, designer jeans or sportswear, it won't take you long to click and browse.

Beauty products, I think, fall into two categories: those you buy anyway that you don't want to have to bother to go out for any more and those specially designed for pregnancy. You'll find a good choice of both here, organic or otherwise.

Finally, there are some really attractive websites offering gifts for your friends when they produce (and hopefully for them to give you), so make sure to leave the book open at the right page when they come round (only joking).

Chapter 1

Designer
Maternity Wear

There is a wonderful selection of luxury/designer maternity wear to be found online. The web is a great place to view different looks and work out where you'll buy your basics from and where you'll select your investment pieces.

You may think you don't want to spend too much, it's only for a short while after all (hmmm), but as this is the time when you really want to look great and it's not always so easy to do so (you can't just slip into those skinny size 8 jeans and a pair of heels), I'd like to tempt you to think again. Yes, go for those well-priced basics and essentials you'll wear over and over again, but buy something special now as well, before you desperately need it, so you know that whatever happens – wherever you're invited and whoever you need to meet – you'll have something tucked away that makes you feel fantastic, no matter how big your bump.

Throughout the maternity clothes sections you'll find websites based in the US, offering a sophisticated range of clothing at reasonable prices and willing to ship to you wherever you are in the world. Because, unlike other clothes, maternity fashions need to provide a certain amount of room, these are great websites both to buy from and to get ideas. You'll find that delivery can be a bit pricy, but for the quality you'll be getting very good value for money, so give them a try.

Sites to Visit

www.apeainthepod.com

This is without a doubt one of the most well-known US-based maternity stores, offering both its own well-priced range and designer selections by Tocca, Lilly Pulitzer, Juicy Couture, Diane von Furstenberg, Betsey Johnson and lots more, plus premium denim brands such as Citizens of Humanity and Paige. Take a look at the Celebrity Red Carpet, which includes actresses such as Holly Hunter, Maggie Gyllenhaal and Diane Farr wearing the gowns, then choose something for yourself.

Site Usability:	★★★★★	Based:	US
Product Range:	★★★★★	Express Delivery Option? (UK)	No
Price Range:	Luxury/Medium	Gift Wrapping Option?	No
Delivery Area:	Worldwide	Returns Procedure:	Down to you

www.bellydancematernity.com

As you'd expect, with such a large market (no pun intended) some of the US maternity wear stores are excellent. This one is no exception, with designs by Diane von Furstenberg, Olian, Susana Monaco and Paige and a fab selection in all areas, from dresses to jeans, lingerie, nightwear and swimwear. Order a couple of pieces early to check on the sizing, or email them with any queries. Delivery is expensive, but with a choice like this it's well worth having a good look.

Site Usability:	★★★★★	Based:	US
Product Range:	★★★★★	Express Delivery Option? (UK)	No
Price Range:	Luxury/Medium	Gift Wrapping Option?	No
Delivery Area:	Worldwide	Returns Procedure:	Down to you

www.blossommotherandchild.com

Blossom caters for the fashion-conscious expectant mum, with a collection of glamorous dresses and separates, which combine high-end fashion with comfort and functionality. You'll also find customised jeans by brands such as Rock and Republic and James. The company uses an assortment of luxurious fabrics, such as silk-cashmere, voile and jersey, and expands the collection continuously.

Site Usability: ★★★★	Based: **UK**
Product Range: ★★★★	Express Delivery Option? (UK) Yes
Price Range: uxury/Medium	Gift Wrapping Option? No
Delivery Area: Worldwide	Returns Procedure: Down to you

www.duematernity.com

If there's a maternity designer that Due doesn't stock, it's probably not worth looking for it. This is a superb range of maternity clothing from a company based in the US. There are lots of brands I haven't heard of, but with C & C California, Chip and Pepper and Paige Premium Denim in there, I'm sure you'll find something. Obviously you need to be more careful when buying from so far away, but the choice of easier-to-fit items and nursing tops and lingerie is vast and most of it you won't find available in this country. Give it a go.

Site Usability: ★★★★★	Based: **US**
Product Range: ★★★★★	Express Delivery Option? (UK) Yes, worldwide express
Price Range: Luxury/Medium	Gift Wrapping Option? No
Delivery Area: Worldwide	Returns Procedure: Down to you

www.fortyweeks.co.uk

The aim of maternity designer basics retailer Forty Weeks is to offer you contemporary, streamlined design combined with great fabrics to create a wardrobe that can be worn before, during and after pregnancy. There's a wide selection of colours and styles which would work perfectly with the more formal pieces of your new wardrobe and, unlike many things you buy now, you'll almost certainly want to wear them afterwards. Take advantage of the home visiting service within the London area.

Site Usability: ★★★★	Based: **UK**
Product Range: ★★★	Express Delivery Option? (UK) No
Price Range: Luxury/Medium	Gift Wrapping Option? No
Delivery Area: Worldwide	Returns Procedure: Down to you

www.hommemummy.co.uk

This is where to come if you're looking for simple, elegant maternity wear that will travel well and look great all the time, as everything is made from soft, comfortable, luxury jersey, stretch lace and cord, from tops to trousers and skirts. You can also buy the Essential Maternity Wardrobe here, which includes a go-anywhere trouser, elegant wrap top and glamorous, versatile dress. There are excellent line drawings of all the items to go with the photos, so you can see the shapes more clearly.

Site Usability:	★★★★	Based:	UK
Product Range:	★★★	Express Delivery Option? (UK)	Yes
Price Range:	Luxury/Medium	Gift Wrapping Option?	No
Delivery Area:	Worldwide	Returns Procedure:	Down to you

www.isabellaoliver.com

Isabella Oliver is a maternity wear company for pregnant women who love clothes. The sexy designs in soft jersey fabrics have signature-style details such as ruching and wrapping to flatter new curves and the website includes style tips to pick up on the season's trends. You can see each item as a model shot or drawing and also using the clever catwalk animation. As well as day and evening separates you can buy lingerie, loungewear, sophisticated sleepwear, chic outerwear, sun and swimwear.

Site Usability:	★★★★★	Based:	UK
Product Range:	★★★★	Express Delivery Option? (UK)	Yes
Price Range:	Luxury/Medium	Gift Wrapping Option?	Yes, automatic
Delivery Area:	Worldwide	Returns Procedure:	Free

www.prettypregnant.co.uk

An addition to the South London, Northcote Road boutique, the Pretty Pregnant website offers a mixture of fashion, from excellent dresses for day and evening to casual separates, jeans, lingerie and swimwear. Brands include Bellybutton, Queen Mum, Fragile, Paige Premium Denim, Coralou and Boob. There is a lot to choose from, so take a look round. You can also buy gifts, hosiery and nursing wear here.

Site Usability:	★★★	Based:	UK
Product Range:	★★★★	Express Delivery Option? (UK)	No
Price Range:	Luxury/Medium	Gift Wrapping Option?	No
Delivery Area:	UK, but call for overseas enquiries	Returns Procedure:	Down to you

www.pushmaternity.com

The Push boutique in Islington specialises in designer maternity wear and a high level of customer service. Now you can buy the collection online from labels such as Earl Jean, Tashia, Alex Gore Brown, Cadeau, Citizens of Humanity, Leona Edmiston (gorgeous jersey dresses) and Juicy Couture. There's maternity hosiery and chic baby bags here as well. Select from next-day or standard delivery (UK, though they ship overseas as well) and if you have any queries don't hesitate to give them a call.

Site Usability:	★★★★	Based:	UK
Product Range:	★★★	Express Delivery Option? (UK)	Yes
Price Range:	Luxury/Medium	Gift Wrapping Option?	No
Delivery Area:	Worldwide	Returns Procedure:	Down to you

www.tiffanyrose.co.uk

Here you'll find smart and unusual maternity wear, including dresses and chic separates. It's quite a small range but stylish, so if you're looking for something for a special occasion you should have a click around. There are also beautiful maternity wedding dresses and a sale area where there are usually some good discounts. The company delivers worldwide and offers a next-day and Saturday delivery service for the UK.

Site Usability:	★★★★	Based:	UK
Product Range:	★★★	Express Delivery Option? (UK)	Yes
Price Range:	Luxury/Medium	Gift Wrapping Option?	No
Delivery Area:	Worldwide	Returns Procedure:	Down to you

Chapter 2

Maternity Boutiques

Here you'll find a good choice of maternity clothes, some very reasonably priced, others at a mid price level. As I've said before, I suggest that you have a look round quite early on, so that even if you don't want to shop yet you'll have a pretty good idea of where you want to go when you're ready.

With such a wide choice now available online, and most of it chic and stylish and a million miles away from what I used to wear (and no, I'm not going to tell you – all I'll say is that now I think back I don't know how I could have), there's no excuse not to look great. This is also a great help on 'off days'. Put on something glam and you're almost certain to feel better straight away. At least you can think about how tiring it must have been in the 'old days' when you had to go out and search for something nice. That must make you feel happy, surely?

Sites to Visit

www.bjornandme.com

For choice and value you'd find it hard to beat this website, where the clothes are divided into sections such as Outdoor and Exercise wear/

Formalwear/Petite/Tall and Plus Size. There's also swimwear and lingerie, so whether you're looking for a pair of soft, white, linen trousers or something for the Oscars, you'll almost certainly find it here – the evening and occasionwear is particularly good. This is international designer-styled maternity wear and a very good collection.

Site Usability:	★★★★	Based:	UK
Product Range:	★★★★	Express Delivery Option? (UK)	Yes
Price Range:	Medium	Gift Wrapping Option?	No
Delivery Area:	Worldwide	Returns Procedure:	Down to you

www.bloomingmarvellous.co.uk

There's a wide choice of well-priced but good-quality clothes for expect-ant mothers and babies on this fun, colourful website. Whether you're looking for casual wear or city clothes, you're sure to find something as it has a wide range, from sophisticated skirts and tops to lots of modern, casual options. There's also information on how to dress with a bump and a monthly newsletter to sign up for, so make this one of your first stops for browsing when you're expecting a baby.

Site Usability:	★★★★★	Based:	UK
Product Range:	★★★★★	Express Delivery Option? (UK)	No
Price Range:	Medium/Very Good Value	Gift Wrapping Option?	No
Delivery Area:	Worldwide	Returns Procedure:	Down to you

www.bumpmagic.co.uk

There are some good brands on this attractive website, including Arabella B, Fun Mum, Melba, Mama Mio, Amoralie, Preggie Pops and Mexican Bolas. Choose from Lingerie, Clothes, Lotions and Potions and Everything Else to see the different ranges, read the excellent information sections on Pregnancy in Style, Health and Wellbeing and Week by Week Guides, or use one of the forums to share your experience. There's a lot here, with the online shopping being a small part of the website.

Site Usability:	★★★★	Based:	UK
Product Range:	★★★	Express Delivery Option? (UK)	Yes
Price Range:	Medium	Gift Wrapping Option?	Yes
Delivery Area:	Worldwide	Returns Procedure:	Down to you

www.bumpsmaternity.com

Bumps Maternity was established several years ago to offer stylish and out-of-the-ordinary maternity wear, from occasion dressing to casual and holiday. It's only available online and consists of a fun, well-photographed range. This is not a huge selection but definitely merits clicking through as most items are good value and they'll ship all over the world. You can buy maternity lingerie and plus-size clothes here as well.

Site Usability:	★★★★	Based:	UK
Product Range:	★★★	Express Delivery Option? (UK)	Yes
Price Range:	Medium	Gift Wrapping Option?	No
Delivery Area:	Worldwide	Returns Procedure:	Down to you

www.dorothyperkins.co.uk

Dorothy Perkins' clothes and accessories are modern and amazingly well priced, using some natural fabrics and with sizing from 8 to 22 for most items. In the maternity department you'll find mainly casual tops, tunics and trousers. Take a good look at the start of the season if you're likely to want something here as once a product has sold out they probably won't replace it. However, new styles come online each week.

Site Usability:	★★★★	Based:	UK
Product Range:	★★★	Express Delivery Option? (UK)	Yes
Price Range:	Very Good Value	Gift Wrapping Option?	No
Delivery Area:	UK	Returns Procedure:	Down to you

www.fleuruno.co.uk

This is a small collection of maternity wear whose main strength lies in the occasion dresses. So if you have somewhere special to go and you simply can't zip up that slinky little black dress any more, take a look round here. Styles include everything from full-length lace evening gowns to smart little cocktail dresses. Sizes go from 10 up to 20.

Site Usability:	★★★★	Based:	UK
Product Range:	★★★	Express Delivery Option? (UK)	No
Price Range:	Medium	Gift Wrapping Option?	No
Delivery Area:	Worldwide	Returns Procedure:	Down to you

www.formes.com

Formes is a French company offering beautifully styled 'designer' pregnancy wear and selling all over the world. You won't find the full collection here, just an edited range, but it's well worth looking through. Unlike a lot of the maternity shops, here you'll find all the information you could possibly want, from complete product detailing to fabric content and full measurements, plus clear pictures.

Site Usability:	★★★★★	Based:	UK
Product Range:	★★★★	Express Delivery Option? (UK)	No
Price Range:	Medium	Gift Wrapping Option?	No
Delivery Area:	Worldwide	Returns Procedure:	Down to you

www.funmum.com

Calling itself 'High Street Fashion with a Bump' will give you a good idea of what you'll find here. This is well-priced, modern maternity shopping where you're bound to find some great essential pieces – funky tops and cargo trousers, jeans and fun evening wear. There's also a small selection of nightwear.

Site Usability:	★★★★	Based:	UK
Product Range:	★★★★	Express Delivery Option? (UK)	No
Price Range:	Medium/Very Good Value	Gift Wrapping Option?	No
Delivery Area:	EU	Returns Procedure:	Down to you

www.jojomamanbebe.co.uk

This is a pretty website offering a good choice for expectant mothers, babies and young children. The drop-down menus on the Home Page take you quickly and clearly to everything you might be looking for, whether it's maternity occasionwear or safety gates for young children. There's a range of underwear and swimwear as well. The site has some excellent present ideas and offers gift vouchers and boxes to make your life easier.

Site Usability:	★★★★★	Based:	UK
Product Range:	★★★★	Express Delivery Option? (UK)	No
Price Range:	Medium	Gift Wrapping Option?	No
Delivery Area:	Worldwide	Returns Procedure:	Down to you

www.mamasandpapas.co.uk

This company combines great attention to detail, high-quality fabrics and pretty designs in its well-priced maternity section, covering everything from evening wear and separates to sleepwear and swimwear. There's lovely clothing here as well for babies and toddlers, plus a wide range of equipment and lots of present ideas. This is a beautifully photographed website offering loads of advice on what to buy. They deliver to the UK only, but you can click through to the US-based site.

Site Usability:	★★★★★	Based:	UK
Product Range:	★★★	Express Delivery Option? (UK)	No
Price Range:	Medium	Gift Wrapping Option?	No
Delivery Area:	UK, but US site available	Returns Procedure:	Down to you

www.melbamaternity.co.uk

Melba offers a great place to buy high-quality basics for reasonable prices, so take a look round at the t-shirts and tops, which come in a choice of colours, stretch jeans and trousers, easy dresses and skirts, lingerie and swimwear. There are several views of each item, so you can see exactly what you're buying. They'll deliver worldwide and offer express delivery within the UK.

Site Usability:	★★★★★	Based:	UK
Product Range:	★★★	Express Delivery Option? (UK)	No
Price Range:	Medium/Very Good Value	Gift Wrapping Option?	No
Delivery Area:	Worldwide	Returns Procedure:	Down to you

www.mothersbliss.com

This is one of those websites where you really don't know where to start, it's so busy on the Home Page. To make life easy, go to the drop-down menu on the left and click on the product you're looking for, whether it's nursing sleepwear, lingerie or Pretty Pop Drops (first time I've come across these). There's a Baby Shop, Book Shop and Sale area here as well and the prices are very good.

Site Usability: ★★★	Based:	UK
Product Range: ★★★★	Express Delivery Option? (UK)	No
Price Range: Very Good Value	Gift Wrapping Option?	No
Delivery Area: Worldwide	Returns Procedure:	Down to you

www.picchumaternity.com

This is the place if you're searching for a Little Black Dress as the selection is excellent. The site also has a wide range of tops, from chic, strapless and halter numbers to basic t-shirt and polo shirt shapes, flattering stretchy knitwear and a choice of basic skirts and trousers. There's a small but stylish collection of resortwear as well.

Site Usability: ★★★★	Based:	UK
Product Range: ★★★	Express Delivery Option? (UK)	Yes
Price Range: Medium	Gift Wrapping Option?	No
Delivery Area: Worldwide	Returns Procedure:	Down to you

www.seraphine.com

Find excellent maternity wear here on this prettily photographed website where the collection is stylish and different and the prices reasonable. You can choose from the latest looks, maternity essentials and glamorous partywear, as well as lingerie by Elle Macpherson, Nougatine and Canelle, gorgeous layettes for newborn babies and Tommy's Ts. Delivery takes up to five working days. You'll find postage costs for the UK and EU on the website and email them for elsewhere.

Site Usability: ★★★★	Based:	UK
Product Range: ★★★★	Express Delivery Option? (UK)	No
Price Range: Medium/Very Good Value	Gift Wrapping Option?	No
Delivery Area: Worldwide	Returns Procedure:	Down to you

www.tum2tum.co.uk

Get past the name of this online maternity retailer and take a look at the well-priced range of work wear, evening wear, casual separates and leisurewear from brands such as Arabella B, Melba, Piccu and Carriwell. There's a lot to choose from, although some of the pictures don't do the clothes justice (to my mind). However, you may well find something here.

Site Usability: ★★★★	Based:	UK
Product Range: ★★★★	Express Delivery Option? (UK)	No
Price Range: Medium	Gift Wrapping Option?	No
Delivery Area: Worldwide	Returns Procedure:	Down to you

www.venus-maternity.co.uk

This online retailer, based in Bristol, stands out for its selection of holiday separates, from pretty tops and shorts to jersey dresses and linen tailoring. Wardrobe essentials include t-shirts and camis, denim skirts, jeans and wrap-over shirts and there's a small selection of lingerie plus pampering treats. The site has lots of information on maternity dressing, including a list of the essential items you'll need to buy first.

Site Usability: ★★★★	Based:	UK
Product Range: ★★★	Express Delivery Option? (UK)	No
Price Range: Medium	Gift Wrapping Option?	No
Delivery Area: Worldwide	Returns Procedure:	Down to you

www.warehousefashion.com

Here's an ultra-modern, fun and often funky website offering you a good selection of maternity clothing (and one of the few high street stores to do so). You'll find party dresses, sleek and simple wrap dresses, pretty camisoles and leggings and good casual separates. The website is clear and easy to navigate and also extremely reasonable. You have the options of 48-hour or next-day delivery. Go shop.

Site Usability: ★★★★★	Based:	UK
Product Range: ★★★	Express Delivery Option? (UK)	Yes
Price Range: Very Good Value	Gift Wrapping Option?	No
Delivery Area: UK	Returns Procedure:	Freepost or return to store

Chapter 3

Business Bumps

Here's an area that's probably improved more than most as we increasingly take our bumps to work right up to the last minute. None of that sitting around on the sofa for us, thank you very much.

You can buy excellent maternity businesswear, jacket shapes and styles that would flatter anyone at any time and well-fitting trousers and skirts to go with. What to wear underneath? That, of course, very much depends on what you do and how formal you need to look. Buy simple, stretch vests in neutral colours for a dressed-up look, some of the lovely patterned tops and shirts as an alternative and then evening camisoles and wraps. That way your tailoring (which after all at any time is an investment) will take you through the whole day and on to cocktails at six. Oh yes, and did I mention the Little Black Dress? There are lots of those here too.

Sites to Visit

www.arabellab.com

Here you can choose from two styles of jacket, long or short, together with long or short skirt and stretch maternity trousers. There are pretty stretch silk wrap tops and shirts and more basic t-shirts, all of which would work together with the tailored pieces. Check here too for smart evening wear, a small collection of lingerie and nightwear and basic denim jeans and jacket.

Site Usability:	★★★★	Based:	UK
Product Range:	★★★	Express Delivery Option? (UK)	Yes
Price Range:	Medium	Gift Wrapping Option?	No
Delivery Area:	EU	Returns Procedure:	Down to you

www.cravematernity.co.uk

This is a well-designed, friendly and clearly photographed website offering well-cut and versatile separates and dresses in good fabrics and at reasonable prices. You'll find tailoring, evening wear and casual separates, all aimed at the busy woman who wants to carry on with her normal life and look smart throughout her pregnancy and afterwards. This is a website just for maternity clothes, so you're not going to be sidetracked by the children's clothes and accessories you'll find on so many other sites here.

Site Usability:	★★★★	Based:	UK
Product Range:	★★★	Express Delivery Option? (UK)	No
Price Range:	Medium	Gift Wrapping Option?	No
Delivery Area:	Worldwide	Returns Procedure:	Down to you

www.definitelybaby.com

This modern maternity online retailer offers a simple selection of tailoring but one which would take you just about anywhere, including a stylish long jacket, tailored cotton shirt and stretch gabardine trouser. It excels in the evening wear department, with timeless, elegant pieces which include, at time of writing, a black silk chiffon, calf-length skirt with camisole top and sequinned tunic dress. Contact them for overseas orders.

Site Usability:	★★★★	Based:	UK
Product Range:	★★★	Express Delivery Option? (UK)	No
Price Range:	Luxury/Medium	Gift Wrapping Option?	No
Delivery Area:	Worldwide	Returns Procedure:	Down to you

www.kickmaternitywear.com

You can choose from a wide range here and not just for work, but the tailoring styles are excellent so this would be a good place to start. There are at least three styles of jackets with matching trousers or skirts, great tops and shirts to go with, plus excellent separates and knitwear. If you want to invest in a Little Black Dress, this is the place to look as there are plenty to choose from.

Site Usability:	★★★★	Based:	UK
Product Range:	★★★★	Express Delivery Option? (UK)	Yes
Price Range:	Medium	Gift Wrapping Option?	No
Delivery Area:	Worldwide	Returns Procedure:	Down to you

www.mimimaternity.com

This US-based online retailer is particularly strong in well-priced tailoring in some very good fabrics, I think you'll be pleased to find. There's also activewear, with a good choice of yoga, cargo and fleece pull-on pants, zip-front jackets, wraps, tunics and hoodies. So whether you want to look chic at the gym right up to the last minute or just have some stylish separates to lounge about in, you can.

Site Usability:	★★★★★	Based:	US
Product Range:	★★★★	Express Delivery Option? (UK)	No
Price Range:	Medium	Gift Wrapping Option?	No
Delivery Area:	Worldwide	Returns Procedure:	Down to you

www.wondermummy.com

Wondermummy has a special section for businesswear, where there are pinstriped suits, simple tops and skirts, formal trousers and cross-over tops in several colours. Although this is only part of the range, so many maternity boutiques seem to leave out the work angle that this definitely merits a look. Browse 'Active' as well for reasonably priced easy pieces.

Site Usability:	★★★★	Based:	UK
Product Range:	★★★	Express Delivery Option? (UK)	No
Price Range:	Very Good Value	Gift Wrapping Option?	No
Delivery Area:	Most EU	Returns Procedure:	Down to you

Chapter 4

Lingerie and Swimwear

You may be one of those incredibly lucky or incredibly controlled people who manage to keep their figure totally intact (apart from the bump, of course) all the way through pregnancy. In which case lucky, or well done, you. I certainly wasn't and the thought of exposing my not-perfect body with its bump in the truly frumpy ranges of lingerie and swimwear that were around then (I sound very, very old, don't I?) was not great.

Now, in terms of lingerie, there's still a lot of white around, but you can also find wonderful lacy bras and briefs in a choice of colours and neutrals. I have to say that I still think the maternity swimwear ranges could do with some improvement, but the best of it is definitely here. Check out the other maternity clothing websites listed as some of those offer lingerie and swimwear too.

Sites to Visit

www.agentprovocateur.com

If Agent Provocateur is your favourite lingerie destination, you'll be happy to learn that by popular demand it has produced a small but sexy and beautiful maternity lingerie collection, comprising a soft-cup, front-fastening feeding bra available in several colours and prints, matching under-bump knickers and postnatal waist-cinching brief. Do I hear some sighs of relief? Maternity lingerie never looked so good.

Site Usability:	★★★★	Based:	UK
Product Range:	★★★★	Express Delivery Option? (UK)	No
Price Range:	Luxury/Medium	Gift Wrapping Option?	No, but packaging is very attractive
Delivery Area:	Worldwide	Returns Procedure:	Down to you

www.amoralia.com

This is a small but cleverly designed selection of lingerie – just click on the style you like to see the full range. There are maternity and nursing bras, hipster briefs, French knickers and thongs, all available in the sorts of colours you don't associate with maternity lingerie, such as blush, lilac, caramel, ivory and lacy black. They'll deliver worldwide.

Site Usability:	★★★★	Based:	UK
Product Range:	★★★	Express Delivery Option? (UK)	No
Price Range:	Medium	Gift Wrapping Option?	No
Delivery Area:	Worldwide	Returns Procedure:	Down to you

www.bravissimo.com

Bravissimo was started to fill the niche in the market created by those who aren't looking for lingerie or swimwear in minute sizes. It offers a wide selection in D to JJ cup, plus bra-sized swimwear in D to J cup, making it the essential site for the fuller figure. There's also a small collection of soft-cup and nursing bras. The service is excellent and if you have any queries you can email them and they'll come back to you immediately. They'll ship to you speedily anywhere.

Site Usability:	★★★★★	Based:	UK
Product Range:	★★★★	Express Delivery Option? (UK)	Yes, but you need to call them
Price Range:	Medium	Gift Wrapping Option?	No
Delivery Area:	Worldwide	Returns Procedure:	Free

www.bumpband.co.uk

This one definitely wasn't around when I had my babies but it looks like such a great idea. Basically, if you haven't heard of it already, the Bumpband, which can be worn from the early stages of pregnancy as an alternative to maternity wear, gives you much-needed, flattering support and lift and is designed to grow with you as it's higher at the front. It's also a help when you want to breastfeed discreetly. Available in two sizes, in white or black.

Site Usability:	★★★	Based:	UK
Product Range:	★★★	Express Delivery Option? (UK)	No
Price Range:	Medium	Gift Wrapping Option?	No
Delivery Area:	UK	Returns Procedure:	Down to you

www.emily-b.co.uk

Emily B is a new brand of maternity lingerie offering you beautiful luxury bras and briefs. It is the result of the frustration the founder, Emily Barnes, experienced after giving birth to her first child in 2002 when she realised that luxury maternity lingerie was extremely hard to find. Here the look is most important, although at the same time her products offer good support, coverage and comfort. You should definitely have a browse.

Site Usability:	★★★★	Based:	UK
Product Range:	★★★	Express Delivery Option? (UK)	No
Price Range:	Medium	Gift Wrapping Option?	No
Delivery Area:	Worldwide	Returns Procedure:	Down to you

www.figleaves.com

Thank goodness for Figleaves, where you'll find what is almost certainly the best range of nursing/maternity bras and briefs on the net, from simple styles to more glamorous ranges with as much lace and embroidery as you could possibly want. There's also a good choice of maternity swimwear, although this is nothing like as stylish as the lingerie. You can be sure when you buy here that you'll receive a speedy, efficient service with free delivery worldwide.

Site Usability:	★★★★★	Based:	UK
Product Range:	★★★★★	Express Delivery Option? (UK)	Yes
Price Range:	Luxury/Medium/Very Good Value	Gift Wrapping Option?	Yes
Delivery Area:	Worldwide	Returns Procedure:	Free in the UK

www.fromheretomaternity.co.uk

If you want to breastfeed your baby wearing a leopard-print bra, or something black and unbelievably pretty and lacy, this is the place to look. You can find your basic maternity essentials here as well, but to my mind the site's strength is definitely in the bra department, where you will find styles by Elle Macpherson, Bravado, Carriwell and Emma Jane. There's also a small range of swimwear and attractive nightwear.

Site Usability:	★★★★	Based:	UK
Product Range:	★★★	Express Delivery Option? (UK)	Yes
Price Range:	Medium	Gift Wrapping Option?	No
Delivery Area:	Worldwide	Returns Procedure:	Down to you

www.heidiklein.co.uk

Heidi Klein offers beautiful holidaywear all the year round and although the maternity range is small, the items are definitely some of the most stylish you can find. There are pretty and flattering kaftans and sarongs, plus all the accessories you could need for your next trip away to the sun (flip-flops, hats, bags and more). The site offers a same-day delivery service in London and express delivery throughout the UK.

Site Usability:	★★★★	Based:	UK
Product Range:	★★★	Express Delivery Option? (UK)	Yes
Price Range:	Luxury/Medium	Gift Wrapping Option?	Yes
Delivery Area:	Worldwide	Returns Procedure:	Down to you

www.mamastore.se

This Swedish maternity wear company ships throughout Europe. By far the strongest part of the collection is the excellent lingerie by Calista, Daisy Rose and Twin, plus sleepwear, hosiery and swimwear. There's also a wide selection of very (and I mean very) inexpensive separates. You need to allow a week to ten days for delivery.

Site Usability:	★★★★	Based:	Sweden
Product Range:	★★★	Express Delivery Option? (UK)	No
Price Range:	Medium/Very Good Value	Gift Wrapping Option?	No
Delivery Area	EU	Returns Procedure:	Down to you

www.mothernaturebras.co.uk

There's a good selection of maternity and nursing bras, plus support garments such as baby belts and attractive swimwear from this small online retailer and one that's well worth having a look at. I have to confess that I'm not sure why most nursing bras have to come in white only, but if that's what you're happy with then you'll probably like this basic collection, of which the swimwear is the strongest part. The information here is helpful and if you want some advice you can call them.

Site Usability:	★★★★	Based:	UK
Product Range:	★★★	Express Delivery Option? (UK)	No
Price Range:	Medium	Gift Wrapping Option?	No
Delivery Area:	Worldwide	Returns Procedure:	Down to you

www.mytights.co.uk

My Tights has a modern and easy-to-use website, offering the hosiery brands of Aristoc, Charnos, Elbeo, Gerbe, La Perla, Levante and Pretty Polly, to name but a few, plus maternity tights by Spanx and Trasparenze. So whether you want footless or fishnet tights and stockings, support tights, shapewear, knee highs or suspenders, you'll find it all here and provided you order before 3pm you'll probably get it the next day.

Site Usability:	★★★★★	Based:	UK
Product Range:	★★★★	Express Delivery Option? (UK)	Yes
Price Range:	Luxury/Medium	Gift Wrapping Option?	No
Delivery Area:	Worldwide	Returns Procedure:	Down to you

www.sexykaftans.com

There were so many kaftans around last summer that you're almost certainly aware by now that this is a must-have for summer holidays. They're also perfect when you have a bump. Whether they're in fashion or not (and I'm sure they will be for a while), they're great for wearing over a swimsuit when you want something with a bit more cover than a sarong. Here's an excellent collection – long, short, colourful or neutral and beautifully embroidered. You'll definitely find yours here. Delivery is worldwide.

Site Usability:	★★★	Based:	UK
Product Range:	★★★	Express Delivery Option? (UK)	Yes
Price Range:	Medium	Gift Wrapping Option?	No
Delivery Area:	Worldwide	Returns Procedure:	Down to you

www.tightsplease.co.uk

Whether you want fishnets and crochet tights, bright colours, knee highs, stay-ups, stockings or footsies, you'll find them all here, plus leg warmers, socks and flight socks, maternity and bridal hosiery. This website caters for all your hosiery needs and with names such as Aristoc, Pretty Polly and Charnos offered, you should never run out again. As an extra benefit delivery is free in the UK and takes only 1 to 2 days.

Site Usability:	★★★★★	Based:	UK
Product Range:	★★★★★	Express Delivery Option? (UK)	Automatic
Price Range:	Luxury/Medium	Gift Wrapping Option?	No
Delivery Area:	Worldwide	Returns Procedure:	Free

www.white-orchid.com

White Orchid is a small online boutique offering a selection of gorgeous, seductive nightwear, with a limited but attractive maternity line of nightdresses and pyjamas in colours such as palest pink, pale blue and lavender. The prices are quite high, but everything here is very high quality and hand finished, so if you want to treat yourself, take a look.

Site Usability:	★★★★	Based:	UK
Product Range:	★★★	Express Delivery Option? (UK)	No
Price Range:	Luxury	Gift Wrapping Option?	No
Delivery Area:	Worldwide	Returns Procedure:	Down to you

Chapter 5

Sportswear to Lounge In

For those days when you can't be bothered to get up, dress smart (even if it's smart/casual) and go out and you really, really want to be comfortable, take a look round here. There's some very good sports/casual wear available on the web, both here and in the other maternity clothes sections, although some of them are based in the US.

Don't let that put you off; this type of clothing lends itself to buying from overseas as it doesn't have to fit perfectly. As long as you're realistic about your size and check the retailer's sizing charts, you shouldn't have to return things. You will have to pay duty, although you usually still gain pricewise as the values are so good in the States and most websites don't try to charge you an arm and a leg for shipping.

Sites to Visit

www.euphoriamaternity.com

Here's another US-based maternity website with a marvellous choice in all areas, from chic tops and trousers to pretty dresses and an excellent selection of sportswear, including zip-front jackets and pull-on pants. There's also nursing lingerie and nightwear and pampering gifts for mothers-to-be and for after the birth. Use the TruFit sizing chart to help you buy the right size. The shipping cost will depend on how much you spend and which service you choose.

Site Usability:	★★★★★	Based:	UK
Product Range:	★★★★★	Express Delivery Option? (UK)	Yes
Price Range:	Medium	Gift Wrapping Option?	No
Delivery Area:	Worldwide	Returns Procedure:	Down to you

www.fitmaternity.com

Once again the US comes up trumps with this excellent website specialising in maternity activewear. It offers everything from a great yoga and basic fitness collection to sports bras, swimwear, maternity tennis dresses and fitness unitards. There's lots of information on exercise and pregnancy, plus a special offer section.

Site Usability:	★★★★	Based:	US
Product Range:	★★★★	Express Delivery Option? (UK)	No
Price Range:	Medium	Gift Wrapping Option?	No
Delivery Area:	Worldwide	Returns Procedure:	Down to you

www.frenchsole.com

If you've been looking for the perfect ballet flat to relax in, you need search no more. French Sole is well known for offering a wide range of styles, from the classic two-tone pump to this season's must-have animal print and metallic versions and each season it brings out new styles. There are excellent driving shoes and travel slippers here as well.

Site Usability:	★★★★	Based:	UK
Product Range:	★★★★	Express Delivery Option? (UK)	No
Price Range:	Medium	Gift Wrapping Option?	No
Delivery Area:	Worldwide	Returns Procedure:	Down to you

www.imaternity.com

You may think initially that you don't want to order maternity wear from overseas. However, when you weigh up the prices here you should definitely consider it as you'll find excellent value, even though you will have to pay duty. Activewear is a good area for ordering from abroad as fit is even easier than most other clothes due to the amount of stretch in the majority of garments.

Site Usability:	★★★★★	Based:	US
Product Range:	★★★★★	Express Delivery Option? (UK)	No
Price Range:	Very Good Value	Gift Wrapping Option?	No
Delivery Area:	Worldwide	Returns Procedure:	Down to you

www.jdsports.co.uk

While you're taking a look at the gorgeous infants' shoes and mini trainers here, you might like to consider your own feet and give them a real treat by ordering something like the Nike Air Capri or soft-soled Puma Sokuto. The range of trainers and casual sports shoes is good and you definitely won't regret it.

Site Usability:	★★★★★	Based:	UK
Product Range:	★★★★★	Express Delivery Option? (UK)	No
Price Range:	Medium	Gift Wrapping Option?	No
Delivery Area:	UK	Returns Procedure:	Down to you

www.queenbee.com.au

Just to offer you something a bit different, this online retailer is based in Australia, so there are some brands here that you're unlikely to come across anywhere else. There's colourful activewear (think berry, olive and navy blue), with hoodies and sweatshirts, plus yoga pants and jeans, great 2 Chix and I Maternity logo t-shirts and some really pretty dresses. The site has a currency converter (useful as everything is priced in Australian dollars) and delivery is not overpriced.

Site Usability:	★★★★	Based:	Australia
Product Range:	★★★★	Express Delivery Option? (UK)	No
Price Range:	Medium	Gift Wrapping Option?	No
Delivery Area:	Worldwide	Returns Procedure:	Down to you

Chapter 6

Bags for Everything

I have to confess to a few twinges of jealousy here. As a major collector of handbags, and remembering the pale-blue quilted baby bag I used to carry around with me, I'm simply amazed by the incredible selection on offer now (not that there's anything wrong with pale blue quilted, but it wasn't stylish as many of the ones you'll find below are). The baby bag is no longer just a necessity but is obviously big business.

I'm sure you'll be pleased to know that there's not only a well-priced choice in just about every colour and shape – from totes to messenger bags, backpacks and slings – but if you want to you can buy your own premium-quality, limited-edition designer fabric or soft leather baby bag, or chic black, nylon tote that would take you anywhere (baby or otherwise), and the rolling Samsonite Baby Wardrobe with its own mini coathangers.

Sites to visit

www.alexandrabee.com

For a baby bag that's a cross between just that and a chic tote/handbag, plus being an investment at the same time, take a look here at a range of bags handmade in Italy which definitely have that designer feel. There's plenty of room and pockets inside and each bag is available in a choice of leathers and prints. Expect to spend around £200 and buy something that's made to last.

Site Usability:	★★★★	Based:	UK
Product Range:	★★★	Express Delivery Option? (UK)	No
Price Range:	Luxury/Medium	Gift Wrapping Option?	No
Delivery Area:	Worldwide	Returns Procedure:	Down to you

www.angelcots.co.uk

There's a full range of Samsonite changing bags here, including carry cases and weekenders. Look out for the ultimate rolling Samsonite Baby Wardrobe, a baby garment bag which can be hung up on arrival and comes complete with small coat hangers and a fold-out, zip-off section for bottles, etc. There are cute bags in the Sammies range (also Samsonite), Brevi and Samsonite travel cots, safety products and lots of ideas for nursery furniture.

Site Usability:	★★★★★	Based:	UK
Product Range:	★★★★	Express Delivery Option? (UK)	No
Price Range:	Luxury/Medium	Gift Wrapping Option?	No
Delivery Area:	UK	Returns Procedure:	Down to you

www.caboodlebags.co.uk

This is a small range of well-priced and efficient baby changing bags, available in a range of chic colours such as black, charcoal, red and beige. All three styles include a changing mat and bottle pocket and are easily wiped down or washable. If you don't want to invest too much at first but you do want to know you're buying tried and tested quality, buy here.

Site Usability:	★★★★	Based:	UK
Product Range:	★★★	Express Delivery Option? (UK)	No
Price Range:	Medium/Very Good Value	Gift Wrapping Option?	No
Delivery Area:	Worldwide	Returns Procedure:	Down to you

www.changingbags.co.uk

Changing Bags is somewhere you must look before you invest in your essential baby bag Whether you're after a shoulder bag, buggy bag, backpack, or dad's bag (great idea), there's lots on offer. Basic brands are Avent, Allerhand, Caboodle, Oi Oi and Skip Hop, to name just a few, and the prices are very reasonable.

Site Usability:	★★★★	Based:	UK
Product Range:	★★★	Express Delivery Option? (UK)	No
Price Range:	Medium/Very Good Value	Gift Wrapping Option?	No
Delivery Area:	UK	Returns Procedure:	Down to you

www.ebags.co.uk

This is a large handbag, luggage and business case website where you will also find some very good baby bags by Samsonite, Kipling, Oi Oi, Little Packrats and Pink Lining (by designer Charlotte Pearl). I have to confess that I hadn't come across the last two until now, but some of the range is really attractive and quite different from what you'll find elsewhere. The site offers accessories such as extra changing mats, blankets and Kipling's quilted 'warm-up' bags as well.

Site Usability:	★★★★★	Based:	UK
Product Range:	★★★★★	Express Delivery Option? (UK)	Yes
Price Range:	Luxury/Medium	Gift Wrapping Option?	No
Delivery Area:	UK	Returns Procedure:	Down to you

www.happybags.co.uk

If you've just had a baby or you know someone who has it would be well worth your while taking a look at this website, from a retailer specialising in baby bags. You'll find the kind of bag that holds all the paraphernalia you need if you go out, with multiple compartments to keep everything separate, and that you can use as a shoulder bag if you want or attach to your high-tech buggy. There's lots of choice, from the Million Dollar Baby Bag (extremely expensive) to the excellent Skip Hop bag which comes in lots of colours.

Site Usability:	★★★	Based:	UK
Product Range:	★★★	Express Delivery Option? (UK)	Yes
Price Range:	Luxury/Medium	Gift Wrapping Option?	Yes
Delivery Area:	Worldwide	Returns Procedure:	Down to you

www.hennabecca.co.uk

There's just one product here and it's essential for anyone who's just had a baby and doesn't want to lose the chic, stylish look she's worked hard to maintain. So, this bag not only looks good and comes in canvas, print and leather versions but it also works hard as the perfect baby bag, with three detachable interior compartments, long zip pulls, bottle holder and loads of other special details.

Site Usability: ★★★★	Based:	UK
Product Range: ★★★	Express Delivery Option? (UK)	Yes
Price Range: Luxury	Gift Wrapping Option?	Yes
Delivery Area: Worldwide	Returns Procedure:	Down to you

www.pinklining.co.uk

Pink Lining is a distinctive fashion label which aims to provide bags which are beautiful, functional and practical. The range includes wallets, wash bags, weekend bags and the signature Yummy Mummy nappy bags. Expect exclusively designed fabrics with leather trims, often enhanced with intricate appliqué detail and whimsical embroidered slogans, and cleverly thought-out pockets for mobiles, BlackBerrys, pens and keys. All the bags have the signature shocking-pink lining.

Site Usability: ★★★★★	Based:	UK
Product Range: ★★★★	Express Delivery Option? (UK)	No
Price Range: Luxury/Medium	Gift Wrapping Option?	No
Delivery Area: Worldwide	Returns Procedure:	Down to you

www.storksak.co.uk

I have to confess that if I was going the baby route again (which I most certainly am not), this would probably be my first port of call. StorkSak creates wonderful 'baby' bags which look like nothing of the sort. They come in black, quality nylon with leather straps and excellent fittings, although if you're not a black addict like me, you can have your bag in rose, sky or modern print. Shapes are tote, classic shoulder-shaped, smart weekend or modern slouch and they offer all the accessories you need.

Site Usability: ★★★★★	Based:	UK
Product Range: ★★★	Express Delivery Option? (UK)	Yes
Price Range: Luxury/Medium	Gift Wrapping Option?	No
Delivery Area: Worldwide	Returns Procedure:	Down to you

Chapter 7

The Pamper Place

This section is for you because you deserve to be pampered, both before and after you produce. I know that everything seems to centre on the baby, and most men (in particular), or friends who haven't had kids just don't understand how exhausting the whole process can be. It's not just the first three months of the pregnancy or the last three months, let alone the first few months when your baby has arrived – you need a fuss constantly.

This is an excellent time for a bit of pampering. You definitely need those wonderful bath and body products, scented candles and silky body lotions to help you feel your best all the time. They're small things, I know, but they can make a great, uplifting difference. Be pampered. Allow yourself nothing less.

Sites to Visit

www.bathandunwind.com

Bath & Unwind specialises in luxury products that help you to relax (and unwind) after a hard day's work. The company aims to provide the highest quality bath and spa products from around the world, including brands such as Aromatherapy Associates, Korres, Nougat, Burt's Bees and Jane Packer. Delivery is free (UK) provided you spend over a certain amount and they'll ship to you anywhere in the world. There is also a gift selector and an express service for the next time you forget that special present.

Site Usability: ★★★★	Based:	UK
Product Range: ★★★★	Express Delivery Option? (UK)	Yes
Price Range: Medium	Gift Wrapping Option?	No
Delivery Area: Worldwide	Returns Procedure:	Down to you

www.bathrobics.com

At Bathrobics there are three toiletries specially formulated to care for your health and well-being during pregnancy: Arnica and Aloe Leg Gel, Rosehip and Passionfruit Stretch Mark Cream and Organic Rosewater and Pomegranate Body Wash. These are combined into kits such as the Pregnancy Pampering Spa Kit and Bathrobics Beauty Spa so that you can create your own spa ritual at home. They include exercise instruction books and relaxation CDs alongside the toiletries.

Site Usability: ★★★★	Based:	UK
Product Range: ★★★	Express Delivery Option? (UK)	Yes
Price Range: Medium	Gift Wrapping Option?	No
Delivery Area: Worldwide	Returns Procedure:	Down to you

www.blisslondon.co.uk

Sign up for Bliss Beut emails and stay in the 'Glow'. Does that give you some idea of the tone from New York and London's hottest spa? If you don't have the time to visit the spas themselves you can at least now buy the products online and relax at home with your own treatments, shower gels and shampoos with simple names like Body Butter, Rosy Toes and Glamour Glove Gel.

Site Usability: ★★★★	Based:	UK
Product Range: ★★★	Express Delivery Option? (UK)	Yes
Price Range: Medium	Gift Wrapping Option?	No
Delivery Area: Worldwide	Returns Procedure:	Down to you

www.boots.com

Not only can you buy your basic bathroom cupboard items here, plus fragrance from most of the major brands, but in the Brand Boutique you will find the full ranges by Chanel, Clarins, Clinique, Dior, Estée Lauder, Elizabeth Arden and Lancôme, plus ultra-modern brands Ruby and Millie, Urban Decay and Benefit. Delivery is free when you spend £40 and returns are free too. This excellent service is simply not publicised enough.

Site Usability:	★★★★★	Based:	UK
Product Range:	★★★★★	Express Delivery Option? (UK)	Yes
Price Range:	Medium/Very Good Value	Gift Wrapping Option?	Yes
Delivery Area:	UK	Returns Procedure:	Free

www.cologneandcotton.net

This is a special website offering some unusual and hard-to-find bath and body products and fragrance by Diptyque (if you haven't already tried its candles you really should, they're gorgeous), Cath Collins, La Compagnie de Provence (try the hand wash) and Cote Bastide. There are also fragrances by Annik Goutal, Coudray and Rosine and for the bathroom you'll find fluffy towels and bathrobes.

Site Usability:	★★★★★	Based:	UK
Product Range:	★★★★	Express Delivery Option? (UK)	Yes
Price Range:	Luxury/Medium	Gift Wrapping Option?	Yes
Delivery Area:	Worldwide	Returns Procedure:	Down to you

www.crabtree-evelyn.co.uk

Well known and sold throughout the world, Crabtree & Evelyn offers a wide range of bath, body and spa products from classic fragrances such as Lily of the Valley to the ultra-modern La Source. Everything is cleverly and attractively packaged and offered on the well-designed and easy-to-use website. Particularly good as gifts are the pretty boxes containing miniatures of the most popular products.

Site Usability:	★★★★★	Based:	UK
Product Range:	★★★★★	Express Delivery Option? (UK)	Yes
Price Range:	Medium	Gift Wrapping Option?	No
Delivery Area:	Worldwide	Returns Procedure:	Down to you

www.garden.co.uk

The Garden Pharmacy's list of top brands seems to be growing by the day. Here you'll find Chanel, Elizabeth Arden, Lancôme, Revlon, Clinique and Clarins online, together with Vichy, Avene, Caudalie and Roc. Then there are spa products by I Coloniali, L'Occitane, Roger et Gallet and Segreti Mediterranei (and no doubt a few more will have appeared by the time you read this). The list of fragrances on offer is huge. The site also provides free gift wrapping and 24-hour delivery.

Site Usability:	★★★★	Based:	UK
Product Range:	★★★★★	Express Delivery Option? (UK)	Yes
Price Range:	Medium	Gift Wrapping Option?	Yes
Delivery Area:	Worldwide	Returns Procedure:	Down to you

www.hqhair.com

If you haven't used it already you should try this fun and incredibly useful website. Here, along with clever beauty products and jewellery (and absolutely everything you could need for your hair, including Blax, Nexxus and Paul Mitchell products), you'll discover Anya Hindmarch, Kate Spade and Lulu Guinness exquisite cosmetic bags and lots of beauty accessories, including high-quality make-up and hairbrushes.

Site Usability:	★★★★★	Based:	UK
Product Range:	★★★★	Express Delivery Option? (UK)	No
Price Range:	Medium	Gift Wrapping Option?	No
Delivery Area:	Worldwide	Returns Procedure:	Down to you

www.moltonbrown.co.uk

The range of Molton Brown's bath, skincare, make-up and spa products seems to increase daily and you want to try every single one. The packaging is lovely and the products not only look and smell wonderful but are not overpriced. Delivery is quick and you frequently get sent delicious trial-sized products with your order. This is a great site for gifts, travel-size products and that extra body lotion and bath gel you simply won't be able to resist.

Site Usability:	★★★★★	Based:	UK
Product Range:	★★★★★	Express Delivery Option? (UK)	No
Price Range:	Medium	Gift Wrapping Option?	Yes
Delivery Area:	Worldwide	Returns Procedure:	Down to you

www.mumstheword.com

Mumstheword.com was created to bring you some of the best natural and organic pregnancy product ranges. The focus is on skincare, beauty and well-being products made specifically for pregnant women. Although most of the products featured are natural or organic, not all of them are, so you can decide which product suits your lifestyle best. Stretch-mark skincare, essential oils, morning sickness relief, pampering gifts, books and diaries are just some of the things you'll discover here.

Site Usability:	★★★★	Based:	UK
Product Range:	★★★★★	Express Delivery Option? (UK)	Yes
Price Range:	Medium	Gift Wrapping Option?	Yes
Delivery Area:	EU	Returns Procedure:	Down to you

www.naturalmagicuk.com

Unlike almost all conventional candles (which contain paraffin wax and synthetic oils), Natural Magic candles are made from clean, pure vegetable wax, scented with the best-quality organic aromatherapy oils. They're also twice the size of the average candle (1kg) with three wicks and up to 75 hours of burn time. Each candle has a specific therapeutic task, such as uplifting, inspiring, soothing and de-stressing, and all are beautifully packaged and perfect for treats and gifts.

Site Usability:	★★★★★	Based:	UK
Product Range:	★★★	Express Delivery Option? (UK)	Yes
Price Range:	Medium	Gift Wrapping Option?	No
Delivery Area:	Worldwide	Returns Procedure:	Down to you

www.skinstore.co.uk

Skinstore offers two ranges that have been specially created for pregnancy and early motherhood. The first is Benev, which concentrates on anti-aging and is free from synthetic chemicals, fragrances and preservatives. The

35

second is Belli Cosmetics, which combines medically proven treatments with the holistic benefits of aroma, taste and massage therapies. What's great about this website is that you can access the online chat facility and 'talk' to an expert before you buy if you want advice.

Site Usability:	★★★★★	Based:	UK
Product Range:	★★★★★	Express Delivery Option? (UK)	No
Price Range:	Luxury/Medium	Gift Wrapping Option?	No
Delivery Area:	EU	Returns Procedure:	Down to you

www.spacenk.co.uk

Nars, Stila, Darphin, Laura Mercier, Eve Lom, Diptyque, Frederic Fekkai and Dr Sebagh are just some of the 60-plus brands offered on the website of this retailer, famous for bringing unusual and hard-to-find products to the UK. (So you don't have to go to New York any more to buy your Frederic Fekkai shampoo – shame.) This is also an excellent place for gifts as it offers a personalised message and gift wrapping service and next-day delivery if you need it.

Site Usability:	★★★★★	Based:	UK
Product Range:	★★★★	Express Delivery Option? (UK)	Yes
Price Range:	Luxury/Medium	Gift Wrapping Option?	Yes
Delivery Area:	Worldwide	Returns Procedure:	Down to you

Chapter 8

Healthcare and Vitamins

I'm definitely not going to tell you what to buy here. You may like to take your daily dose of vitamins, you may be told by your doctor that you need certain supplements, or you may read about the latest energy-giving tea that every mum-to-be should know about. Whatever it is, you'll probably find it below.

The only advice I would give is that if you're in any doubt at all, ask your doc.

Sites to Visit

www.chemistdirect.co.uk

Chemist Direct operates out of London and is a member of the National Pharmaceutical Association. There's a wide range of products here, from vitamins and health supplements to baby products, toiletries, holiday and sun care. They're also happy to fill your prescriptions for you and the prices are excellent (always check against an offline chemist if you're not sure about the cost). You send payment online and your prescription by post, after which they'll despatch your order to you immediately.

Site Usability:	★★★★	Express Delivery Option? (UK)	Yes
Product Range:	★★★★	Gift Wrapping Option?	No
Price Range:	Medium	Returns Procedure:	Down to you
Delivery Area:	UK		

www.goldshield.co.uk

As well as all the vitamins and supplements you would expect from a health food store, here you can buy food and snacks, such as assortments of fruit and nuts, crystallised ginger, dried fruit, pistachios and pumpkin seeds and everything for making your own yoghurt. There are also not quite so 'healthy' (but very tempting) snacks, including chocolate-coated ginger and brazils. There's lots of information on all the different sections, plus health books.

Site Usability:	★★★★	Express Delivery Option? (UK)	No
Product Range:	★★★★	Gift Wrapping Option?	No
Price Range:	Medium	Returns Procedure:	Free
Delivery Area:	Worldwide		

www.goodnessdirect.co.uk

There's a vast range here, with 3000-plus health foods, vitamins and items selected for those with special dietary needs. You can search for foods that are dairy free, gluten free, wheat free, yeast free and low fat, plus organic fruit, vegetables (in a selection of boxed choices), fish and meat. You'll also find frozen and chilled foods, so you can do your complete health shopping from this retailer. Don't be worried by the amount of choice, the website is easy to navigate and order from.

Site Usability:	★★★★	Based:	UK
Product Range:	★★★★★	Express Delivery Option? (UK)	No
Price Range:	Medium	Gift Wrapping Option?	No
Delivery Area:	UK	Returns Procedure:	Down to you

www.hollandandbarrett.com

This famous-name health supplement and information retailer has a simple and easy-to-use website, offering products within sections such as Sports Nutrition, Digestive Aids, Weight Management and Women's

Products. You do really need to know what you're looking for, as you'll find the details on each individual product only when you click on it. However, the order system is simple, so if you want something specific, take a look.

Site Usability:	★★★	Based:	UK
Product Range:	★★★★	Express Delivery Option? (UK)	No
Price Range:	Medium	Gift Wrapping Option?	No
Delivery Area:	Worldwide	Returns Procedure:	Down to you

www.marnys.com

On this website you can find organic products such as muesli, toasted sesame seeds, brown lentils, texturised soya, flax seeds, pumpkin and sunflower seeds as well as salt crystal lamps. There's also a wide range of supplements, vitamins and minerals, divided into sections such as Royal Jelly, Korean Ginseng and Bee Pollen as specific products and Weight Control, Cardiovascular System and Hormonal System as areas.

Site Usability:	★★★★	Based:	Spain
Product Range:	★★★★★	Express Delivery Option? (UK)	No, but fast delivery is automatic
Price Range:	Medium	Gift Wrapping Option?	No
Delivery Area:	Worldwide	Returns Procedure:	Down to you

www.pharmacy2u.co.uk

All your regular medicines and healthcare essentials are available on this site, plus plenty of advice and suggestions. If you can't be bothered or don't have the time to go out to the chemist, this is definitely the site for you. It's very clear and well laid out and I doubt whether there would be anything you couldn't find. You can also arrange for your prescriptions to be filled. They are members of the Royal Pharmaceutical Society of Great Britain and the National Pharmaceutical Association.

Site Usability:	★★★★★	Express Delivery Option? (UK)	No
Product Range:	★★★★★	Gift Wrapping Option?	No
Price Range:	Medium	Returns Procedure:	Down to you
Delivery Area:	Worldwide for most products		

Chapter 9

Natural Beauty Products

*A*s we seem to be going greener by the day, I felt it appropriate to offer you the best of the natural and organic beauty product websites. So if you're a fan of aromatherapy, Bach Flower Remedies and pure skincare and body products, you'll know where to find them online.

Some of these products have always been difficult to find on the high street – you've had to search out a particular shop, probably a distance from where you normally want to go – so the web lends itself perfectly to this type of shopping. This is particularly so as for the most part these are products that are easy to pack and send. Now you can browse the full range online.

Sites to Visit

www.airandwater.co.uk

Here you can discover the properties of essential oils with the natural soaps, beauty products, aromatherapy boxes, carrier and massage oils. Or enhance your home with oil burners, incense, resins, candles and va-porisers and find Bach Flower Remedies and the Rescue Remedy range of herbal supplements. Suppliers include Edom Health and Beauty Products, Meadows Aromatherapy and Arran Aromatics.

Site Usability: ★★★★	Based:	UK
Product Range: ★★★★	Express Delivery Option? (UK)	Yes
Price Range: Medium	Gift Wrapping Option?	No
Delivery Area: EU	Returns Procedure:	Down to you

www.baldwins.co.uk

G. Baldwin & Co is London's oldest and most established herbalist. If you pay a visit to its shop you'll find yourself stepping back in time, encountering wooden floors, high, old-fashioned counters and shelves stacked with herbs, oils and ointments. You can shop online from the complete ranges of both Bach Flower Remedies and the Australian Bush Flower Essences, Baldwin's own-brand aromatherapy oils, natural soaps, creams and bath accessories and herbs, seeds, roots and dried flowers.

Site Usability: ★★★★	Based:	UK
Product Range: ★★★★	Express Delivery Option? (UK)	Yes
Price Range: Medium	Gift Wrapping Option?	No
Delivery Area: Worldwide	Returns Procedure:	Down to you

www.fushi.co.uk

Fushi was established just over four years ago as a lifestyle-brand of holistic health and beauty products. Expanding on the philosophy that inner health promotes outer well-being, Fushi has developed a range of natural products including herbal remedies, cosmetic ranges and aromatherapy oils, most of which are organic. Use the product finder to treat specific ailments or select by product range. There's lots of information, so be prepared to spend some time here.

Site Usability: ★★★★★	Based:	UK
Product Range: ★★★★	Express Delivery Option? (UK)	No
Price Range: Medium	Gift Wrapping Option?	No
Delivery Area: Worldwide	Returns Procedure:	Down to you

www.mandala-aroma.com

Mandala Aroma is a luxury organic aromatherapy company set up by former fashion buyer and qualified aromatherapist Gillian Kavanagh. Here you'll discover bath oils, body treatment oils and aromatherapy candles, all under the headings of Wisdom, Love, Courage and Strength. Click on the item of your choice and you'll find out more about its ingredients and benefits.

Site Usability:	★★★★★	Based:	UK
Product Range:	★★★	Express Delivery Option? (UK)	No
Price Range:	Medium	Gift Wrapping Option?	No
Delivery Area:	Worldwide	Returns Procedure:	Down to you

www.michelinearcier.com

Micheline Arcier promises to use only the purest essential oils in its preparations. All its bath, body, face oils and face creams are based upon unique formulas that have been gently evolved by Madame Arcier herself over the last 40 years. The Debut de Vie range is specially designed for mothers and babies and includes such luxuries as Vie Nouvelle Body Oil and Lavande Bath Oil. There are lots of other treats here as well.

Site Usability:	★★★★	Based:	UK
Product Range:	★★★	Express Delivery Option? (UK)	No
Price Range:	Luxury/Medium	Gift Wrapping Option?	No
Delivery Area:	Worldwide	Returns Procedure:	Down to you

www.mumstheword.com

Mumstheword.com was created to bring some of the best natural and organic pregnancy ranges direct to mums-to-be. The focus is on skincare, beauty and well-being. Although most of the items are natural or organic, not all of them are, so you can decide which product suits your lifestyle best. There are full details about all of the products on offer to assist you in your choice.

Site Usability:	★★★★	Based:	UK
Product Range:	★★★★	Express Delivery Option? (UK)	Yes
Price Range:	Medium	Gift Wrapping Option?	Yes
Delivery Area:	EU	Returns Procedure:	Down to you

www.mysanatural.com

Quite a lot of online retailers offering natural and environmentally friendly products think that we want to see them looking as natural as possible. Personally I don't think we do – buying lotions and potions online should always be a treat. Here at Mysa the natural and treat elements meet beautifully – think Pink Grapefruit Hand and Body Lotion, Ginger Loofah Soap or Sweet Jasmine Body Scrub and you'll get the idea. Packaging is chic and minimal and there are great gift sets too.

Site Usability:	★★★★★	Based:	UK
Product Range:	★★★	Express Delivery Option? (UK)	Yes
Price Range:	Medium	Gift Wrapping Option?	No
Delivery Area:	Worldwide	Returns Procedure:	Down to you

www.naturalcollection.com

All the products on this website are seriously natural, from fairly traded laundry baskets to organic cotton bed linen. There is also a Personal Care selection which includes brands such as Organic Options (natural soaps), Faith in Nature (aromatherapy body care), Barefoot Botanicals (skin and body care) and lots of natural pampering products and gift ideas. In the Wellbeing section you can order Sage Organics vitamins and minerals and Bath Indulgence Spa sets.

Site Usability:	★★★★★	Based:	UK
Product Range:	★★★★★	Express Delivery Option? (UK)	Yes
Price Range:	Medium	Gift Wrapping Option?	No
Delivery Area:	Worldwide	Returns Procedure:	Down to you

www.nealsyardremedies.com

This is probably one aromatherapy and herbal remedy retailer you have heard of. From the first shop located in Neal's Yard in the heart of London's Covent Garden, Neal's Yard Remedies has grown into one of the country's leading natural health retailers. On its attractive website you can buy a wide range of its products, from aromatherapy and body care to luxurious bath products and homeopathic remedies, plus attractively packaged gift sets.

Site Usability:	★★★★	Based:	UK
Product Range:	★★★★	Express Delivery Option? (UK)	Yes
Price Range:	Medium	Gift Wrapping Option?	No
Delivery Area:	Worldwide	Returns Procedure:	Down to you

www.nicetouch.co.uk

Nice Touch offers REN, Aromatherapy Associates, Dermalogica, Trilogy botanical skincare, Xen-Tan self-tanning range, St Tropez, Pacifica soy candles and prettily packaged, earth-friendly baby products. The company prides itself on helping you make informed choices about the products that you put on your skin. There's all the information you need about each brand, including the ingredients of the products, their suitability for your skin type and the ethics of the companies which make them. It's an excellent website.

Site Usability:	★★★★★	Based:	UK
Product Range:	★★★★	Express Delivery Option? (UK)	No
Price Range:	Medium	Gift Wrapping Option?	No
Delivery Area:	Worldwide	Returns Procedure:	Down to you

www.origins.co.uk

You may well have heard of Origins, specialists in natural skincare. The company uses aromatic plants, earth and sea substances and other resources to make its products as close to nature as they can be. Now you can buy the full range online, including the luxurious Ginger Souffle Whipped Body Cream, Jump Start Body Wash and Pomegranate Wash cleanser. You really do want to try them all.

Site Usability:	★★★★★	Based:	UK
Product Range:	★★★★	Express Delivery Option? (UK)	Yes
Price Range:	Medium	Gift Wrapping Option?	No
Delivery Area:	UK	Returns Procedure:	Down to you

www.potions.org.uk

Potions & Possibilities produces natural toiletries and aromatherapy products, ranging from soaps and bath oils to restorative balms and creams. Everything is blended and created using the highest-quality essential oils.

You can find the award-winning products in Bloomingdales (in the US) and Fenwicks in the UK, among other stores. Choose from bath sizzlers, bath and shower gels, shampoos, fragrance and gift collections.

Site Usability:	★★★★	Based:	UK
Product Range:	★★★	Express Delivery Option? (UK)	Yes
Price Range:	Medium	Gift Wrapping Option?	No
Delivery Area:	Worldwide	Returns Procedure:	Down to you

www.primrose-aromatherapy.co.uk

This attractively laid-out website is just about aromatherapy (rather than offering you lots of other products as well). The selection of essential oils is huge, with pictures of the fruits, flowers and herbs themselves rather than dinky little bottles. For each product there's a great deal of information on the properties and how to use them. They will ship all over the world and you need to contact them if you want courier delivery.

Site Usability:	★★★★	Based:	UK
Product Range:	★★★	Express Delivery Option? (UK)	Yes
Price Range:	Medium	Gift Wrapping Option?	No
Delivery Area:	Worldwide	Returns Procedure:	Down to you

www.pureskincare.co.uk

All of the products here are 100% natural and suitable for vegetarians. There's also brief information next to each brand name to show which brands are organic or contain organic ingredients, rather than those which are purely 'natural'. Brands available include Balm Balm, Akamuti, Aubrey Organics, Dr Bronner, Suki and Trovarno Organics. Products range from general skin and hair care to specialist skincare and travel sizes.

Site Usability:	★★★★★	Based:	UK
Product Range:	★★★★	Express Delivery Option? (UK)	No
Price Range:	Medium	Gift Wrapping Option?	No
Delivery Area:	UK	Returns Procedure:	Down to you

www.theorganicpharmacy.com

The Organic Pharmacy is dedicated to health and beauty using organic products and treatments. Fully registered with The Royal Pharmaceutical

Society of Great Britain, it chooses to specialise in herbs, homeopathy and organic skincare. It promises no artificial preservatives, colourings or fragrances and everything it offers is handmade in small batches. Look for cosmetics, skincare and gorgeously fragranced candles, plus mother and baby care.

Site Usability:	★★★★★	Based:	UK
Product Range:	★★★★	Express Delivery Option? (UK)	No
Price Range:	Luxury/Medium	Gift Wrapping Option?	No
Delivery Area:	Worldwide	Returns Procedure:	Down to you

www.youraromatherapy.co.uk

This is a clear and modern aromatherapy website, where you can immediately see all the products on offer, including essential and massage oils, aromatherapy kits, candles and accessories, vaporisers and ionisers and body care for all the family. There is a good gift section and an attractive selection of candles.

Site Usability:	★★★★★	Based:	UK
Product Range:	★★★★	Express Delivery Option? (UK)	No
Price Range:	Medium	Gift Wrapping Option?	No
Delivery Area:	Worldwide	Returns Procedure:	Down to you

Chapter 10

Organic Foods

If you like your food to be organic, particularly fruit and veg, you'll probably already know how expensive they are in the supermarkets. So why not look online? There are lots of marvellous places now offering organic food on the web (where else?) and not just fruit and veg but meat, fish, bread and loads of other products. Probably the best way to buy your greens is to use one of the box services, where you receive a shipment every week, the size determined by you. In any case, have a look round here and make your choice.

Sites to Visit

www.abel-cole.co.uk

Abel & Cole delivers delicious boxes of fresh organic fruit and veg, organic meat, sustainably sourced fish and loads of other ethically produced foods, buying as much as possible from UK farms. It offers regular selection boxes of fresh produce, and providing you live in the South of England you can order all of its other food and drink too, including locally baked bread. For those who live outside the main area there are two selections of organic fruit and vegetables.

Site Usability:	★★★★	Based:	UK
Product Range:	★★★	Express Delivery Option? (UK)	No
Price Range:	Medium	Gift Wrapping Option?	No
Delivery Area:	UK	Returns Procedure:	Down to you

www.caleyco.com

Caledonian Foods represents a collective of top-quality Scottish suppliers and aims to bring you fresh food, full of flavour, of the highest quality, with complete traceability and provenance. With a network of over 100 independent food producers, all the food is fresh, free-range, organic and wild. You can select from meat and game, fish and shellfish, such as oysters, smoked salmon and hand-dived scallops, cheeses, desserts and truffles, wines, whiskeys and gifts.

Site Usability:	★★★★★	Based:	Scotland
Product Range:	★★★★	Express Delivery Option? (UK)	No
Price Range:	Medium	Gift Wrapping Option?	No
Delivery Area:	UK	Returns Procedure:	Down to you

www.graigfarm.co.uk

Now in its 19th year, Graig Farm Organics is an award-winning pioneer of organic meats and other organic foods in the UK. The range is extensive and includes meat (organic beef, lamb, mutton, pork, chicken and turkey, as well as local game and goat meat), ready meals, fish, baby food, dairy, bread, groceries, vegetables and fruit. There are also soups and salads, alcoholic drinks, a gluten-free range, and even pet food, plus herbal remedies and essential oils.

Site Usability:	★★★★	Based:	UK
Product Range:	★★★★	Express Delivery Option? (UK)	No
Price Range:	Medium	Gift Wrapping Option?	No
Delivery Area:	UK	Returns Procedure:	Down to you

www.organics-4u.co.uk

Organics4u supplies top-quality organic vegetables, fruit and dry goods direct to your home or place of work anywhere in the UK. The fruit and vegetables are brought to you in boxes of various sizes and you can choose to have them delivered weekly, fortnightly or monthly. The site also offers dry goods boxes, containing items such as pasta, spices, pulses and oil, although you can buy these products separately if you want to.

Site Usability: ★★★★	Based:	UK
Product Range: ★★★	Express Delivery Option? (UK)	No
Price Range: Medium	Gift Wrapping Option?	No
Delivery Area: UK	Returns Procedure:	Down to you

www.rhug.co.uk

This organic online farm offers meat produced on the Rhug Estate Farm in Corwen, North Wales. It offers Welsh lamb, beef and chicken, plus groceries such as herbs and spices, cheese and excellent-looking cookies. There are also non-organic sausages and savoury and sweet handmade pies, such as plum, and steak and ale. Delivery is free on orders over £100.

Site Usability: ★★★★	Based:	UK
Product Range: ★★★★	Express Delivery Option? (UK)	No
Price Range: Medium	Gift Wrapping Option?	No
Delivery Area: UK	Returns Procedure:	Down to you

www.riverford.co.uk

Riverford Organic Vegetables is situated along the Dart Valley in Devon and delivers fresh organic vegetable boxes direct from the farm to homes across the south of the UK. It started organic vegetable production in 1987 and has become one of the country's largest independent growers, certified by the Soil Association. Simply enter your postcode to check that the site delivers to your area (and find out which day), then select which of the fruit and vegetable boxes is most suitable for you.

Site Usability: ★★★★	Based:	UK
Product Range: ★★★★	Express Delivery Option? (UK)	No
Price Range: Medium	Gift Wrapping Option?	No
Delivery Area: UK (South)	Returns Procedure:	Down to you

www.somersetorganics.co.uk

Depending on the season, Somerset Organics provides its own organic Angus beef, rare breed Berkshire pork and organic lamb, all of which are farmed by themselves at Gilcombe Farm. The company also stocks a full range of meats and poultry reared on local organic farms, plus non-organic free-range meats. The dairy range includes stilton, brie and vintage cheddar, plus milk and cream, and you can order your fruit and veg boxes here as well.

Site Usability:	★★★★	Based:	UK
Product Range:	★★★★	Express Delivery Option? (UK)	No
Price Range:	Medium	Gift Wrapping Option?	No
Delivery Area:	UK	Returns Procedure:	Down to you

www.thelocalfoodcompany.co.uk

Here you'll be ordering fresh, organic (and non-organic) Devon food, including bread rolls, cakes and biscuits (with some gluten free), cheeses, deli and fresh meat boxes, smoked salmon and duck, fruit and veg, drinks, and lots of other delicious-sounding goods. For most items they tell you which farm has supplied them and give you some information about them, which is excellent. The site offers hamper and gift ideas, plus household and non-food items as well.

Site Usability:	★★★	Based:	UK
Product Range:	★★★★	Express Delivery Option? (UK)	No
Price Range:	Medium	Gift Wrapping Option?	No
Delivery Area:	UK	Returns Procedure:	Down to you

www.thesussexwinecompany.co.uk

The Sussex Wine Company is an independent online wine merchant, which lists quality wine and spirits from around the world, all produced with attention to detail both in the vineyard and the winery. The organic wines start from £5.95 and some of the estates listed are Albet I Noya of Spain, Battle of Bosworth of Maclaren Vale in Australia, Bodegas Vina Ljalba of Rioja in Spain and Touchstone Organic from Argentina. The company aims for next-day delivery where possible.

Site Usability:	★★★★★	Based:	UK
Product Range:	★★★★	Express Delivery Option? (UK)	Yes, whenever possible
Price Range:	Luxury/Medium	Gift Wrapping Option?	No
Delivery Area:	UK	Returns Procedure:	Down to you

www.westcountryorganics.co.uk

There's a wide choice of organic food and drink here, from meat, vegetables and fruit, beer, wine and vegetarian products to pies, tofu, fish and cheese. This is an easy-to-navigate though unsophisticated website, so don't expect lots of beautiful 'foodie' pictures. However, with such an excellent selection of, in particular, vegetables, which you order using the box service, you should have a look round and give it a try.

Site Usability:	★★★★	Based:	UK
Product Range:	★★★★	Express Delivery Option? (UK)	You set the day for delivery
Price Range:	Medium	Gift Wrapping Option?	No
Delivery Area:	UK	Returns Procedure:	Down to you

Chapter 11

Gorgeous Gifts for New Mums

Inevitably if you have a friend who's just had a baby you're going to want to give/send them something. Your first idea will probably be flowers and you'll want to send them immediately, but stop for just a moment and consider.

Sometimes it's a better idea to wait a day or so until mum and baby have arrived home as, without a doubt, lots of flowers will have arrived at the hospital and will start to fade in the heated atmosphere. Have them delivered to the new baby's home and provided you don't choose something with a short shelf life, they'll last for a week or so.

Alternatively you can give something different, such as a fruit basket, bottle of champagne, special hamper or pampering gift. I'm a firm believer that new mothers need special presents at (sorry, but I'm going to say it) an absolutely marvellous but also very stressful time – after all, they did all the work, didn't they?

Sites to visit

www.albumania.com

Here's a website where you can find a unique kind of present. At Albumania you design your own photo album, box file, guest book, address book or diary. You just download a photograph (digitally), choose the colour of binding and ribbon, all online, then you can see exactly what the cover of your book will look like. While you're ordering you have the option of adding pages and a ribbon-tied card with your personal message. All the books are gift boxed and take about two weeks.

Site Usability:	★★★★★	Based:	UK
Product Range:	★★★	Express Delivery Option? (UK)	No
Price Range:	Medium	Gift Wrapping Option?	No
Delivery Area:	Worldwide	Returns Procedure:	Down to you

www.arenaflowers.com

Arena Flowers offers a pretty selection of hand-tied floral arrangements as new baby gifts, which you can accompany with a teddy bear, Prestat chocolates or a balloon. As there's such a wide range over all the categories I suggest you select by flower type or by the amount you want to spend. The sites offer a free UK next-day delivery service, plus a same-day service throughout the UK (which is free in London and the South East).

Site Usability:	★★★★★	Based:	UK
Product Range:	★★★★★	Express Delivery Option? (UK)	Yes
Price Range:	Medium	Gift Wrapping Option?	No
Delivery Area:	UK	Returns Procedure:	Down to you

www.astleyclarke.com

Originally I planned to put this wonderful online jeweller into the Perfect Gifts for Babies chapter, as it does have a small but lovely selection of bracelets perfect for new baby and christening presents. Then I decided that it really belonged here, where husbands and new grandparents can have a browse for something special for a new mum. Designers such as Coleman Douglas, Talisman Unlimited, Vinnie Day, Flora Astor and

Catherine Prevost offer truly special pieces. Prices start at around £50, then go skywards.

Site Usability:	★★★★★	Based:	UK
Product Range:	★★★★★	Express Delivery Option? (UK)	Yes
Price Range:	Luxury/Medium	Gift Wrapping Option?	Yes
Delivery Area:	Worldwide	Returns Procedure:	Down to you

www.babeswithbabies.com

This is a lovely place to buy a gift for a new mum (or if you are one, to treat yourself). It offers pretty, polka-dot mama and baby pyjamas, chic nursing tops, Superfluffie alpaca slippers, pampering gift sets and incredibly elegant baby bags as just some of its ideas. You can book baby portrait sessions and buy gift vouchers here as well.

Site Usability:	★★★★★	Based:	UK
Product Range:	★★★★	Express Delivery Option? (UK)	Yes, but call to arrange
Price Range:	Medium	Gift Wrapping Option?	Automatic
Delivery Area:	Worldwide	Returns Procedure:	Down to you

www.boutiquetoyou.co.uk

Boutique to You specialises in personalised gifts and jewellery perfect for new mums. It has also been responsible for introducing some cult jewellery brands from the USA, including Mummy & Daddy Tags, Lisa Goodwin New York and Fairy Tale Jewels. On the website there's a wish-list facility so you can send 'wish mails' to your nearest and dearest with hints of what you'd like to receive.

Site Usability:	★★★★	Based:	UK
Product Range:	★★★★	Express Delivery Option?	(UK) No
Price Range:	Medium	Gift Wrapping Option?	Yes
Delivery Area:	Worldwide	Returns Procedure:	Down to you

www.dreambabyuk.co.uk

There are lots of different types of new and expecting mum gifts here, so whether she's into natural, spa or the beautifully fragranced type of pampering, you'll find it on this site. There's also the *Booties Keepsake Book*, which comes in blue or pink (of course), *Beatrix Potter My First Year* book and Natalia New Parent Survival Kit. There are lots of other gifts here, including teddies and champagne, new baby gifts and food hampers.

Site Usability:	★★★★★	Based:	UK
Product Range:	★★★★	Express Delivery Option? (UK)	Yes
Price Range:	Luxury/Medium	Gift Wrapping Option?	No
Delivery Area:	Worldwide except for container roses and bouquets	Returns Procedure:	Email them first

www.fruit-4u.com

This company will put together the most mouthwatering mix of fresh fruit and present it beautifully in a basket so that you can send it as a gift. You'll find names such as the Exotic Fruit Basket and the Supreme Fruit Basket, both packed with perfect class 1 seasonal fruits. You can add cheese, wine, teddies and champagne to your selected basket.

Site Usability:	★★★★	Based:	UK
Product Range:	★★★	Express Delivery Option? (UK)	Yes
Price Range:	Medium	Gift Wrapping Option?	No
Delivery Area:	UK	Returns Procedure:	Down to you

www.janepackerdelivered.com

Here are the most beautifully presented, modern flowers to send as a gift or, if you want to give yourself a treat, to yourself. The range in her stores is much larger than what's offered online, but here you'll find roses, hyacinths, pink parrot tulips, orchids and mixed bouquets, all presented in her unique, chic style. You can buy Jane Packer's books, fragranced bath and body gifts, champagne and chocolates and gift vouchers here as well.

Site Usability:	★★★★★	Based:	UK
Product Range:	★★★	Express Delivery Option? (UK)	Yes
Price Range:	Luxury/Medium	Gift Wrapping Option?	Beautiful packaging
Delivery Area:	UK	Returns Procedure:	Only if faulty

www.jomalone.co.uk

Virtually anything from Jo Malone's wonderfully luxurious collection of pampering treats will make a lovely gift, from her Lime Basil and Mandarin Cologne to her Amber and Lavender shampoo and conditioner. This type of gift giving is not just about the products, it's about the whole atmosphere of relaxation and luxury they create. And as the packaging is gorgeous too, you need do no more than place your order and have it sent out for you (or better still, of course, deliver it yourself).

Site Usability:	★★★★★	Based:	UK
Product Range:	★★★★★	Express Delivery Option? (UK)	Yes
Price Range:	Luxury/Medium	Gift Wrapping Option?	Yes
Delivery Area:	UK	Returns Procedure:	Down to you

www.myfirstday.co.uk

There are so many wonderful gifts you can choose as a memento of a baby's birth, most of which fit into a specific category such as flowers, hampers or silver. Here's something totally different and very unusual, which I think is a lovely idea. Each day since mid-summer's day 2005, landscape photographer Gavan Goulder has taken stunning photographs of the Cornish coastline, so you can buy a beautifully framed photograph to mark the day of your (or a friend's) baby's birth. Take a look.

Site Usability:	★★★★★	Based:	UK
Product Range:	★★★	Express Delivery Option? (UK)	No
Price Range:	Luxury/Medium	Gift Wrapping Option?	No
Delivery Area:	Worldwide	Returns Procedure:	Down to you

www.passionleaf.com

If you'd like to give fruit as a gift but don't really want to send the same as everyone else, take a look here. Passionleaf creates quite amazing, real fruit bouquets (which currently it can deliver only within the M25) using strawberries, melons, oranges and pineapples, cut into pretty shapes and packed into wicker tubs. Just to look at this website will make your mouth water. You can add balloons and chocolate strawberries to your gift. Call to order.

Site Usability:	★★★	Based:	UK
Product Range:	★★★★	Express Delivery Option? (UK)	Yes
Price Range:	Luxury/Medium	Gift Wrapping Option?	No
Delivery Area:	UK within M25	Returns Procedure:	Down to you

www.savonneriesoap.com

This is a beautiful website with an extremely luxurious feel. You can buy exquisitely packaged handmade soaps (think Flower Garden and Honey Cake and Natural soap decorated with a shell), bath and body products such as Geranium and Bergamot Oil and Petit Grain bath crystals, plus a range of perfect gift boxes containing a selection of the products.

Site Usability:	★★★★	Based:	UK
Product Range:	★★★	Express Delivery Option? (UK)	Yes
Price Range:	Medium	Gift Wrapping Option?	Yes
Delivery Area:	Worldwide	Returns Procedure:	Down to you

www.thewhitecompany.com

This is one place I immediately turn to for gifts for friends who've just had a baby and for babies as well. It's a collection that just seems to get better all the time, with beautiful photography, reasonable prices and excellent service combining to make you want to buy much more than you set out to. Take a look at the supersoft towelling robes and pretty toiletry sets, or luxurious cushions and throws for mums. For babies there are cashmere shawls, satin-edged polar fleece blankets and gift sets.

Site Usability:	★★★★★	Based:	UK
Product Range:	★★★★★	Express Delivery Option? (UK)	Yes
Price Range:	Medium	Gift Wrapping Option?	Yes
Delivery Area:	Worldwide	Returns Procedure:	Down to you

www.virginiahayward.com

Established in 1984, Virginia Hayward offers a beautifully presented traditional range of gifts and hampers which would be perfect for new mothers. There's a wide choice of food- and wine-related gifts, plus pampering presents which you can send for mothers and babies. You can choose from a named or standard delivery and they'll deliver to BFPO addresses.

Site Usability:	★★★★★	Based:	UK
Product Range:	★★★★	Express Delivery Option? (UK)	Yes
Price Range:	Luxury/Medium	Gift Wrapping Option?	No
Delivery Area:	UK	Returns Procedure:	Down to you

www.vitaltouch.com

The New Parent Survival Kit is just one of the gifts you can order from this aromatherapy-based website which includes baby massage oil and New Parent Instant Revitaliser (I wish I'd been given that one). If you want something different and special, you can call them and they'll put a gift together for you. All of the products can be beautifully wrapped and sent out on your behalf with your personal message.

Site Usability:	★★★★	Based:	UK
Product Range:	★★★	Express Delivery Option? (UK)	No
Price Range:	Medium	Gift Wrapping Option?	Yes
Delivery Area:	Worldwide	Returns Procedure:	Down to you

www.winedancer.com

You can, of course, just walk into your local wine merchant and buy your bottle of bubbly then and there. Or you could do something a bit different and send a bottle of Veuve Clicquot in its very own ice bucket with your personalised card, or a boxed mini bottle of Laurent Perrier with a candle and bath essence. Alternatively you can arrange to have a personalised label created for a gift containing two or three bottles.

Site Usability:	★★★★	Based:	UK
Product Range:	★★★★	Express Delivery Option? (UK)	Yes
Price Range:	Luxury/Medium	Gift Wrapping Option?	No
Delivery Area:	Worldwide	Returns Procedure:	Down to you

Chapter 12

Baby Showers

aby showers have become a part of the event calendar and although helping expectant parents plan for a baby has been a tradition for centuries, the current types of celebration have reached us more recently from across the pond.

They've always served several purposes, allowing friends and family to share in the joy and excitement of the forthcoming baby and giving support for mums-to-be. They're also an opportunity to give both fun and practical gifts.

When I had my children (sorry, back to that again) we didn't go down the baby shower route – you were flooded with flowers and gifts once the baby was born, which was great, of course. However, the way things are done now, it's much easier to give something essential, useful and well thought out rather than something last minute.

On the websites below you'll find lots of ideas for baby showers at a range of prices, plus a great deal of advice and information – so if you're not clued up on this area yet, you soon will be.

**Your siteguide.com password is SG012. Please use this as the media code when subscribing for your free year's login.

Sites to Visit

www.babygiftgallery.co.uk

If you are organising a baby shower then Baby Gift Gallery will be delighted to host your gift list. The range here is lovely, so be prepared to take your time, and in particular take a look at the Doudou et Compagnie House of Barbotine gift boxes, Emile et Rose gifts and pretty keepsake boxes and photo albums. Then you might want to browse through baby gift boxes which you can customise yourself and babywear by Bob and Blossom, Emile et Rose, Inch Blue, Little Blue Dog, Toby Tiger and more.

Site Usability:	★★★★★	Based:	UK
Product Range:	★★★★★	Express Delivery Option? (UK)	Yes – call them
Price Range:	Luxury/Medium	Gift Wrapping Option?	Yes
Delivery Area:	Worldwide	Returns Procedure:	Down to you

www.babyshowerhost.co.uk

This is a very pretty website to browse around, offering well-priced items for baby showers which are all in themes, such as Little Angel, Mod Mums and Polka Dot Baby. Once you've established your theme you then choose from the complete range, which includes table stationery, banners, balloons, confetti and invites, plus announcement cards, favour bags and games. There are pretty gift ideas here as well.

Site Usability:	★★★★★	Based:	UK
Product Range:	★★★★★	Express Delivery Option? (UK)	Yes
Price Range:	Medium/Very Good Value	Gift Wrapping Option?	No
Delivery Area:	EU	Returns Procedure	Down to you

www.kittysash.com

If you don't want to buy everything for your baby shower in one place, this would be a perfect one to order high-quality baby shower invitations. The range is small but you can personalise it as you wish. You can also order your thank-you cards, cute birth announcements and pretty different christening invitations.

Site Usability: ★★★★	Based:	UK
Product Range: ★★★	Express Delivery Option? (UK)	No
Price Range: Medium	Gift Wrapping Option?	No
Delivery Area: UK		

www.mybabyshower.co.uk

The minute you click on to this pretty website you want to see more. It's beautifully designed and very clear, with links to everything you need from the Home Page. As far as products go, just click on Favours, Games, Gifts, Nappy Cakes (I have difficulty with this one) and Party Accessories to find a small, well-priced (but unfortunately not so well-photographed) range.

Site Usability: ★★★	Based:	UK
Product Range: ★★★	Express Delivery Option? (UK)	No
Price Range: Medium/Very Good Value	Gift Wrapping Option?	No
Delivery Area: UK	Returns Procedure	Down to you

www.puddleduckandrhubarb.com

This is a place where you'll find perfect gifts for baby showers and babies on a lovely website with an irresistible name. Just choose from the range of soft toys and keepsake boxes, cushions, comforters or fleecy slippers or, if you want something special and unique, one of the handmade, limited-edition gifts.

Site Usability: ★★★★★	Based:	UK
Product Range: ★★★	Express Delivery Option? (UK)	No
Price Range: Medium	Gift Wrapping Option?	Yes
Delivery Area: Worldwide, excluding US and Canada	Returns Procedure	Down to you

www.showermybaby.co.uk

If you're not quite sure what you're doing when you reach this website, read the 'Shower my Baby Quick Tip Guide', which will help send you on your way. Then you can choose from one of the complete (reasonably priced) packs, the pretty gifts, such as personalised plates and keepsake tins, and themed party stationery. There's an ethnic baby range here as well.

Site Usability: ★★★★	Based:	UK
Product Range: ★★★★	Express Delivery Option? (UK)	Yes
Price Range: Medium/Very Good Value	Gift Wrapping Option?	No
Delivery Area: UK	Returns Procedure	Down to you

www.snowflakeshowers.co.uk

The aim of Snowflake Showers is to equip you with complete, no-fuss baby shower kits that look like they took months to plan and because the same groups of mums and mums-to-be often attend each other's showers, Snowflake Showers provides small twists and tweaks that make each event slightly different. One of its kits is a Rule Book (just in case you don't know it all already), then there are hand-made invites and thank-you cards, balloons, confetti, table accessories, games and favours.

Site Usability: ★★★★	Based:	UK
Product Range: ★★★	Express Delivery Option? (UK)	No
Price Range: Luxury/Medium	Gift Wrapping Option?	No
Delivery Area: UK	Returns Procedure	Discuss with them if faulty

www.theshowershop.co.uk

This is an excellent website if you're considering having a baby shower, as not only can you find out everything you need to know about them in a delightfully simple and friendly way, but you will find a planning checklist, recipes for scones (afternoon tea, of course), The Ultimate Cheese Fondue and canapés (for an evening shower). You can also buy all the essentials such as invitations and tablewear, making this a good, well-priced, one-stop destination.

Site Usability: ★★★★★	Based:	UK
Product Range: ★★★	Express Delivery Option? (UK)	No
Price Range: Very Good Value	Gift Wrapping Option?	No
Delivery Area: EU	Returns Procedure	Discuss with them if faulty

Section 2
The Baby Book

Having searched the net for the best of the baby websites for you I've frankly been astonished by what's on offer. Here I go again, saying that there isn't anything you can't find online and, once again, I really mean it.

I'm not just talking about pretty romper suits, cots and wonderful gift ideas, although there are plenty of those, as you'll see from the websites below. But you'll also find every type of pram and buggy imaginable, from the traditional Silver Cross pram to one of the new, high-tech travel systems which convert from a buggy to a carrycot to a car seat. Forget the days when you had to wait for the attention of a salesperson (whom you'd hope would know everything) to come and serve you in a crowded shop. Now more information than you could possibly want or need is online to help you make your choice.

Children's furniture is another case in point. Take a look at the beautiful French-style, Houston Cream or Magellan Cherry beds, cots wardrobes and chests from www.baby-pages.co.uk and you'll see what I mean. You can let your imagination run wild and spend a small (large) fortune here or just buy one beautiful piece that'll last a lifetime – the styling and quality are simply superb.

Just one point here – although many of the baby equipment websites offer a wide selection of products (from buggies to car seats to complete room sets), I've listed most of them only once, under the section where they have the strongest presence. I do, however, tell you about the other products on offer in each case, so to find the full choice available in every area, make sure you have a good read through.

Chapter 13

Birth Announcements

You may like simple, traditionally printed cards or something colourful and far more modern. Either way you'll find a compre-hensive selection of possibilities here.

In most cases you can get your cards printed extremely fast, which is, of course, what you're going to need. Just one word of advice: because all of these sites rely on you in-putting the details, make sure you check the proof you're given really thoroughly and then get someone else to check it as well. Once they go to print it'll be too late and really frustrating if you find even the smallest mistake.

Sites to Visit

www.announceit.co.uk

Here you can find birth announcement cards in a large variety of styles and designs, folded or flat cards personalised to your specification, with ribbons, photos, hand-finished embellishments and contemporary and stylish graphics. You can also create cards for christening and baptism invitations and naming ceremonies and there's a small range of photo albums and other gifts.

Site Usability:	★★★★	Based:	UK
Product Range:	★★★★	Express Delivery Option? (UK)	No
Price Range:	Medium	Gift Wrapping Option?	No
Delivery Area:	Worldwide		

www.announcement-of-birth.co.uk

On this easy-to-use website you start by choosing the style of card you want, whether landscape, portrait or folded, then click on the quantity you need, enter your text and upload your image and you're done. The specification for each style of card is very clear and they can be used not only for birth announcements but for invitations and thank-you cards as well. They'll produce a large-format banner for you too.

Site Usability:	★★★★	Based:	UK
Product Range:	★★★	Express Delivery Option? (UK)	No
Price Range:	Medium/Very Good Value	Gift Wrapping Option?	No
Delivery Area:	UK		

www.babysayshello.com

This is a simple but clever website for birth announcements. Just choose a design from one of the templates, fill in the details of your baby's birth, download your favourite picture and you're away. Printing is speedy and they'll deliver worldwide. You can also have your announcement online on your personal web page where your friends and family can send you their best wishes to create your online 'guest book'.

Site Usability:	★★★★★	Based:	UK
Product Range:	★★★	Express Delivery Option? (UK)	No
Price Range:	Medium	Gift Wrapping Option?	No
Delivery Area:	Worldwide		

www.giftcorporation.com

Here's a collection of beautiful personalised candles for all occasions, including births and christenings. Once you've chosen your design (and there's a wide choice), you give them the baby's name and the date of birth as well as, for some candles, a photograph and/or a poem that you'd like included. You need to allow at least three weeks for your candles to arrive and they deliver all over the world.

Site Usability:	★★★★★	Based:	UK
Product Range:	★★★★★	Express Delivery Option? (UK)	No
Price Range:	Medium	Gift Wrapping Option?	No
Delivery Area:	Worldwide		

www.heritage-stationery.com

Heritage Stationery offers a traditional, personal service, creating high-quality stationery, mostly printed on the in-house letterpress which enables the company to offer a delivery time of 48 hours. The company specialises in traditional birth announcement cards, photo birth announcement cards, christening invitations and correspondence cards, plus social and wedding stationery. It also offers leather photograph albums, which can be personalised.

Site Usability:	★★★★★	Based:	UK
Product Range:	★★★★★	Express Delivery Option? (UK)	Yes
Price Range:	Luxury/Medium	Returns Procedure:	Only if faulty
Delivery Area:	UK		

www.letterpress.co.uk

The Letter Press specialises in traditional, high-quality stationery, offering a full service from birth announcements, personal stationery, wedding and evening invitations to reply cards, orders of service, menus, place cards and thank-you cards. The designs are based on simple, classical styles, which you can either adopt as they are or use as a starting point for your own design. You can add or adapt any of the features shown on the website, using decorative motifs, borders or ribbons, different ink or typefaces.

Site Usability:	★★★★★	Delivery Area:	UK
Product Range:	★★★★★	Based:	UK
Price Range:	Luxury/Medium	Express Delivery Option? (UK)	No

www.paperplain.net

Click through to the children's stationery here to find enchanting birth announcement cards, from traditionally embossed to the lovely toile Bunny Cards. Or choose from the Infant Cards range where you buy cards with pretty designs at the top to print yourself on your home computer. There are also children's party invitations, personalised foldover cards and thank-you cards. Where you are choosing to personalise an item, you'll need to approve a proof before they'll print.

Site Usability: ★★★	Delivery Area:	Worldwide
Product Range: ★★★	Based:	UK
Price Range: Medium/Very Good Value	Express Delivery Option? (UK)	No

www.storkpost.co.uk

Stork Post has sourced various ranges of high-quality cards from card houses and designers across Europe. Design features include transparent overlays, premium-quality inserts, pearl finishes, bows, ribbon and cord. For extra luxury, cards can be embossed or have a textured finish. Each card has a full design description – you personalise your cards and (if you want) download a picture. Delivery takes approximately ten days.

Site Usability: ★★★★★	Delivery Area:	UK
Product Range: ★★★★	Based:	UK
Price Range: Luxury/Medium	Express Delivery Option? (UK)	No

www.sweetbabyface.co.uk

This is an innovative website offering you the facility to create both greetings cards and birth announcements using your own digital pictures and personalised photo calendars which you can start on any month. The process is simple. You just click on the 'building blocks' and go through the clear instructions – you can start from scratch, continue from where you left off last time or reorder something you've already created. Give it a try.

Site Usability: ★★★★	Delivery Area:	UK – call them for overseas
Product Range: ★★★	Based:	UK
Price Range: Medium/Very Good Value	Express Delivery Option? (UK)	No

www.whole-caboodle.co.uk

At The Whole Caboodle you'll find enchanting designs for birth announcements, printed on high-quality paper and trimmed in pink or blue ribbon. Then there are matching christening invitations and scrolls, plus handmade photograph albums and keepsake boxes. This is a beautiful, modern and unfussy collection created with a huge amount of care.

Site Usability: ★★★★★	Delivery Area:	UK
Product Range: ★★★★★	Based:	UK
Price Range: Luxury/Medium	Express Delivery Option? (UK)	No

Chapter 14

Baby Equipment

W hat can I say? I'm sure you don't want me to talk about the huge (huge) amount of choice available here, although it's hard not to. I suggest that first you make a clear list so you know what you need. (You'll find plenty of list suggestions on the baby advice websites in Chapter 25 and on many of the websites below.) Then, unless you have clear ideas on what you want and/or don't want to spend hours and hours reading up on all the options, go to www.johnlewis.com where you'll find a really well-researched and edited range to inspect. For reviews, go to www.which.co.uk or look thoroughly through just one of the larger equipment websites.

For items such as buggies and car seats you can go to price comparison websites www.kelkoo.co.uk or www.uk.shopping.com to see who's offering the best price and check through the websites below for some of the fantastic and efficient new products on offer.

Sites to Visit

www.babybathshop.co.uk

For the Hip-O-Boat, Super Sub Sophie, Bubbles for the Tub or Splashy the Penguin, this is definitely the place as there are lots of fun bathtime toys to choose from. Going back to basics you can buy a pack of Pooh Bear Bath Splats (did I say basics?) to make sure your baby doesn't slip in the bath, wash mits, bath slings and the Bumbo Baby Sitter. So everything for bathtime as you can see.

Site Usability: ★★★★	Based:	UK
Product Range: ★★★★	Express Delivery Option? (UK)	No
Price Range: Medium	Gift Wrapping Option?	No
Delivery Area: UK	Returns Procedure	Down to you

www.babycare-direct.co.uk

One of the first places to check out on this friendly website is the Baby-list section, where you'll find helpful lists of what you'll need to have ready when your baby arrives (and what you will probably want to take with you to hospital). Then click through to Baby on the Move, with its wide range of clearly pictured and described buggies, prams and travel systems, and to Safety Equipment, where you'll find everything you'll need under Feeding Time, Baby Bedtime and Bath And Changing.

Site Usability: ★★★★★	Based:	UK
Product Range: ★★★★★	Express Delivery Option? (UK)	No
Price Range: Medium	Gift Wrapping Option?	Yes
Delivery Area: Worldwide	Returns Procedure	Down to you

www.babycity.co.uk

Designed in pale pink and blue, Baby City is a calming, well-laid out website offering lots of products, including baby clothes and accessories, monitors and safety equipment such as cot nets and toy ties. There are also useful but quite hard-to-find products such as nappy wrappers (!), steam sterilisers and bottle warmers and a range of products for premature babies. There are lots of gift ideas here as well.

Site Usability: ★★★★★	Based:	UK
Product Range: ★★★★	Express Delivery Option? (UK)	No
Price Range: Medium	Gift Wrapping Option?	Yes
Delivery Area: Worldwide	Returns Procedure	Down to you

www.babygurgles.co.uk

I have to say that I thought you had just about enough baby equipment websites to browse through when I came to this site, but when I read the question 'What is a Buggy Snuggle?' in the margin I knew you'd want to know. It is, of course, a cute version of just what you'd expect it to be, available in lots of different prints. There are other lovely things here, such as The Bug in a Rug Baby Wrap, Miracle swaddling blanket, Wheelie Bug toddler rides and lots of other basic and essential equipment. Take a look.

Site Usability:	★★★★★	Based:	UK
Product Range:	★★★★	Express Delivery Option? (UK)	No
Price Range:	Medium	Gift Wrapping Option?	No
Delivery Area:	UK	Returns Procedure	Down to you

www.babymonitorsdirect.co.uk

Baby Monitors Direct offers a wide range of easy-to-use baby monitors and safety products. The range includes digital audio, video and breathing monitors and it specialises in the new video monitors where you both hear and see your baby. All orders over £95 include free next-working-day delivery (to UK mainland) and a one-year guarantee.

Site Usability:	★★★★★	Based:	UK
Product Range:	★★★★★	Express Delivery Option? (UK)	Yes
Price Range:	Medium	Gift Wrapping Option?	No
Delivery Area:	UK	Returns Procedure	Down to you

www.babysecurity.co.uk

Yes, you can buy baby security items from most of the large online equipment retailers, but if you want to visit a specialist in this area then take a look at this website You can buy baby monitors, stair gates, safety glass film, cupboard locks, edge guards, outlet plugs and much more. There's also an excellent 'What's New' section where you can view all the latest products.

Site Usability:	★★★★★	Based:	UK
Product Range:	★★★★★	Express Delivery Option? (UK)	Yes
Price Range:	Medium	Gift Wrapping Option?	No
Delivery Area:	UK	Returns Procedure	Down to you

www.bambinomio.com

This is the place to buy all those baby essentials: cotton nappies and nappy covers, hypo allergenic and non-biological washing powder, laundry bags, muslin squares and special, cotton-lined swim nappies. You can find this brand in many of the online baby stores or you can order everything directly here. Delivery is extremely reasonable and they deliver worldwide.

Site Usability:	★★★★★	Based:	UK
Product Range:	★★★	Express Delivery Option? (UK)	No
Price Range:	Medium	Gift Wrapping Option?	No
Delivery Area:	Worldwide	Returns Procedure:	Down to you

www.hippychick.com

Hippychick specialises in discovering and developing innovative and original products for babies, such as the Clevamama baby bath towel, Art and Eater suits (guess), Hipseat baby carrier and Shoo shoes. You could find some of these products in the shops, but Hippychick has brought them together all in one easy-to-navigate website, where there's plenty of information on all the products and buying couldn't be easier.

Site Usability:	★★★★★	Based:	UK
Product Range:	★★★★	Express Delivery Option? (UK)	Yes
Price Range:	Medium	Gift Wrapping Option?	Yes
Delivery Area:	Worldwide	Returns Procedure:	Down to you

www.johnlewis.com

Click straight through to the Nursery section at John Lewis's excellent online store and I know you won't be surprised to find that you can buy just about everything here. As well as lovely furniture for nurseries there's excellent equipment: humidifiers, baby monitors, steam and microwave sterilisers, bottles, bibs and accessories. Typically with John Lewis you won't find a huge amount of choice but a well-edited range – they go quite simply for the best at each price level and have done a great deal of research for you.

Site Usability:	★★★★★	Based:	UK
Product Range:	★★★★	Express Delivery Option? (UK)	Yes
Price Range:	Luxury/Medium	Gift Wrapping Option?	No
Delivery Area:	UK	Returns Procedure:	Down to you

www.kiddicare.com

Kiddicare is a large, independent retailer of baby and nursery equipment and nursery furniture. It claims to keep everything in stock, ready to send out to you. You can buy Avent sterilisers and feeding bottles, Grobags, buggies and travel cots, highchairs, rockers and baby swings, plus equipment for the home including playpens, stair gates, cots, changing units and nursery furniture. Delivery is free to most of the UK and takes about four working days.

Site Usability:	★★★★★	Based:	UK
Product Range:	★★★★★	Express Delivery Option? (UK)	No
Price Range:	Medium	Gift Wrapping Option?	No
Delivery Area:	UK	Returns Procedure:	Down to you

www.kiddies-kingdom.com

This is a well-laid out website which helps you get to the product you're looking for with no fuss. So you can choose from highchairs, prams and pushchairs, buggy boards and travel systems, Moses baskets, cots and cribs, furniture and monitors and much, much more. The site offers all the premium brands and there's free delivery in the UK if you spend over £50, which you're almost certain to do.

Site Usability:	★★★★★	Based:	UK
Product Range:	★★★★★	Express Delivery Option? (UK)	Yes, automatic
Price Range:	Luxury/Medium	Gift Wrapping Option?	No
Delivery Area:	UK	Returns Procedure:	They collect most items

www.mamasandpapas.co.uk

This company combines great attention to detail, high-quality fabrics and pretty designs throughout its website. There's lovely clothing here for babies and toddlers, plus a wide range of equipment, with everything from car seats and travel cots to room sets and lots of gift ideas. This is a beautifully photographed website offering loads of advice on what to buy. They only deliver to the UK but you can click through to the US-based site.

Site Usability:	★★★★★	Based:	UK
Product Range:	★★★	Express Delivery Option? (UK)	No
Price Range:	Luxury/Medium	Gift Wrapping Option?	No
Delivery Area:	UK, but US site available	Returns Procedure:	Down to you

www.mothercare.com

It's hard to know where to put Mothercare, as it offers such a wide range of everything for mothers, babies and young children. There is some incredibly well-priced maternity wear, pushchairs, buggies and all sorts of travel systems, everything for the nursery, plus feeding and safety equipment, toys and gifts. The emphasis here is on simplicity and good pricing. There are excellent checklists for hospital bags, baby's first wardrobe and travel solutions and a great deal more information as well.

Site Usability:	★★★★★	Based:	UK
Product Range:	★★★★	Express Delivery Option? (UK)	No
Price Range:	Very Good Value	Gift Wrapping Option?	No
Delivery Area:	UK – enquire for overseas orders	Returns Procedure:	Down to you or to store

www.preciouslittleone.com

Here's an excellent baby equipment website offering, among other things, footmuffs, pushchairs and accessories with plenty of details to help you choose. There are also car seats and a good range for the nursery, including the high-quality Saplings range of furniture, most of which will take your child from baby to older years. You can even buy giant themed sticker sets for room decorating.

Site Usability:	★★★★★	Based:	UK
Product Range:	★★★★	Express Delivery Option? (UK)	No
Price Range:	Medium	Gift Wrapping Option?	No
Delivery Area:	Worldwide	Returns Procedure:	Down to you

www.snugnights.co.uk

Snug Nights specialises in mattress protectors for all sizes of bed, including cots. The soft cotton towelling cot sheets have a breathable polyurethane membrane on the underside as well as being waterproof. You can also buy Safebaby Sleeper units and machine-washable changing mats here, plus anti-allergy mattress covers for beds 2'6" and up.

Site Usability:	★★★	Based:	UK
Product Range:	★★★	Express Delivery Option? (UK)	No
Price Range:	Medium	Gift Wrapping Option?	No
Delivery Area:	Worldwide	Returns Procedure:	Down to you

www.tesco.com

You may not immediately think of Tesco when you're considering buying baby equipment online. However, when you discover that the site offers baby monitors, security essentials, car seats, buggies, cots and other equipment on its easy-to-navigate website, plus the fact that you can compare up to four items together so that you see not just the price but the essential details of each on one page, you may well be tempted to take a look here. Expect very good prices and excellent service.

Site Usability: ★★★★★		Based:	UK
Product Range: ★★★★		Express Delivery Option? (UK)	Yes
Price Range: Very Good Value		Gift Wrapping Option?	No
Delivery Area: UK		Returns Procedure:	Return to store or arrange collection

www.thebaby.co.uk

Don't be put off by the tremendous range here, including Mountain Buggy Prams, Simon Horn and Wigwam Kids furniture, Stevenson Rocking Horses and so much more. Whatever you're looking for, for your baby or child, you'll probably find it, whether you need travel accessories, full room sets or baby accessories such as highchairs and monitors. They offer a next-day delivery service and will ship worldwide, although some items are restricted by weight.

Site Usability: ★★★		Based:	UK
Product Range: ★★★★★		Express Delivery Option? (UK)	Yes
Price Range: Luxury/Medium		Gift Wrapping Option?	Yes
Delivery Area: Worldwide		Returns Procedure:	Down to you

www.tommeetippee.co.uk

This is an extremely well-known brand for babies. On the attractive website you can find most of the products, ranging from feeding equipment such as breast pumps, bottles and teats, electric and cold water sterilisers, to soothers, teethers, excellent baby monitors and baby toys, plus its own brand of Cotton Bottoms nappies. It's a beautifully laid out website with helpful information – well worth having a look at.

Site Usability: ★★★★	Based:	UK
Product Range: ★★★	Express Delivery Option? (UK)	No
Price Range: Medium	Gift Wrapping Option?	No
Delivery Area: UK	Returns Procedure:	Down to you

www.twoleftfeet.co.uk

This is a fantastic baby equipment website claiming to offer the largest selection in the UK. Browse through the sections offering cots and baby bedding, pushchairs, prams and the latest buggies, car seats, cribs and rocking horses and just about everything in between. Premium brands include Silver Cross, Bebe Confort, Chicco, Britax and Maclaren. You'll also find lovely children's furniture here.

Site Usability: ★★★★★	Based:	UK
Product Range: ★★★★★	Express Delivery Option? (UK)	Yes
Price Range: Medium	Gift Wrapping Option?	No
Delivery Area: Most EU, plus the USA	Returns Procedure:	Down to you

Chapter 15

Organic and Eco-friendly Baby Products

Closely following the trend for 'green' products are these websites offering every organic item you can think of for babies, from skincare to clothes and organic and eco-friendly nappies. Some of the ranges are a bit too natural for me (in colour and style, I mean), but others are gorgeous, with soft, fleecy jackets, pure cotton velour sleepsuits and fragrant, natural skincare.

The nappies I'm not going to comment on, that one's totally up to you. Either way, if you want the disposable kind, totally organic or something in between, you can buy it all online. Most supermarkets offer a good choice as well.

Sites to Visit

www.adili.com

This is a beautifully designed organic fashion website, offering clothes for adults as well as babies and young children. In the babies' section you can buy hand-loomed jackets and reversible patchwork dungarees, plus enchanting snuggle and sleepsuits, sleeping bags, bibs and organic cotton nappies. The girls' and boys' clothing ranges go up to five years.

Site Usability:	★★★★★	Based:	UK
Product Range:	★★★★	Express Delivery Option? (UK)	Yes
Price Range:	Medium	Gift Wrapping Option?	No
Delivery Area:	Worldwide	Returns Procedure	Down to you

www.aravore-babies.com

Aravore Babies' clothes and bedding are made from 100% certified organic cotton grown by small farmers in Paraguay. Beautifully made and incredibly soft, each item has its own particular charm and identity. The essential collection includes luxuriously soft baby wraps and blankets, matching hats, mittens and booties and exquisitely knitted cardigans and ponchos. Each season new items are introduced into the collection as well as a small selection of limited-edition items.

Site Usability:	★★★★★	Based:	UK
Product Range:	★★★★★	Express Delivery Option? (UK)	Yes – call them to arrange
Price Range:	Medium	Gift Wrapping Option?	No
Delivery Area:	Worldwide	Returns Procedure	Down to you

www.beamingbaby.co.uk

Some of the organic websites are very green and not as inspiring as they could be to buy from. This one is totally different – attractive and easy to use, it positively makes you want to stop and browse the product range. Shop here for nappies, organic and natural baby wipes, bedding and Moses baskets, cotton organic towels, bath and baby products and baby clothes.

Site Usability:	★★★★★	Based:	UK
Product Range:	★★★	Express Delivery Option? (UK)	Yes
Price Range:	Medium	Gift Wrapping Option?	No
Delivery Area:	UK	Returns Procedure	Down to you

www.earthlets.co.uk

Here you'll find a wide range of organic baby products at very reasonable prices. They're not trying to seduce you with an ultra-sophisticated website but just offer you a full, natural range, from cloth nappies and accessories such as organic cotton wool, to natural toiletries, home safety products such as protective corners and bath thermometers, and plenty of other essentials for feeding, sleeping and playtime.

Site Usability:	★★★	Based:	UK
Product Range:	★★★★	Express Delivery Option? (UK)	No
Price Range:	Medium/Very Good Value	Gift Wrapping Option?	No
Delivery Area:	UK	Returns Procedure:	Down to you

www.ecotopia.co.uk

Ecotopia, established in 2002 with assistance from the Prince's Trust, prides itself on supplying a massive range of interesting and useful environmentally friendly and natural products. So you'll find biodegradable and reusable nappies by Bambino Mio and Moltex; Natracare, Lavera and Green Baby natural bath and beauty products; a small range of organic cotton baby clothes; and handmade rubberwood toys.

Site Usability:	★★★★	Based:	UK
Product Range:	★★★★	Express Delivery Option? (UK)	No
Price Range:	Medium/Very Good Value	Gift Wrapping Option?	No
Delivery Area:	Worldwide	Returns Procedure:	Down to you

www.globalkids.co.uk

Globalkids is a family-run business set up to make the benefits of organic clothing more widely available and affordable. The range has grown to include baby bedding, natural skincare, fair trade toys, books and crafts. The excellent baby basics include towels, vests and sleepsuits and there are cute clothes for toddlers as well.

Site Usability:	★★★★	Based:	UK
Product Range:	★★★★	Express Delivery Option? (UK)	No
Price Range:	Very Good Value	Gift Wrapping Option?	Yes
Delivery Area:	Worldwide	Returns Procedure:	Down to you

www.greenbaby.co.uk

Through its friendly and extremely busy website, Greenbaby offers its core ranges of supersoft, organic cotton clothing and nappies (both eco-disposable and organic washable). There are natural bath products, teats, bottles, bibs and sterilisers, laundry products and just about all the other essentials you could need. There's also a lovely range of sheepskin rugs, seat liners, bootees and mittens.

Site Usability:	★★★★	Based:	UK
Product Range:	★★★★	Express Delivery Option? (UK)	Yes, but call them
Price Range:	Medium	Gift Wrapping Option?	No
Delivery Area:	Worldwide	Returns Procedure:	Down to you

www.hejhog.co.uk

This is a good website to use for natural and organic products, although the information is rather sparse until you get to the actual products themselves. The brands on offer are Engel, Mini Milou, Lana, Simply Soaps, for bath and skincare, Badger Balms, Naturally Fresh deodorants and Hedgerow Herbal wash grains and bath bags. It is worth looking at as there are some lovely products and they deliver worldwide, but more information would be great.

Site Usability:	★★★	Based:	UK
Product Range:	★★★★	Express Delivery Option? (UK)	Yes
Price Range:	Medium	Gift Wrapping Option?	No
Delivery Area:	Worldwide	Returns Procedure:	Down to you

www.huggababy.co.uk

Huggababy was founded in 1995 by Margaret Hastings, who designed the Huggababy carrier as a solution for her baby who didn't want to be put down. It has now grown into a multi-product company, with all the items being sourced in the UK. Natural products include the original baby carrier, plus organic lambskins, handmade leather shoes, soft merino wool sleeping bags, cot blankets and nappies.

Site Usability:	★★★★	Based:	UK
Product Range:	★★★	Express Delivery Option? (UK)	No
Price Range:	Medium	Gift Wrapping Option?	No
Delivery Area:	Worldwide	Returns Procedure:	Down to you

www.lulasapphire.com

Focusing on safety, functionality and style, Lula Sapphire is more than just a baby and toddler shop – it's designed for new parents who want high-quality everyday essentials that nurture growth, foster imagination and care about the environment. You'll find unique designs, including award-winning swaddling blankets, bouncers and chairs, monitors, thermometers, breast pumps and baby gyms, plus organic skincare and eco-friendly nappies.

Site Usability:	★★★★★	Based:	UK
Product Range:	★★★★★	Express Delivery Option? (UK)	Yes
Price Range:	Medium	Gift Wrapping Option?	Yes
Delivery Area:	Worldwide for most items	Returns Procedure:	Down to you

www.mini-organic.co.uk

Yes, this is, literally, organics for the minis, so expect to find lots of natural, unbleached and naturally dyed (and very, very cute) baby clothes from bodysuits, kimono daysuits and stripy rompers to fleece hoodie tops, cords and cargo pants. Sizing runs from 0 to 2 years and you can clearly see what's available right now in each item and colour. There are organic bathtime products here too.

Site Usability:	★★★★★	Based:	UK
Product Range:	★★★	Express Delivery Option? (UK)	Yes
Price Range:	Medium/Very Good Value	Gift Wrapping Option?	Yes
Delivery Area:	EU and USA		

www.spiritofnature.co.uk

On this attractively designed website you can order organic baby and children's clothing up to eight years. The range includes pretty basics such as velour rompers, stripy t-shirts, rain clothing, organic fleece, underwear, nightwear and eco-friendly biodegradable nappies. There's also a collection of high-quality wooden toys for babies, toddlers and pre-schoolers designed to encourage motor skills, hand–eye coordination and imagination through play, using vibrant, non-toxic colours containing no PVC or plastic.

Site Usability:	★★★★★	Based:	UK
Product Range:	★★★★	Express Delivery Option? (UK)	Yes, if you call them before 2pm
Price Range:	Medium/Very Good Value	Gift Wrapping Option?	No
Delivery Area:	Worldwide	Returns Procedure:	Down to you

www.thegreenparent.co.uk

This is the magazine for anyone who wants to follow the organic and eco-friendly way of life, as it covers all aspects of the family from birth to alternative education, eco house and nutrition. Each issue contains a range of features and regular items, including book reviews, food and drink, health and beauty, ethical fashion and green travel. You can order the magazine to be sent out to you or read it online and you can buy the recommended products here as well.

Site Usability:	★★★★★	Based:	UK
Product Range:	★★★	Express Delivery Option? (UK)	No
Price Range:	Medium/Very Good Value	Gift Wrapping Option?	No
Delivery Area:	Worldwide	Returns Procedure:	Down to you

www.totsbots.com

Coming from a generation that moved firmly (and with great speed) away from reusable nappies, it seems to me that the world has turned completely on its head and more and more people are switching back to them. At totsbots.com you'll find a range of reusable nappies in lots of different colours and with colourful printed wraps and fleeces to put on top. Also waterproof and laundry bags, nappy pins and booster liners.

Site Usability:	★★★	Based:	UK
Product Range:	★★★	Express Delivery Option? (UK)	No
Price Range:	Medium	Gift Wrapping Option?	No
Delivery Area:	UK	Returns Procedure:	Down to you

Chapter 16

Specially for Twins and Close-in-Age Tinies

This is an area I really do know something about – not that I had twins, but my first two boys are only thirteen months apart. Don't ask me why I did it, I really haven't a clue, and now I can only wonder at my intrepidness (I thought I'd use that rather than daftness or madness). Twins are one thing, but choosing to have two so close is something entirely different.

There are now some excellent products for twins, particularly in the buggy area as high-tech tandem or side-by-side buggies have developed hugely in the past few years. They seem to be much lighter, easier to travel with and much, much easier to fold down than before. There are also some excellent products for close-in-age babies, such as the clever BuggyPod which you'll find below. Now I could have done with one of those.

Sites to Visit

www.2became4.com

Visit this website particularly if you have a tiny already and you're expecting another as it sells the BuggyPod, which attaches to your existing buggy so you can carry both without having to invest in a double buggy. The site also has lots of other essential gear for twin and triplet travel, including some well-priced Marco double side-by-side and tandem buggies.

Site Usability:	★★★★★	Based:	UK
Product Range:	★★★★	Express Delivery Option? (UK)	No
Price Range:	Medium	Gift Wrapping Option?	No
Delivery Area:	Worldwide	Returns Procedure:	Down to you

www.babyequipmentcomplete.com

There's a good range of buggies and travel systems here, plus cots, bathtime essentials, car seats, bouncers and bedding for singles. There's also an excellent choice of tandem and side-by-side buggies for twins, including those by Maclaren, Chicco, Cosatto, Jane and Outnabout, and a wide range of prices from just over £100 to around £300. The information is not over detailed but clear and simple and there are some good sale discounts.

Site Usability:	★★★★★	Based:	UK
Product Range:	★★★★	Express Delivery Option? (UK)	Yes
Price Range:	Medium	Gift Wrapping Option?	No
Delivery Area:	UK	Returns Procedure:	Down to you

www.jusonne.co.uk

Jusonne has a large selection of special products for twins, including cot dividers, stroller connectors, bottle props, twin float and swim rings, twin carriers, wagons and travellers and even a twin Moses basket. As you'd expect it also has an excellent selection of side-by-side or tandem buggies (and triple buggies too), which would be perfect for twins or tinies close in age.

85

Site Usability:	★★★★	Based:	UK
Product Range:	★★★★★	Express Delivery Option? (UK)	No
Price Range:	Medium	Gift Wrapping Option?	No
Delivery Area:	Worldwide	Returns Procedure:	Down to you

www.tamba.org.uk

This is the Twins and Multiple Births Association, the nationwide UK charity providing information and mutual support networks for families of twins, triplets and more. It operates a national Freephone helpline, Twinline, a confidential, support, listening and information service for all parents of twins, triplets and more. If you're expecting twins you should definitely have a look round here.

www.twinsmagazine.com

This US-based website has a real wealth of information in the 'Expecting Twins' and 'Twins Resources' sections. You can read the articles, contact other organisations and browse the bookshelf where you'll find titles such as *The Multiples Manual* and *The Art of Parenting Twins*. Although they will ship to the UK, it's extremely expensive, so I suggest you go to www.amazon.com and order the books there.

www.twinsonline.co.uk

Twinsonline is a UK-based website which offers information, advice and moral support to parents and anyone pregnant with twins. It covers most aspects of parenting from pregnancy and birth to the first few days. There's also a section which deals with twin specifics which are common problems that can occur at any age.

www.twinsthings.co.uk

Obviously you don't have to buy two of everything here, but the emphasis on this website is definitely on double changing bags (designed for double buggies), twin cots, twin and triplet reins, twin slogan t-shirts and other gifts. Having said that, it's extremely well stocked with loads of other baby essentials you don't easily find elsewhere, such as bottle warmers, cup holders, ID wristbands and toy ties, so whether you're producing one or more, you'll probably find ideas here.

Site Usability:	★★★★	Based:	UK
Product Range:	★★★★	Express Delivery Option? (UK)	Yes — call them
Price Range:	Medium	Gift Wrapping Option?	No
Delivery Area:	UK, but call for overseas enquiries	Returns Procedure:	Down to you

www.twinsuk.co.uk

Here's an excellent resource offering lots of practical advice and information and set up by parents of twins, so they really should know what they're talking about. The information runs from pregnancy to pre-school and includes product reviews, plus an excellent online shop where you can buy just about everything, including feeding accessories, buggies, gifts and well-priced clothing. If you're expecting twins you'll need this site.

Site Usability:	★★★★★	Express Delivery Option? (UK)	No
Product Range:	★★★★★	Gift Wrapping Option?	No
Price Range:	Medium/Very Good Value	Returns Procedure:	Down to you, but they charge a
Delivery Area:	Worldwide		restocking fee
Based:	UK		

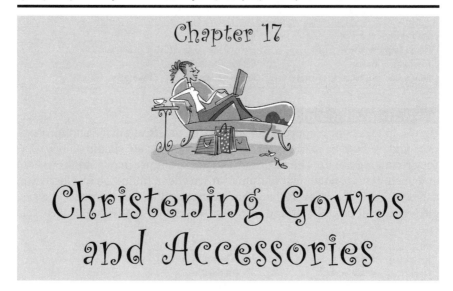

Chapter 17

Christening Gowns and Accessories

I f you aren't lucky enough to have been handed down a real heirloom christening gown (I wasn't), you may want to go for broke here – and you certainly can: you can spend hundreds of pounds at some of the designers below.

Alternatively you may feel you'd like to buy something a bit more reasonable and you'll find a beautiful selection of really good-value (and high-quality) gowns, rompers, shawls, jackets and accessories to look through. You can have great fun here and get totally carried away.

Sites to Visit

www.christening-gowns.com

This website comes to you from fantastic children's online retailer Mischief Kids. Here you can buy from the Heirloom Christening Collection of British-made gowns and rompers at a wide choice of prices. The site also offers all the accessories (jackets, shawls, hats and bootees) to go with the gowns and you can have them embroidered as well.

Site Usability:	★★★★	Based:	UK
Product Range:	★★★★★	Express Delivery Option? (UK)	Yes
Price Range:	Luxury/Medium	Gift Wrapping Option?	No
Delivery Area:	Worldwide	Returns Procedure:	Down to you

www.christeningwear.co.uk

This is a beautifully designed website for christening gowns and so it should be, for here you'll find true designer quality at designer prices. Whichever style you choose, when you click on 'larger view' you get a great deal of detail so you can clearly see embroidery, buttons, bows and ribbons. Everything here is designed by Pamela Kennedy (who started by designing wedding dresses). This would be a wonderful place to choose something really special.

Site Usability:	★★★★★	Based:	UK
Product Range:	★★★	Express Delivery Option? (UK)	No
Price Range:	Luxury	Gift Wrapping Option?	No
Delivery Area:	Worldwide	Returns Procedure:	Down to you

www.honfleur.co.uk

Honfleur claims to hold stock of all its christening gowns and accessories so you won't have to wait for one to be specially made for you. The range is well priced, with gowns starting at around £80. The company offers the collections of Collins and Hall, Little Darlings and Christine Ann and has a special winter christening selection. It's a busy website but well worth having a look round.

Site Usability:	★★★	Based:	UK
Product Range:	★★★★	Express Delivery Option? (UK)	Yes
Price Range:	Medium	Gift Wrapping Option?	No
Delivery Area:	Worldwide	Returns Procedure:	Down to you

www.poshtotsonline.co.uk

From the picture on this retailer's Home Page you can immediately see that it offers some beautiful baby clothes. Click through to the online shop and the christening section and although I have to say that the pictures don't really do the collection justice, there's a lot to look through, including pretty cotton knitted jackets, bibs and bonnets. Prices for dresses start at around £60.

Site Usability:	★★★	Based:	UK
Product Range:	★★★★	Express Delivery Option? (UK)	Yes
Price Range:	Medium/Very Good Value	Gift Wrapping Option?	No
Delivery Area:	Worldwide	Returns Procedure:	Down to you

www.sundaybest.com

Here you'll find christening robes by Rosemary Taylor, Collins and Hall, Claire de Lune and Sarah Louise, with a wide choice of styles and prices from around £60 to £400. It's great to be able to see all of these in one place and to be able to choose from the classic, sweet and simple to beautifully embroidered silk and lace without having to switch to another website.

Site Usability:	★★★★	Based:	UK
Product Range:	★★★★★	Express Delivery Option? (UK)	Yes, worldwide express
Price Range:	Luxury/Medium	Gift Wrapping Option?	No
Delivery Area:	Worldwide	Returns Procedure:	Down to you

www.susanlawson.co.uk

Susan Lawson designs beautiful, high-quality christening gowns which you can see in detail on her website and then request delivery anywhere in the world. These are real heirloom gowns, some of which are limited editions, made of silk, lace and embroidered organza. You can buy embroidered shawls, jackets and handmade silk booties here as well.

Site Usability:	★★★★★	Based:	UK
Product Range:	★★★★	Express Delivery Option? (UK)	No
Price Range:	Luxury/Medium	Gift Wrapping Option?	No
Delivery Area:	Worldwide	Returns Procedure:	Down to you in agreement with them

Also look at the following websites for christening gowns and accessories:

www.balloonsweb.co.uk
www.thekidswindow.co.uk
www.mamasandpapas.co.uk
www.babycity.co.uk

Chapter 18

Baby and Pre-school Toys

There are two kinds of baby toy websites: those that think you should be teaching your child from the year dot (and you probably should, to some extent) and those who think that toys are just that: fun things to play with. From what I can see a bit of both is essential, although the best of all options is obviously to combine the fun with the learning – something most of these websites seem to do well.

So here you can see plenty of choice and click through from the toys to the learning games with ease. It's a wonderful area to choose treats for your child and a great place for gifts as well.

Sites to Visit

www.amazon.co.uk

I doubt that you still think of Amazon as just an amazing place to buy books, but just in case you do you ought to take a look at its baby toy department (in Games and Toys). You may be horrified by the fact that the first page shows you only 24 out of almost 3000 items, but my advice is to take a look at the menu on the left and choose the amount you roughly want to spend (unless you know the specific brand, which I never do). There's always going to be almost too much to see at Amazon, but who can complain?

Site Usability: ★★★★★	Based:	UK
Product Range: ★★★★★	Express Delivery Option? (UK)	Yes
Price Range: Luxury/Medium/Very Good Value	Gift Wrapping Option?	Yes
Delivery Area: Worldwide	Returns Procedure:	Down to you

www.babydazzlers.com

This company aims to offer you toys that combine the elements of fun with teaching, so as well as lots of toys and craft kits to buy there's a great deal of advice on what you should be choosing (and what your child should be doing) at each stage from birth to five years. It's an excellent resource (as well as a great shop) and I just wish it had been around when I had my kids.

Site Usability: ★★★★★	Based:	UK
Product Range: ★★★★★	Express Delivery Option? (UK)	Yes, but call them
Price Range: Medium	Gift Wrapping Option?	Yes
Delivery Area: UK and call for overseas	Returns Procedure:	Down to you

www.baby-toys.co.uk

Here you can find Imogene Rabbit, Twaddles Osgood and Thelonious Monkey, Ziggles, Garden to Go and Wrap Along Bee, so if you're not quite yet into the brainteasers and early learning ideas you can order from most of the websites in this section, order something gorgeous from here that will probably become a lifelong friend for your child. (Tigger and Giraffe, are you listening?)

Site Usability: ★★★★★	Based:	UK
Product Range: ★★★★	Express Delivery Option? (UK)	No
Price Range: Medium	Gift Wrapping Option?	No
Delivery Area: Worldwide	Returns Procedure:	Down to you

www.beyondtherainbow.co.uk

This is a marvellous website for toys and games for your pre-schooler. Not only is it colourful, fun and well laid out, but there's a wide selection, in sections such as Bashing and Banging (great for small boys), Pull and Push Along Toys and Activity Toys, as well as the straightforward learning variety. There are some great wall charts to help to learn to tell the time and to spell, plus the Maths Bus. Delivery is free on orders over £50.

Site Usability:	★★★★★	Based:	UK
Product Range:	★★★★★	Express Delivery Option? (UK)	Yes
Price Range:	Luxury/Medium	Gift Wrapping Option?	No
Delivery Area:	UK	Returns Procedure:	Down to you

www.brightminds.co.uk

There's no messing around here. This online retailer is right on the early learning button, with over 1000 games, puzzles, flash cards, books, CD Roms and charts to help your child develop essential literacy, numeracy and creative skills. Select the area you're interested in, be it maths, English, science or history (or geography, foreign languages or music) and go from there.

Site Usability:	★★★★★	Based:	UK
Product Range:	★★★★★	Express Delivery Option? (UK)	Yes
Price Range:	Medium	Gift Wrapping Option?	No
Delivery Area:	Worldwide	Returns Procedure:	Down to you

www.dillongreen.co.uk

Dillon Green specialises in soft toys and other treats for babies, with Steiff and Jelly Cat being the main brands. Then there are microwavable bears (they're filled with treated wheat grains and lavender flowers so you can warm them up safely), Minimink gorgeous fake-fur scarves, hats and bootees, Miamoo products such as Cuddle Cream and Splashy Wash. Finally, for mums, you'll find Mama Mio pregnancy body treats.

Site Usability:	★★★★★	Based:	UK
Product Range:	★★★	Express Delivery Option? (UK)	Yes
Price Range:	Medium	Gift Wrapping Option?	No
Delivery Area:	Worldwide	Returns Procedure:	Down to you

www.elc.co.uk

The baby and toddler section at the Early Learning Centre's colourful website is well worth having a look round, as you'll find a wide range perfect for starting your baby off. There are bath toys, Blossom Farm baby toys, buggy and cot toys and just about every other type of baby toy you can think of. The site makes it easy for you to choose by listing type of toy or themes such as Action and Adventure and Art and Music.

Site Usability:	★★★★★	Based:	UK
Product Range:	★★★★★	Express Delivery Option? (UK)	Yes
Price Range:	Medium/Very Good Value	Gift Wrapping Option?	No
Delivery Area:	UK	Returns Procedure:	Free – collection or Freepost

www.gamleys.co.uk

Action Man, Bratz Dolls, Dora the Explorer (love that one), Little Tikes, My Little Pony, Peppa Pig, Pixel Chix (!?), Pocoyo, Polly Pocket and Power Rangers are just some of the brands on offer here. Then for tinies there are pre-school toys by Fisher Price, Mega Bloks, Teletubbies and Tomy. Provided you stick to the clear menus of categories and brands, you shouldn't get lost; go off on a tangent and you almost certainly will be.

Site Usability:	★★★★★	Based:	UK
Product Range:	★★★★★	Express Delivery Option? (UK)	No
Price Range:	Medium	Gift Wrapping Option?	No
Delivery Area:	UK	Returns Procedure:	Down to you

www.izziwizzikids.co.uk

I really like this website. At moments when you just can't look at another colourful and busy online retailer where there's (probably) too much choice, you can calm down here. Izzi Wizzi specialises in toys for babies up to one year old. For each product (Tooting Teddy or Old MacDonald's Noisy Barn, for example) it gives you just the right amount of information. You can browse by age, product type or category and they deliver throughout the EU.

Site Usability:	★★★★	Based:	UK
Product Range:	★★★	Express Delivery Option? (UK)	Yes
Price Range:	Medium	Gift Wrapping Option?	No
Delivery Area:	EU	Returns Procedure:	Down to you

www.minimarvellous.co.uk

Don't be surprised when the address for this website changes to bloom-ingmarvellous.co.uk, as this is the 'mini' section of the excellent baby and maternity clothing company of the same name. The site has a good range of toys for kids of two to eight years, including activity toys, arts and crafts, playsets, early learning, books and DVDs. Expect good prices, a good choice and really good service here.

Site Usability:	★★★★★	Based:	UK
Product Range:	★★★★★	Express Delivery Option? (UK)	No
Price Range:	Medium/Very Good Value	Gift Wrapping Option?	No
Delivery Area:	Worldwide	Returns Procedure:	Down to you

www.smartbabyzone.co.uk

Smart Baby Zone provides a range of toys under headings such as Smart Toys, Smart Music and Smart PC. They are designed not only to entertain your child but also to encourage them to discover and explore their surroundings and develop new skills. The categories have been sub-divided by age to make choosing as easy as possible. Once you click on an item you can see exactly which development category it's designed for.

Site Usability:	★★★★★	Based:	UK
Product Range:	★★★★	Express Delivery Option? (UK)	Yes
Price Range:	Medium	Gift Wrapping Option?	No
Delivery Area:	UK and email for overseas deliveries	Returns Procedure:	Down to you

www.theentertainer.com

This is one of the largest independent toy retailers in the UK, with a huge range and an excellent, easy-to-navigate website where you can search by brand, type of toy, age group or price. Once you've decided what you want to buy and registered both your address and any addresses to which you want your orders despatched, you simply select from the standard or express delivery services, give your payment details and you're done.

Site Usability:	★★★★★	Based:	UK
Product Range:	★★★★★	Express Delivery Option? (UK)	Yes
Price Range:	Medium	Gift Wrapping Option?	No
Delivery Area:	Worldwide	Returns Procedure:	Down to you

www.toysbymailorder.co.uk

Toys by Mail Order specialises in toys, gifts, games, nursery items and jigsaw puzzles for children of all ages. You can search the range of wooden toys and soft toys for baby and toddler gifts, the many items stocked for older boys and girls, plus traditional family games. The site offers fast delivery, a gift wrapping service and personalised messages for special occasions. As well as all this you'll find Manhattan bootees, puppets, dolls, puzzles and games for when they're a little older.

Site Usability:	★★★★	Based:	UK
Product Range:	★★★★★	Express Delivery Option? (UK)	Yes, two-day service
Price Range:	Medium	Gift Wrapping Option?	No
Delivery Area:	Worldwide	Returns Procedure:	Down to you

Chapter 19

Travel Made Easy

First choose the type of pram, buggy or travel system that you want. Needless to say, this will take quite a lot of research, but it's important to do it properly as you'll spend as much money here as on anything else and you definitely don't want to get it wrong.

Some of the baby magazines (and *Which?*) have comprehensive features detailing the latest travel options for babies which are well worth reading, particularly as they are independent. Otherwise you can do all your research online at one of the larger baby stores.

Once you've decided which one you want to go for, you'll want to use a price-comparison website such as www.kelkoo.co.uk or www.uk.shopping. com to see where the best deals are – you'll be surprised at the wide range of prices offered. I know I've mentioned this before, but it's a good thing to keep in mind.

The same goes for car seats and any other type of branded equipment – it's always worthwhile checking prices to find the latest deals.

Sites to Visit

www.activebambino.co.uk

ActiveBambino specialises in the high-quality LittleLife baby carrier, travel bed and travel cot product range. So you'll find perfect products for the walking, hiking and general active life enthusiast in the LittleLife Ultralight, Voyager and Cross Country structured carriers. There are also excellent child and parent backpacks, compact travel cots and all the relevant accessories. This is a small but excellent range.

Site Usability:	★★★★★	Based:	UK
Product Range:	★★★	Express Delivery Option? (UK)	Yes
Price Range:	Medium	Gift Wrapping Option?	No
Delivery Area:	UK	Returns Procedure:	Down to you

www.baby-pages.co.uk

Baby Pages offers you the choice of prams and travel systems by Silver Cross, Bebe Confort, Quinny, Micralite, Bugaboo and Britax. Then there are accessories such as bags, buggy liners and blankets, buggy pods, baby hoodies, sheepskin liners and rain hoods. There's also a good range of car seats right up to 12 years and furniture ranges by Boori and Kidsmill.

Site Usability:	★★★★★	Based:	UK
Product Range:	★★★★★	Express Delivery Option? (UK)	Most items are sent next-day in UK
Price Range:	Luxury/Medium	Gift Wrapping Option?	No
Delivery Area:	UK	Returns Procedure:	Down to you

www.babyslingsandoutdoorthings.com

You should take a look at this website as it carries some excellent products for getting you and your baby 'out and about'. There's the clever ring shawl, wraparound and pouch slings, structured baby carriers and Ergo New Generation backpacks and totes. This is very much the perfect place to make your life simpler if you want to go walking and hiking and take your baby along.

Site Usability:	★★★	Based:	UK
Product Range:	★★★	Express Delivery Option? (UK)	No
Price Range:	Medium	Gift Wrapping Option?	No
Delivery Area:	Worldwide, but contact for delivery outside EU	Returns Procedure:	Down to you

www.babytravelshop.com

Wouldn't you just know that someone would snap up this completely obvious URL? Anyway, thank goodness the site is as good as its name, offering all the basic travel essentials you could need. There are baby bags, accessories such as cooler fans and kettles to go (plus adaptors and first aid kits), bottle insulators and steriliser bags, shades, harnesses, Baby Banz sunglasses and sunhats. A must if you're going travelling soon.

Site Usability:	★★★★	Based:	Ireland
Product Range:	★★★★	Express Delivery Option? (UK)	No
Price Range:	Medium/Very Good Value	Gift Wrapping Option?	No
Delivery Area:	Worldwide	Returns Procedure:	Down to you

www.johnlewis.com

Click straight through to the Nursery section at John Lewis's excellent online store and I know you won't be surprised to find that you can buy just about everything here. Typically with John Lewis you won't find a huge amount of choice but a well-edited range – the company goes quite simply for the best at each price level and has done a great deal of research for you. Combine this with the good service and you may well take the easy option and buy here.

Site Usability:	★★★★★	Based:	UK
Product Range:	★★★★	Express Delivery Option? (UK)	Yes
Price Range:	Luxury/Medium	Gift Wrapping Option?	No
Delivery Area:	UK	Returns Procedure:	Return to store or free

www.kidstravel2.com

This is a family online retailer specialising in the travel needs of parents and children, whether they're going by car, plane, bike, boat or on foot. So you can buy excellent in-car organisers, travel puzzles and games, kitbags and holdalls and perfect girls' vanity cases. It's a friendly website with a growing range of 'child-tested' products, so take a look before your next journey. Delivery is free on all mainland UK orders over £25.

Site Usability: ★★★	Based:	UK
Product Range: ★★★	Express Delivery Option? (UK)	Yes
Price Range: Medium/Very Good Value	Gift Wrapping Option?	Yes
Delivery Area: Worldwide	Returns Procedure:	Down to you

www.mamaway.co.uk

As in 'mam away' (just in case you didn't realise). This website is dedi-cated to anyone who wants to breastfeed their baby and go about their normal active life as well, so there's a range of casual nursing tops, pretty lacy nursing bras, sports bras and baby slings. There's also the extremely well-priced and roomy Mamaway bag, which should hold just about everything you'd want to take with you – although you'll have to buy a separate changing mat.

Site Usability: ★★★★	Based:	UK, but all orders are shipped from
Product Range: ★★★		Taiwan so you will pay duty
Price Range: Very Good Value	Express Delivery Option? (UK)	No
Delivery Area: Worldwide	Gift Wrapping Option?	No
	Returns Procedure:	Down to you

www.morrck.co.uk

At Morrck you'll find fleecy all-in-one wrap-around hoodies for tiny babies, perfect for travelling, plus double-layer fleece wraps for toddlers. The website is simply designed, so don't expect sophisticated products or a sophisticated ordering system. However, the ideas look excellent and anything that's going to make travel easier with babies is well worth looking at.

Site Usability: ★★★	Based:	UK
Product Range: ★★★	Express Delivery Option? (UK)	UK
Price Range: Medium	Gift Wrapping Option?	No
Delivery Area: UK	Returns Procedure:	Down to you

www.sugarandspicebaby.co.uk

This is a slightly calmer baby gear website than some, as it's not trying to offer you absolutely everything (although there are plenty of products to choose from). As well as the normal buggies and travel gear there are in-car accessories such as bottle heaters and roller sun blinds, travel cots and infant carriers – all very well pictured and clearly described.

Site Usability:	★★★★★	Based:	UK
Product Range:	★★★★	Express Delivery Option? (UK)	Yes
Price Range:	Luxury/Medium	Gift Wrapping Option?	No
Delivery Area:	UK, but call for an overseas quote	Returns Procedure:	Down to you

www.thatcuteage.com

This is quite a basic website but one that offers lots of useful products, including the HandySitt. If you haven't already come across it, it's a portable baby and toddler seat which fixes to your existing chairs and folds flat for travelling. Other brands on offer are Mulberry Bush and Bushbaby fleeces, Grobag sleeping bags, Minimink faux-fur hats and mitts and Skip Hop baby bags.

Site Usability:	★★★★★	Based:	UK
Product Range:	★★★★	Express Delivery Option? (UK)	Yes
Price Range:	Medium	Gift Wrapping Option?	No
Delivery Area:	UK	Returns Procedure:	Down to you

www.tinytotsaway.co.uk

Having spent many years travelling with three small children and loads of kit, I should think this website is an absolute boon for parents today. At Tiny Tots Away you can order your nappies by Huggies, Moltex or Pampers, food and drink by Cow and Gate, Hipp, Farley and more, baby milk, wipes and lotions, plus swim and sun products. Tell them where you're going and when, and provided they deliver to your destination, your problems are solved.

Site Usability:	★★★★★	Express Delivery Option? (UK)	No
Product Range:	★★★★★	Gift Wrapping Option?	No
Price Range:	Medium	Returns Procedure:	Claim if carrier damages products,
Delivery Area:	Most Worldwide		otherwise n/a
Based:	UK		

www.travellingwithchildren.co.uk

I really like what the creator of this website says: 'Once we arrived home again after a stressful week, having established that I'd packed too much and discovered that half the products and equipment I'd taken for Rory were either impractical, inconvenient or not required in the first place, I decided to set about doing something about it before our next trip.' So she did and here's lots of helpful advice and information, plus a whole range of products to make your life easier as you go.

Site Usability:	★★★★	Based:	UK
Product Range:	★★★	Express Delivery Option? (UK)	Yes
Price Range:	Medium	Gift Wrapping Option?	Yes
Delivery Area:	Most worldwide other than USA and Canada	Returns Procedure:	Claim if carrier damages products, otherwise n/a

www.wrapngo.co.uk

Wrap and Go is an innovative coat for both babies and toddlers that allows you to put it on and take it off without having to take your child out of the pushchair or car seat. It's designed without proper sleeves; instead a simple Velcro fastening creates the sleeves, with a zip forming the cosy toes section, and it transforms from an indoor 'blanket' to an outdoor coat very quickly. It comes in three sizes: Small for 0-6 months, Medium for 6-12 months and Large is ideal for 1-2 years.

Site Usability:	★★★	Based:	UK
Product Range:	★★★	Express Delivery Option? (UK)	No
Price Range:	Medium	Gift Wrapping Option?	No
Delivery Area:	UK	Returns Procedure:	Down to you

Chapter 20

Baby Clothes up to Two Years

Oh the fun you can have here, not to mention the money you can spend if you want to. Whether you're buying for your own baby or someone else's, you'll be spoilt for choice. There are hand knits and pure cashmere sweaters, goose-down jackets, beautiful printed romper suits and the softest velour sleepsuits. Then there are the incredible outfits in gorgeous colours that are mirror images of those for older children, beautifully made, handfinished and in expensive fabrics that you'll find hard to resist.

Thankfully you don't have to go from one shop to another to find all these goodies (I know, I've said that before) – you can just sit and click through from the enchanting designer babywear websites to the (often just as enchanting) accessibly priced babywear online retailers.

I've divided this section into Designer Babywear and Baby Boutiques (offering accessibly priced babywear), with the aim of making it easier for you to shop. So I hope you find it helpful. You can also leave the page open at Designer Babywear when grannies and godmothers come to visit (hint, hint).

My advice? Make sure you've decided how much you want to spend first. The temptation here is tremendous.

Designer Babywear

Sites to Visit

www.balloonsweb.co.uk

Just looking at the pictures on this website, in the Catamini and Pamplona sections particularly, makes you want to buy something as they're absolutely enchanting. Balloonsweb specialises in designer children's clothing for the aforesaid brands and also Miss Sixty, Chipie, Jean Bourget, Ikks and Timberland. This is an excellent children's website offering clothes and accessories from newborn to 14 years, plus pretty baby gifts and christening wear.

Site Usability:	★★★★★	Based:	UK
Product Range:	★★★★★	Express Delivery Option? (UK)	No
Price Range:	Luxury/Medium	Gift Wrapping Option?	No
Delivery Area:	Worldwide	Returns Procedure:	Down to you

www.boutiqueenfant.com

Boutique Enfant offers a collection of cashmere knitwear for six-month to twelve-year-old babies and children in a rich and vibrant colour selection for older children and marshmallow colours for the baby range. The emphasis is on traditional designs and you can mix and match from the range of knits as well as buy blankets and toys. If you're looking for a special present, the site offers a high-quality gift wrapping service and they'll ship worldwide. There are exquisite handsmocked girls' dresses here as well.

Site Usability:	★★★★★	Based:	UK
Product Range:	★★★★	Express Delivery Option? (UK)	No
Price Range:	Luxury	Gift Wrapping Option?	Yes
Delivery Area:	Worldwide	Returns Prodecure	Down to you

www.littlefashiongallery.com

Little Fashion Gallery is based in France and has a range of beautiful, luxury clothes and accessories for children aged 0–6. As well as offering brands such as American Apparel, Antik Batik, Caramel Baby and Child and Bonnie Baby, this is an excellent destination for gifts which they're happy to ship worldwide. You can also read the *Little Fashion Gallery* magazine online, which tells you all about the childrenswear trends for the season and has a variety of other articles.

Site Usability:	★★★★	Based:	UK
Product Range:	★★★★★	Express Delivery Option? (UK)	Yes
Price Range:	Luxury	Gift Wrapping Option?	Yes
Delivery Area:	Worldwide	Returns Procedure	Free

www.mariechantal.com

This is an exquisite collection of baby and childrenswear designed by Marie Chantal of Greece. As you would expect, the prices are quite steep, but you'll be hard put to find this quality of fabric and modern use of colour and design in many other children's stores. The clothing is available in two sections: babies and toddlers (although some of these go up to age eight). If you want something really special, you should take a look here.

Site Usability:	★★★★	Based:	UK
Product Range:	★★★★	Express Delivery Option? (UK)	No
Price Range:	Luxury/Medium	Gift Wrapping Option?	No
Delivery Area:	Worldwide	Returns Procedure:	Down to you

www.masterandmiss.com

AraVore, Cut 4 Cloth, D'Arcy Brown, Ikks, Mini a Ture and Tiny Tulips are some of the original children's clothing brands offered here, with the range extending from baby clothes to children up to ten years. There's lots to choose from, including colourful knitwear, traditional separates and some pretty nightwear from eighteen months to eight years.

Site Usability:	★★★★	Based:	UK
Product Range:	★★★★	Express Delivery Option? (UK)	Yes
Price Range:	Luxury/Medium	Gift Wrapping Option?	No
Delivery Area:	UK	Returns Procedure:	Down to you

www.rachelriley.com

The next time you're asked where someone could find a really special out-
fit for your little one, point them in the direction of Rachel Riley, where
you'll discover a truly lovely collection for infants, teens and grown-ups
as well. Everything here is exquisite, with a marvellous attention to style
and detail. And as you'd expect, nothing is inexpensive. So if you can't
afford to kit out your child totally from here, at least you can ask a
godmother or granny to contribute something really special.

Site Usability:	★★★★	Based:	UK
Product Range:	★★★★	Express Delivery Option? (UK)	Yes
Price Range:	Luxury	Gift Wrapping Option?	No
Delivery Area:	Worldwide	Returns Procedure:	Down to you

www.thekidswindow.co.uk

The Kids Window is a real children's department store, offering children's
clothing brands from designers such as Catfish, Inside Out, Marie Chantal
and Budishh, a full range of baby equipment, activity toys such as trampolines, swings and slides and lots of toys and games. You can search
on this website by age, gender, season and brand. Or click through to
each section of the range.

Site Usability:	★★★★★	Based:	UK
Product Range:	★★★★★	Express Delivery Option? (UK)	Yes
Price Range:	Luxury/Medium	Gift Wrapping Option?	Yes
Delivery Area:	Worldwide	Returns Procedure:	Down to you

www.weegooseberry.com

Wee Gooseberry has aimed itself at the tiny end of the designer market,
with most of the clothes going up to 24 months. There's a wonderful
choice of brands including Levi, Catamini, Bob and Blossom (love it),
Ellepi, Kidorable rainwear (love that too), Mini Mink, Ickle Pickle and
Snuggle Sac. It also has fancy dress costumes for tinies, a wide range of
shoes and some lovely gift ideas. Buy from here.

Site Usability:	★★★★★	Based:	UK
Product Range:	★★★★★	Express Delivery Option? (UK)	Yes
Price Range:	Luxury/Medium	Gift Wrapping Option?	Yes
Delivery Area:	Worldwide	Returns Procedure:	Down to you

Baby Boutiques

Sites to Visit

www.alfieandlulu.com

This is a lovely childrenswear store based in the Wirral, in Cheshire, and offering cute, well-priced baby things such as bright, striped Babygros, dictionary-definition t-shirts and rompers (think Genius, Happy or Cheeky), faux-fur gilets, hoody jackets with bear ears and mini Converse trainers. It's not a huge range, but what there is is fun and different.

Site Usability:	★★★★	Based:	UK
Product Range:	★★★	Express Delivery Option? (UK)	Yes
Price Range:	Medium/Very Good Value	Gift Wrapping Option?	No
Delivery Area:	Worldwide	Returns Procedure:	Down to you

www.aztecstore.com

Here you'll find a simple, pretty range of clothes and accessories for girls and boys up to age eight, with a separate section for babies and toddlers. There are dresses, ra-ra skirts, smock tops and capri pants, lovely trimmed cardigans and swimsuits with ruched frills and wraps to match (for the girls, of course). For boys the selection is also traditional, with appliqued knitwear, gingham shorts and shirts and fun Hawaiian print swim trunks. Everything is reasonably priced.

Site Usability:	★★★★	Based:	UK
Product Range:	★★★	Express Delivery Option? (UK)	Yes
Price Range:	Medium	Gift Wrapping Option?	No
Delivery Area:	Worldwide	Returns Procedure:	Down to you

www.bloomingmarvellous.co.uk

Blooming Marvellous offers everything for the newborn baby, including sets of Babygros and vests in pink or blue, pointelle blankets, bootees and padded outdoor suits. It's not a huge range for babies, but what the site specialises in are extremely well-priced essential basics. You can sign up for the monthly email newsletter full of parenting advice and tips, promotions and competitions and you'll always get an excellent service.

Site Usability:	★★★★★	Based:	UK
Product Range:	★★★★★	Express Delivery Option? (UK)	No
Price Range:	Medium/Very Good Value	Gift Wrapping Option?	No
Delivery Area:	Worldwide	Returns Procedure:	Down to you

www.bugsandfairies.co.uk

When I first came across this website and realised that every item here was handcrafted, I immediately assumed that it would also be very expensive. Well, I was wrong and I think that to find such a collection of gorgeous, classic pieces at this quality (and these prices) is quite exceptional. If you have a little girl and you think she'd be interested in the pink 'party' cardigan with crocheted corsage, teamed with a heavenly cream tutu, then you'll need to shop here now.

Site Usability:	★★★★★	Based:	UK
Product Range:	★★★★★	Express Delivery Option? (UK)	Yes, call to arrange
Price Range:	Medium	Gift Wrapping Option?	No
Delivery Area:	Worldwide	Returns Procedure:	Down to you

www.emmyandally.com

If you'd like to take a look at a different and fun collection of clothes for tinies, stop here for a moment. Yes, I know this retailer is based in the USA, but when you consider the fact that they're really not charging very much extra to ship worldwide and that the clothes are cute and very well priced, you might like to take a look. The range for girls here is sweet and different, there are lovely baby shoes and also a great range of baby bags, some of which you can find here in the UK and some of which you can't.

Site Usability:	★★★★★	Based:	US
Product Range:	★★★★★	Express Delivery Option? (UK)	No
Price Range:	Medium	Gift Wrapping Option?	No
Delivery Area:	Worldwide	Returns Procedure:	Down to you

www.gagagoogoo.co.uk

I almost couldn't get past the name of this website, but then when I had a look I could see it was offering something original and clever (which almost certainly only the adults will understand). This is a range of baby and toddler t-shirts up to two years and packs of bibs with famous and witty sayings on them, such as 'Go ahead and make my day' (Clint Eastwood), 'Here's looking at you, kid' (Humphrey Bogart) and 'I have nothing to declare but my genius' (Oscar Wilde).

Site Usability:	★★★★★	Based:	UK
Product Range:	★★★	Express Delivery Option? (UK)	Yes
Price Range:	Medium	Gift Wrapping Option?	No
Delivery Area:	Worldwide	Returns Procedure:	Down to you

www.jojomamanbebe.co.uk

This is a pretty website offering a good choice for babies and young children. The drop-down menus on the Home Page take you quickly and clearly to everything you might be looking for, whether it's baby essentials, nightwear or towelling snugglers. There are also some excellent Polartec all-in-ones for colder weather. Delivery is free in the UK, there are some good gift ideas and they offer gift vouchers and gift boxes as well.

Site Usability:	★★★★★	Based:	UK
Product Range:	★★★★	Express Delivery Option? (UK)	No
Price Range:	Medium	Gift Wrapping Option?	No
Delivery Area:	Worldwide	Returns Procedure:	Down to you

www.kentandcarey.co.uk

Kent and Carey has been in the business of supplying beautifully made, classic children's clothes for more than 15 years. For babies there are cute Babygros and sweet nightwear in pretty fabrics. For slightly older girls, Peter Pan printed tops, tiered skirts and print tied trousers and for boys check shirts, long shorts and traditional 'grown-up style' knitwear. The pictures are lovely and the prices are good as well.

Site Usability:	★★★★	Based:	UK
Product Range:	★★★	Express Delivery Option? (UK)	No
Price Range:	Medium	Gift Wrapping Option?	No
Delivery Area:	Worldwide	Returns Procedure:	Down to you

www.littlebluedog.co.uk

At Little Blue Dog you'll find a unique collection of baby t-shirts, Babygros, sleepsuits and accessories made from premium-quality cotton. Everything here is handprinted with quirky, design-led images such as the Lazing Lion and (yes, ok) Little Blue Dog to make them just that little bit different. The range is well priced, with sleepsuits and baseball tops at around £14.99.

Site Usability:	★★★★	Based:	UK
Product Range:	★★★	Express Delivery Option? (UK)	Yes, if you call them
Price Range:	Very Good Value	Gift Wrapping Option?	Yes
Delivery Area:	Worldwide	Returns Procedure:	Down to you

www.littletrekkers.co.uk

If this is the moment when you realise your newly walking (and getting into things and splashing in puddles) toddler is going to be getting wet and dirty from now on, you definitely ought to take a look here. You'll find extremely good-value waterproofs, from splashsuits, jackets and dungarees to skiwear and fleece for babies and kids up to age eight. There's also weatherproof and summer pool footwear and lots of other ideas for babies and young children.

Site Usability:	★★★★★	Based:	UK
Product Range:	★★★★	Express Delivery Option? (UK)	Yes
Price Range:	Medium/Very Good Value	Gift Wrapping Option?	No
Delivery Area:	Worldwide	Returns Procedure:	Down to you

www.mamasandpapas.co.uk

This company combines great attention to detail, high-quality fabrics and pretty designs in its babywear section, covering everything from a gorgeous selection for the newborn which it has called 'welcome to the world', excellent, well-priced basics and exquisite and innovative clothes for girls and boys. This is a beautifully photographed website offering loads of advice on what to buy. They deliver to the UK only but you can click through to the US-based site.

Site Usability:	★★★★★	Based:	UK
Product Range:	★★★★★	Express Delivery Option? (UK)	No
Price Range:	Medium	Gift Wrapping Option?	No
Delivery Area:	UK, but US site available	Returns Procedure:	Down to you

www.monkeyandme.co.uk

Here you'll find cute t-shirts, dresses and skirts for tinies, with some items up to five years, in pretty colours and with slogans such as 'My Daddy Rocks', 'Glamour Puss', 'I want Chips, Chocolate and Cake'. Everything is reasonably priced and although there are some toys and gifts here too, the site's strength is definitely in the t-shirts. They offer next-day delivery within the UK and are happy to ship worldwide.

Site Usability:	★★★★	Based:	UK
Product Range:	★★★	Express Delivery Option? (UK)	Yes
Price Range:	Very Good Value	Gift Wrapping Option?	No
Delivery Area:	Worldwide	Returns Procedure:	Down to you

www.nippazwithattitude.co.uk

You definitely need a sense of humour for this one as some of the slogans won't be for everyone, but if you want to put your 2–3-year-old in a Day-Glo orange t-shirt with 'Mayhem' or 'Wreckin' Services' written across the front, then this is the place you'll find it. There are some cute things here as well, such as t-shirts and rompers with 'You don't have to Sleep to Dream' and 'Easy Tiger', but be prepared for some not everyone will appreciate.

Site Usability:	★★★	Based:	UK
Product Range:	★★★	Express Delivery Option? (UK)	Yes
Price Range:	Very Good Value	Gift Wrapping Option?	No
Delivery Area:	Worldwide	Returns Procedure:	Down to you

www.notjustpinkandblue.com.

Inspired by a mum looking for clothes for her baby that weren't (yes you've guessed it) just white, pink or blue, here you can see a good collection of separates for 0-2-year-old babies, including lovely, bright-coloured and well-priced sleepsuits, butterfly-patterned pinafore dresses, stripy t-shirts and a good choice of outerwear.

Site Usability:	★★★★	Based:	UK
Product Range:	★★★	Express Delivery Option? (UK)	No
Price Range:	Very Good Value	Gift Wrapping Option?	No
Delivery Area:	Worldwide	Returns Procedure:	Down to you

www.pumpkinpatch.co.uk

Pumpkin Patch is an easy website to shop from, as it's clearly divided into Baby Patch, Kids Patch (9 months to 4 years and 5 to 11 years), Patch Extras (hats, bags, socks and tights) and Urban Angel (8-14 years). The clothes are extremely well priced and the collection is best for babies and tinies. UK delivery only from this website, although there are specific sites for New Zealand and Australia.

Site Usability:	★★★★	Based:	UK
Product Range:	★★★★	Express Delivery Option? (UK)	No
Price Range:	Very Good Value	Gift Wrapping Option?	No
Delivery Area:	UK	Returns Procedure:	Down to you

www.snuglo.co.uk

Slogans really seem to be the thing right now. Here you'll find them on bibs – 'I don't do greens', 'What's for Pudding?' – t-shirts – 'I love Football', 'Kiss me Quick' – vests, rompers, hats (which all seem to say 'cute', or 'Bad Hair Day'), hoodies and even pants. Sizing is for babies and then kids 2-8 years and there's a huge choice of colours and slogans. All orders are packed as gifts and you can add your personal message and have your order sent out for you.

Site Usability:	★★★★	Based:	UK
Product Range:	★★★★	Express Delivery Option? (UK)	No
Price Range:	Medium	Gift Wrapping Option?	Yes
Delivery Area:	Worldwide	Returns Procedure:	Down to you

Chapter 21

Baby Footwear

The best thing about nearly all the baby footwear here is that the soles are designed to be non-slip. I know you may think that that should be obvious, but it isn't always. Having said that, I'm sure that the 'non-slipness' (not a word, I know) has helped many children to slide their strollers where they're not supposed to go (I was going to tell you the story about my middle son's voyage at two years old down a couple of steps in our farmhouse but he'll probably not be pleased so I'll leave it at that).

Anyway, gorgeous soft leather with delightful designs, sheepskin boots, fleece slippers and mini sports shoes are just some of the choices you'll have to make here. I'll leave you to it.

Sites to Visit

www.daisy-roots.com

The shoes here go from babies up to four years and from adorable pale blue or pink Bill Amberg sheepskin boots to fleecy slippers and soft personalised shoes. The main part of the range is for tinies and there's a great deal of choice, with rather less in the up-to-four range. The site offers gift boxing on all the shoes, so this would also be a good place for baby gifts.

Site Usability:	★★★★	Express Delivery Option? (UK)	No
Product Range:	★★★	Gift Wrapping Option?	Yes
Price Range:	Medium/Very Good Value	Returns Procedure:	Down to you. No returns on
Delivery Area:	Worldwide		personalised goods
Based:	UK		

www.inch-blue.com

Inch Blue boots are designed for comfort and growing space. Made exclusively from natural leather, they'll let your baby's feet breathe and with soft suede soles they won't slip. They're not just for babies – Inch Blue makes boots for toddlers and children aged up to four years as well. The best-selling designs include paws, frogs, delightful ballet shoes and oriental birds. There is also a collection, called Rosie and Romeo, of gorgeous Babygros, bibs and changing mats, plus attractive gift sets.

Site Usability:	★★★★	Based:	UK
Product Range:	★★★★	Express Delivery Option? (UK)	No
Price Range:	Medium/Very Good Value	Gift Wrapping Option?	No
Delivery Area:	Worldwide	Returns Procedure:	Down to you

www.jellybabys.co.uk

There are lots of other baby products on this well-laid out site, but I particularly like the range of baby shoes, which for boys includes flats, baseball, learner (as in driver) and football and for girls blossom, fairy and magic star. You can find these shoes elsewhere, but here they're well laid out together on one page, there are different views which can all be sized up and there's just the right amount of information.

Site Usability:	★★★★★	Based:	UK
Product Range:	★★★★	Express Delivery Option? (UK)	No
Price Range:	Medium/Very Good Value	Gift Wrapping Option?	Yes
Delivery Area:	Worldwide and free in the UK	Returns Procedure:	Down to you

www.muddypuddles.com

Waterproofs, wellies, thermal socks and booties, hats, gloves, brollies for tinies, ski wear and even a wellie peg are all to be found on this innovative and clever site aimed at children up to five, with a very few items going up to eight (such as ski tops). This is an essential website for just about anyone with young children, so take a good look round as you could easily give some of the flowered wellies, funny socks and bootees as gifts.

Site Usability:	★★★★	Based:	UK
Product Range:	★★★★	Express Delivery Option? (UK)	No
Price Range:	Medium/Very Good Value	Gift Wrapping Option?	No
Delivery Area:	Worldwide	Returns Procedure:	Down to you

www.ollipops.com

It's just as well that Ollipops has a red 'Start Here' sign on the Home Page as there's so much there it would be hard to know where to go otherwise. So, click on to The Shop and then go through to the range of shoes, by Starchild, Bobux, Sole Mania or Aquashoe. Most of the shoes are for tinies, but Aquashoe go from infants to adults, so you can pick up a pair for yourself as well.

Site Usability:	★★★★	Based:	UK
Product Range:	★★★★★	Express Delivery Option? (UK)	No, but delivery is free for most items
Price Range:	Medium	Gift Wrapping Option?	No
Delivery Area:	Worldwide	Returns Procedure:	Down to you

www.robeez.co.uk

This is the UK website for fast-expanding, Canadian-based children's retailer Robeez, which specialises in high-quality leather, skid-resistant, soft-soled shoes. The website is beautifully clear and easy to navigate – choose from girls or boys, 0-2 or 2-4, then go shopping. There are shoes decorated with puppies, cherries, bows or hearts, bootees with plush linings, the Holiday Collection with bows or snowflakes and everything in a wide range of colours. It's a gorgeous collection and perfect for gifts.

Site Usability:	★★★★★	Based:	UK
Product Range:	★★★★★	Express Delivery Option? (UK)	Yes
Price Range:	Medium	Gift Wrapping Option?	Yes
Delivery Area:	Worldwide	Returns Procedure:	Down to you

www.shimmyshoes.com

These are pretty, handmade shoes for babies up to 24 months. It's not a large range (although it's growing all the time), but one which has been designed with huge care and attention. Each shoe has a name to reflect its design, such as Cheeky Monkey, Flower Power, Pretty as a Princess and High Flier. What makes it really special is that when you click on a shoe you not only get a big picture but several views, so you know exactly what you're buying. Now why don't they all do that?

Site Usability:	★★★★★	Based:	UK
Product Range:	★★★	Express Delivery Option? (UK)	No
Price Range:	Very Good Value	Gift Wrapping Option?	Yes
Delivery Area:	Worldwide	Returns Procedure:	Down to you

www.thebabyshoeshop.co.uk

The Baby Shoe Shop (which is part of website 'Kidsbits') specialises in retailing soft shoes for babies and toddlers, from quality manufacturers such as Daisy Roots, Shoo Shoo, Pitter Patter, Inch Blue and Star Child. It also sells rubber wellies from Aigle and neoprene beach shoes from the Wetsuit Factory. There are cute ballet pumps with satin ribbons, a gorgeous choice of little soft shoes for boys and girls and kids' wetsuit shoes for running in and out of the water.

Site Usability:	★★★★	Based:	UK
Product Range:	★★★	Express Delivery Option? (UK)	No
Price Range:	Medium/Very Good Value	Gift Wrapping Option?	No
Delivery Area:	UK	Returns Procedure:	Down to you

Chapter 22

Premature Baby Clothes

If you have a very early baby, this is the place you'll almost certainly need to shop as these retailers specialise in tiny sizes, in some cases from 1lb upwards.

I have to confess that I didn't realise when I started writing this book that premature babies account for approximately 8% of total births, but I'm delighted (and surprised) at the amount of choice there is for them.

The only comment overall that I have is that most of them should change their names to sound more gentle (and move away from prem, preem and eeny), but then, that's just me. The products are excellent and that's the thing that counts, of course.

Sites to Visit

www.clothes4prematures.co.uk

This is an unsophisticated website offering clothes for real tinies weighing from 1-3lbs in the Early Bird range and then from 3-12lbs in the main range. Both groups are quite small, but each contains everything you need, from simple vests and sleepsuits to fleece and velour Babygros, hats, boots and mitts and the essential Tiny Traveller - a unique baby carrier that fits snugly into first-stage car baby seats to keep tiny babies safe.

Site Usability: ★★★		Based:	UK
Product Range: ★★★		Express Delivery Option? (UK)	No
Price Range: Medium		Gift Wrapping Option?	No
Delivery Area: UK		Returns Procedure:	Down to you

www.earlybaby.co.uk

For a website specialising just in early baby clothes and gear (and created by a mother of two premature babies), this is a real pleasure to browse round. There is an attractive Home Page, with lots of original choice in each category, including colours that firmly move away from the usual pink, blue and white, to orange, fuchsia and purple. In the Early Info section you'll find lots of helpful advice written by Julie Ironside, whose site this is, plus links to other sites you may find useful.

Site Usability: ★★★★★		Based:	UK
Product Range: ★★★★★		Express Delivery Option? (UK)	Yes
Price Range: Medium/Very Good Value		Gift Wrapping Option?	No
Delivery Area: Worldwide – free in the UK		Returns Procedure:	Down to you

www.peenyweeny.co.uk

Here I go again: this is an excellent website with a really good range of premature clothes for babies, but please someone, tell me where this name comes from? I find it hard to take it seriously. Anyway, now that's done, I can tell you that you'll find a good choice of early baby clothes from absolute tinies up to 12lbs. There are essentials too, such as tiny car seats, thermal wraps, special baby carriers and sheepskins.

Site Usability: ★★★★		Based:	UK
Product Range: ★★★★★		Express Delivery Option? (UK)	No
Price Range: Medium/Very Good Value		Gift Wrapping Option?	No
Delivery Area: Worldwide		Returns Procedure:	Down to you

www.preciousprems.co.uk

There are two ranges here: the Precious Prems range, which goes up to 8lbs, and the Chuckleberries range from 2-6lbs. Both offer sweet options for early babies in the form of vests, sleepsuits, tops, trousers, jackets, hats and bibs. As this website has been created by parents who have had two premature babies, you should find everything you need.

Site Usability:	★★★	Based:	UK
Product Range:	★★★	Express Delivery Option? (UK)	No
Price Range:	Medium	Gift Wrapping Option?	No
Delivery Area:	UK	Returns Procedure:	Down to you

www.tinybabyandco.com

Tiny Baby and Co has a busy website for early babies where you select your clothes by colour and size, going from 2.5lbs to 8lbs. Some of the pictures could definitely be better, but the prices are good and there's a choice of vests, sleepsuits, Babygros, blankets and accessories which all go together in different colour groups. In the Neonatal Care section you'll find a small range created for ease of access and dressing.

Site Usability:	★★★	Based:	UK
Product Range:	★★★	Express Delivery Option? (UK)	No
Price Range:	Very Good Value	Gift Wrapping Option?	No
Delivery Area:	UK	Returns Procedure:	Down to you

Chapter 23

Perfect Gifts for Babies

I t usually follows that, when you're producing, your friends are as well and it's lovely to give something pretty and useful as a gift, particularly if you don't have to go out to the shops to buy it. In fact, you absolutely would not be able to find this range on the high street – you might find a lot of other ideas, but nothing like the choice below, which has been put together to make it easier for you.

There are beautiful baby baskets, personalised items, places where you can buy ready-created 'baby hampers' and sites where you can choose everything to be included. Then there are clever ideas such as bouquets made of baby clothes (take a look, they're really pretty), cashmere blankets and personalised bathrobes. You'll be amazed at what you can find.

Sites to Visit

www.andreabrierley.com

This is a lovely place to buy something special and quite different. Andrea Brierley has created a range of prints of illustrated names decorated with gorgeous colourful designs of animals, roundabouts, farmyards, fairytale castles and the like. They're not expensive and something you can't buy anywhere else. She'll also undertake an original watercolour commission for you if you get in touch with her. You need to email or call to order.

Site Usability:	★★★★	Based:	UK
Product Range:	★★★	Express Delivery Option? (UK)	No
Price Range:	Medium	Gift Wrapping Option?	No
Delivery Area:	UK	Returns Procedure:	Down to you

www.aspinaloflondon.com

There are some lovely gift ideas here for babies, all in Aspinal's signature high-quality leather and well-thought-out designs. Choose from contemporary and traditional photo albums covered in pretty pastel shades, baby shower gift books, suede photo frames, photo wallets and keepsake boxes. Most items can be personalised and everything can be beautifully gift boxed and sent out with your personal message.

Site Usability:	★★★★★	Based:	UK
Product Range:	★★★★★	Express Delivery Option? (UK)	Yes
Price Range:	Luxury/Medium	Gift Wrapping Option?	Yes
Delivery Area:	Worldwide	Returns Procedure:	Down to you

www.babas.uk.com

All of Babas' beautiful handmade baby bedding and accessories are individually made for you and packed in their own unique calico packaging. You can choose from cot sets, crib sets and Moses baskets, sleeping bags and towels in the range of contemporary designs with names such as Noah's Ark, Teddy Triplets and Splashy Duck. Everything is beautiful and different from what you'll find elsewhere, and perfect for baby gifts.

Site Usability:	★★★★	Based:	UK
Product Range:	★★★	Express Delivery Option? (UK)	No
Price Range:	Medium	Gift Wrapping Option?	Yes
Delivery Area:	Worldwide	Returns Procedure:	Down to you

www.babiesbaskets.com

Babiesbaskets is a retailer offering (you guessed) 'basket' gift sets for new babies and they go right up to the luxury end of the spectrum, although prices start off quite reasonably. There's the 'Loveheart' baby basket containing a Babygro, cardigan, pram shoes, fleece and photo album and the ultimate 'Fudge' baby basket, which offers as well a cableknit blanket, hand-embroidered towel and Babygro, and handmade photo album. Everything is beautifully packaged.

Site Usability: ★★★★	Based:	UK
Product Range: ★★★★	Express Delivery Option? (UK)	Yes
Price Range: Luxury/Medium	Gift Wrapping Option?	Yes
Delivery Area: Worldwide	Returns Procedure:	Down to you

www.babybare.co.uk

Here's another prettily designed and easy-to-navigate website specialising in gifts for the new baby. There are ready-to-send gift sets for boys and girls at a variety of price levels, china gifts such as cups and mugs, money boxes and piggy banks, soft personalised fleece pram blankets and lots more. If you aren't keen on the site's ready-made sets, you can put your own together and include soft toys, bath wear, sleepsuits, blankets and shawls.

Site Usability: ★★★★	Based:	UK
Product Range: ★★★	Express Delivery Option? (UK)	Yes
Price Range: Luxury/Medium	Gift Wrapping Option?	Yes
Delivery Area: Worldwide	Returns Procedure:	Down to you

www.babyblooms.co.uk

At BabyBlooms you'll be ordering handmade bouquets, created from specially designed BabyBlooms' garments. Small bouquets include a range of socks and a hat, while the larger bouquets also feature bodysuits and sleepsuits, creatively formed into flower buds. This may sound slightly strange, but everything here is really pretty and, needless to say, will last much longer than flowers.

Site Usability: ★★★★	Based:	UK
Product Range: ★★★★	Express Delivery Option? (UK)	Yes
Price Range: Medium	Gift Wrapping Option?	Yes
Delivery Area: Worldwide	Returns Procedure:	Down to you

www.babycelebrate.co.uk

This is a Cheshire-based, high-quality baby gift website where there are delightful ideas for newborn and slightly older babies with names such as Baby Play Basket and Luxury Baby on the Go. For slightly older children aged up to two there are pretty printed cutlery sets and lunch boxes, plus colourful soft and wooden toys. As everything is designed to be a gift, the products are all beautifully presented, so you could have them sent out direct from the retailer.

Site Usability:	★★★★	Based:	UK
Product Range:	★★★	Express Delivery Option? (UK)	Yes
Price Range:	Luxury/Medium	Gift Wrapping Option?	Yes
Delivery Area:	Worldwide	Returns Procedure:	Down to you

www.babygiftbox.co.uk

Babygiftbox offers a lovely range of ideas. You can choose from Welcome Home baby boxes with names such as Flower Power and Lullaby, soft lambswool or fleece and cashmere blankets, and christening gifts such as silver charms, chiming spoons and hand-knitted heirloom cot blankets. There's also the Yummy Mummy Gift Set to make sure that the new mum isn't forgotten.

Site Usability:	★★★★	Based:	UK
Product Range:	★★★★	Express Delivery Option? (UK)	Yes
Price Range:	Medium	Gift Wrapping Option?	Yes
Delivery Area:	UK	Returns Procedure:	Down to you

www.babygiftgallery.co.uk

The range of baby gifts on offer here is very wide so be prepared to take your time. In particular take a look at the christening gifts of sterling silver bangles, Doudou et Compagnie House of Barbotine Gift Boxes, Emile et Rose, keepsake boxes and photo albums. Then you might want to browse through baby gift boxes which you can customise yourself and babywear by Bob and Blossom, Emile et Rose, Inch Blue, Little Blue Dog, Toby Tiger and more. It is a lovely website for baby gifts, so do take a look.

Site Usability: ★★★★	Based:	UK
Product Range: ★★★★	Express Delivery Option? (UK)	Yes – call them
Price Range: Luxury/Medium	Gift Wrapping Option?	Yes
Delivery Area: Worldwide	Returns Procedure:	Down to you

www.bellini-baby.com

Every time I think 'that's enough, no more baby gift websites' I come across another that you simply have to know about and this is one of those. Perfect for luxury, expensive gifts, Bellini Baby offers you the opportunity of buying beautiful baskets and hampers (most of which include champagne, so they're for you too) with Takinou of France soft toys, Bebe-Jou soft cotton terry baby dressing gowns, pampering essentials and chocolates, all gorgeously wrapped and hand-tied with ribbon.

Site Usability: ★★★★★	Based:	UK
Product Range: ★★★★	Express Delivery Option? (UK)	They aim for next day for all UK orders
Price Range: Luxury	Gift Wrapping Option?	Yes
Delivery Area: Worldwide	Returns Procedure:	Down to you

www.blueberrybarn.co.uk

This is, in the main, a hamper and gift website for lots of different occasions. Just click through to the Mum and Baby department and you'll find a good range of ideas, most of which can be wrapped and personalised (and they make those options very clear). Choose from such ideas as the 'Guess How Much I Love You' baby book, Peter and Jemima activity basket and Baby Welcome Gift Box, to name but a few.

Site Usability: ★★★★★	Based:	UK
Product Range: ★★★★	Express Delivery Option? (UK)	No
Price Range: Medium	Gift Wrapping Option?	Yes
Delivery Area: UK	Returns Procedure:	Down to you

www.fuzzybuzzys.co.uk

Fuzzybuzzys produces personalised fleece blankets for babies, made from the softest lambskin fleece and 100% double-brushed cotton. The blankets are machine washable, quick-dry, colourfast (they promise) and will not shrink or fray with use. You choose from the range of colours, prints and appliqués and then personalise your blanket with the baby's name.

Site Usability:	★★★★	Based:	UK
Product Range:	★★★	Express Delivery Option? (UK)	No
Price Range:	Medium/Very Good Value	Gift Wrapping Option?	Yes
Delivery Area:	Worldwide	Returns Procedure:	Only if faulty

www.gltc.co.uk

A great range of gifts and ideas for babies and young children of all ages is available here, including personalised cutlery, clocks and adventure books, baby and toddler sleeping bags, magic lanterns and colourful wall hangings. There's the Squishy, Squirty Bath Book, Jungle soft toy bowling set and Toy House Play Mat, plus loads more clever suggestions. There are also some innovative storage ideas.

Site Usability:	★★★★	Based:	UK
Product Range:	★★★★	Express Delivery Option? (UK)	Yes
Price Range:	Medium	Gift Wrapping Option?	No
Delivery Area:	Worldwide	Returns Procedure:	Down to you

www.letterbox.co.uk

Letterbox is more of a traditional toy shop, where you can buy gifts and toys for children of all ages. These include activity toys, dressing-up out-fits, pretty room accessories (painted chests of drawers and fairy mobiles) and traditional games. There are also baby gifts such as personalised cushions and towels and bathrobes from ages 6–12 months upwards.

Site Usability:	★★★★	Based:	UK
Product Range:	★★★★★	Express Delivery Option? (UK)	Yes
Price Range:	Medium	Gift Wrapping Option?	No
Delivery Area:	Worldwide	Returns Procedure:	Down to you

www.milkychops.com

Here you will discover some lovely gift ideas, such as delightful hand-painted stools (which you can personalise if you want to), cute t-shirts and hand-knitted beanies, plus pretty felt decorations. This is not a large range but a creative selection of handmade and hand-painted creations where you may just find the perfect gift.

Site Usability: ★★★	Based:	UK
Product Range: ★★★	Express Delivery Option? (UK)	No
Price Range: Medium	Gift Wrapping Option?	No
Delivery Area: Worldwide	Returns Procedure:	Down to you

www.morelloliving.co.uk

I was delighted to find this beautifully designed website, where you can browse a range of well-photographed, clear pictures of lovely accessories and gifts for children, including knitted animals, finger puppets, wooden letters, photo frames, scented candles and much more. Take a look round now, as from the personalised paintings to the Create-it Fairy Princess kit I'm sure you'll be as enchanted as I was.

Site Usability: ★★★★★	Based:	UK
Product Range: ★★★★★	Express Delivery Option? (UK)	No
Price Range: Medium	Gift Wrapping Option?	No
Delivery Area: UK	Returns Procedure:	Down to you

www.roomersgifts.com

Embroidered baby blankets, hand-painted personalised toy boxes and door plaques, personalised bracelets and friendship rings, plus other unique gifts for babies and children are just some of the things you'll find here. This is not a traditional baby gift website, but one where you're more likely to find something they'll love to own a bit later on, such as a named treasure box.

Site Usability: ★★★	Based:	UK
Product Range: ★★★	Express Delivery Option? (UK)	No
Price Range: Medium	Gift Wrapping Option?	No
Delivery Area: Worldwide	Returns Procedure:	Down to you

www.timetin.com

If you want to give something completely different from the normal run of baby gifts, take a look here. You can use your baby Timetin to gather information on what life was like around the time of your baby's birth, remind yourself of the names you considered and make predictions on how you think he or she will develop. The Timetin contains a specially designed 'Time Book', reminder card, sealing labels, Message for the Future envelope and advice on what to put in the tin.

Site Usability:	★★★★	Based:	UK
Product Range:	★★★	Express Delivery Option? (UK)	No
Price Range:	Medium	Gift Wrapping Option?	No
Delivery Area:	Worldwide	Returns Procedure:	N/A

www.tinytotgifts.com

Tiny Tots Gifts is a beautifully laid out website where you can order musical soft toys, Asthma Friendly Cuddly Comforts and the Guess How Much I Love You gift set, of two Nut Brown hares and a story book. You can also buy delightful baby outfits, Funky Feet and Daisy Root baby shoes and bathtime accessories. There's a high-quality gift wrapping service and they'll ship worldwide.

Site Usability:	★★★★★	Based:	UK
Product Range:	★★★★	Express Delivery Option? (UK)	No
Price Range:	Medium	Gift Wrapping Option?	Yes
Delivery Area:	Worldwide	Returns Procedure:	Down to you

www.trulymadlybaby.co.uk

While offering lots of colourful and sometimes innovative baby products, here there's also a section called 'Perfect Pressies', where you can choose something pretty for a new baby without breaking the bank. There are things like the pretty, hardwearing Kaloo Liliblue tableware set, Marcus Lion and Teo Hedgehog soft toys and Katiepie watercolour names. Not everything in this section would make a great gift, but there are lots of other ideas around the site, so have a browse.

Site Usability:	★★★★	Based:	UK
Product Range:	★★★	Express Delivery Option? (UK)	No
Price Range:	Medium/Very Good Value	Gift Wrapping Option?	No
Delivery Area:	Worldwide	Returns Procedure:	Down to you

Chapter 24

Nursery Bedding and First Furniture

O f course, at this stage you're making all the choices here and you can create whatever style of nursery you want without any interference from the kids (which will come later, believe me). However, unless you're prepared for a complete redesign within a few years, if you're buying expensive furniture make sure that it's reasonably able to adapt to older years, such as the styles you can find at The Children's Furniture Company, and not too over decorated.

You can make up for it with curtains, bedlinen and accessories, but great furniture will last for years and years. For example, the wonderful proper-size bunk beds we had for our first two are now my 16-year-old daughter's bed and a spare. She has just started to moan (about a new bed, new furniture and new curtains and I don't blame her), but that's actually 19 years of use in total, so I can't complain.

Sites to Visit

www.aspaceuk.com

At Aspace you can shop by range (Astor, Vermont, Porterhouse, Mill Tree, Key West, Captain's Girl, Bloomsbury, Hudson) or by type of furniture, such as single or bunk beds, desks, wardrobes and chests, duvet sets, mattresses, sleeping bags, bean bags and cushions. In each section there's a great deal to see at a wide range of prices, but there's also a lot of information and help on how to put ranges together.

Site Usability:	★★★★	Based:	UK
Product Range:	★★★★★	Express Delivery Option? (UK)	No
Price Range:	Luxury/Medium	Gift Wrapping Option?	No
Delivery Area:	UK	Returns Procedure:	They'll collect

www.bedroominabox.co.uk

This is such a clever idea. You start with browsing the fabrics with themes like Beside the Sea, Nursery Rhymes and Loop the Loop. Once you've found something you like, you send off for samples. Then when you've made your final decision (and they're delighted to give advice at any stage if you want it), you choose which fabric and style you'd like for your curtains or blinds, for bedding, cushions and lampshades. If you need paint, you can order that as well. Allow 4-6 weeks for delivery.

Site Usability:	★★★★	Express Delivery Option? (UK)	No
Product Range:	★★★★	Gift Wrapping Option?	No
Price Range:	Luxury/Medium	Returns Procedure:	Everything is made for you so only if
Delivery Area:	UK		faulty
Based:	UK		

www.bellemaison.com

Moving away from the traditional children's ranges of furniture, at Belle Maison you'll discover a delightful and inspired collection of handcrafted pieces. In the Junior Belle Maison section you can choose from the Cheeky Charlie, Sweet Dreams or Isabella's Nurseries (plus more), all of which are cleverly designed, stylish, light and airy. There are also pretty canopies, quilts and cushions to go with each set.

Site Usability:	★★★★	Based:	UK
Product Range:	★★★★	Express Delivery Option? (UK)	No
Price Range:	Luxury/Medium	Gift Wrapping Option?	No
Delivery Area:	Worldwide, but call them for overseas deliveries	Returns Procedure:	They'll collect larger items

www.gltc.co.uk

Here's great range of ideas for babies and young children of all ages, including Fairy Ballerina and Sports Champion duvet sets and accessories, reasonably priced traditional children's furniture, innovative storage ideas, play tables, bunk beds, baby and toddler sleeping bags and themed furniture. There's the Squishy, Squirty Bath Book, Jungle soft toy bowling set and Toy House Play Mat too, plus loads more clever suggestions.

Site Usability:	★★★★	Based:	UK
Product Range:	★★★★	Express Delivery Option? (UK)	Yes
Price Range:	Medium	Gift Wrapping Option?	No
Delivery Area:	Worldwide	Returns Procedure:	Down to you

www.helenbroadhead.co.uk

If you like something completely different then take a look round here, where Helen Broadhead offers her original and hand-painted range of furniture. What you need to do first is look on her designs page and choose from the collection, including Under the Sea, Teddy Bears, Jungle, Tank, Pirates or Fairy, then select the piece of furniture you'd like, from tables and chairs to mirrors and chests. Nothing is overpriced and most items would make lovely gifts.

Site Usability:	★★★★	Based:	UK
Product Range:	★★★★	Express Delivery Option? (UK)	No
Price Range:	Medium	Gift Wrapping Option?	Yes
Delivery Area:	Worldwide, but call for overseas deliveries	Returns Procedure:	No returns for bespoke items unless they're faulty

www.hippins.co.uk

The Hippins brand has been around for over a decade, offering a unique mix of groovy children's designer clothing, funky children's furniture, traditional handcrafted wooden toys, personalised presents, unusual ideas for christening gifts, children's birthday presents and everything for new babies, including stylish nursery furniture, baby bedding and nursery accessories. You'll also find the company's own-label children's designer clothing range for ages from birth to eight years, including handmade leather baby shoes.

Site Usability:	★★★	Express Delivery Option? (UK)	No
Product Range:	★★★★★	Gift Wrapping Option?	No
Price Range:	Medium	Returns Procedure:	Down to you. Personalised items are
Delivery Area:	EU		not returnable
Based:	UK		

www.kidsfabrics.co.uk

Here you can buy fabric for children's furnishings by the metre or as
ready-cut kits for curtains, cot bedding and pillow cases. You can also
order linings, header tape, voile and other accessories and a selection of
four samples which they'll send you free of charge. There's a wide choice
of delightful fabrics for children, with themes such as jungle/animals,
appliqued and embroidered fabrics, fairytale, cars and helicopters, outer
space, soldiers and teddies.

Site Usability:	★★★★	Based:	UK
Product Range:	★★★★	Express Delivery Option? (UK)	No
Price Range:	Medium	Gift Wrapping Option?	No
Delivery Area:	Worldwide	Returns Procedure:	Down to you

www.kidsrooms.co.uk

Kids Rooms specialises in children's furniture and accessories for children's bedrooms, nurseries and playrooms. The range includes children's
beds, wardrobes, chest of drawers, bedside cabinets, children's tables
and chairs, toy boxes, bedding, bookends, height charts and much more.
The website is attractive and easy to navigate and the product range is
growing all the time.

Site Usability:	★★★★★	Based:	UK
Product Range:	★★★★	Express Delivery Option? (UK)	No
Price Range:	Medium	Gift Wrapping Option?	No
Delivery Area:	UK	Returns Procedure:	Down to you

www.kidzbedroomdepot.com

Although maybe not as beautifully laid out as some of the other children's
furniture websites, you certainly won't be disappointed in the choice here.
Offering individual items and complete room sets by Scallywag, Little

Tikes, Lea, Thukka, Wigwam Kids and Steve Allen, plus others, you need to call them to arrange delivery, which can be to mainland UK only.

Site Usability:	★★★	Based:	UK
Product Range:	★★★★★	Express Delivery Option? (UK)	No
Price Range:	Luxury/Medium	Gift Wrapping Option?	No
Delivery Area:	UK	Returns Procedure:	They'll collect larger items

www.kingofcotton.co.uk

If you haven't already come across this website you'll probably be delighted to do so now. It doesn't offer cot-sized bed linen and mattresses (as so many of the websites here do), but I think you'll find it hard to beat on price and quality for everything from single beds upwards. You can invest in the best Siberian goose down if you want to for duvets and pillows or spend much less, but whatever you buy you can expect excellent service. Try the towels as well.

Site Usability:	★★★★★	Based:	UK
Product Range:	★★★★★	Express Delivery Option? (UK)	No
Price Range:	Medium/Very Good Value	Gift Wrapping Option?	No
Delivery Area:	Worldwide	Returns Procedure:	Down to you

www.linenstore.co.uk

This is another place you may or may not want to let your children loose at (well certainly not with your credit card, anyway). There's an amazing range of children's and nursery bed linen and accessories, including Dennis the Menace, Scooby Doo, RAF, Cosmic Spaceboy and Thomas the Tank Engine (for boys, of course), alongside Magical Fairy, Tinkerbell, Dora the Explorer and Party Girl for girls, plus loads (and I mean loads) more. For the nursery there are pretty designs from Lollipop Lane, plus borders and curtains to match.

Site Usability:	★★★★	Based:	UK
Product Range:	★★★★★	Express Delivery Option? (UK)	No
Price Range:	Medium/Very Good Value	Gift Wrapping Option?	No
Delivery Area:	UK, but there's www.andyslinens.com for USA	Returns Procedure:	Down to you

www.noolibird.com

Let your imagination run wild and decorate your child's bedroom with Farmyard Friends, Fairies, Knights or Safari Animals. At Noolibird you choose your theme and then all the pieces that make it work, from duvet sets and cot liners to borders, ready-made curtains, cot quilts and matching fabrics. As well as the above you can order themed stamps, inks and stamping paints and swatches first to make sure you're happy with your choice.

Site Usability:	★★★★★	Based:	UK
Product Range:	★★★	Express Delivery Option? (UK)	No
Price Range:	Medium	Gift Wrapping Option?	No
Delivery Area:	Worldwide	Returns Procedure:	Down to you

www.nurserywindow.co.uk

Once you arrive at this website you'll find it very hard to leave. There are some seriously lovely things here for children's rooms, from unusual bedding, Moses baskets and high-quality cots and furniture to gift baskets for new babies. Everything is beautifully photographed. Just click on the area of the online shop you're interested in, enter and you'll certainly be hooked. You can also buy matching fabric to the bed linen. Nothing is cheap, but it's all beautiful quality.

Site Usability:	★★★★★	Based:	UK
Product Range:	★★★★	Express Delivery Option? (UK)	No
Price Range:	Luxury/Medium	Gift Wrapping Option?	No
Delivery Area:	UK	Returns Procedure:	Down to you

www.thechildrensfurniturecompany.co.uk

It's well worthwhile having a good look round and investing here, as these are not children's things for the short term but pieces of furniture that will last and last, with childish accents that you can remove and change For instance, there are bunks that can be debunked and safety rails removed, engraved panels which can be swapped for plain ones and brightly coloured panels which flip to reveal more muted tones.

Site Usability:	★★★★★	Express Delivery Option? (UK)	No
Product Range:	★★★★★	Gift Wrapping Option?	No
Price Range:	Luxury/Medium	Returns Procedure:	They charge a collection fee if you
Delivery Area:	UK		change your mind
Based:	UK		

www.tuttibambini.co.uk

Tutti Bambini offers a range of coordinating nursery furniture, including cribs, cots, cot beds, wardrobes, dressers, toy boxes, shelves and cot-top changers. It also sells glider chairs, wooden toys and quality mattresses which are available in four sizes. The cot-top changers are designed to fit on to the top of a cot or cot bed and have raised sides and a padded, vinyl, wipe-clean surface. Take some time when you're looking here as this is a good collection at a wide range of prices.

Site Usability:	★★★★★	Based:	UK
Product Range:	★★★★★	Express Delivery Option? (UK)	Yes for some items
Price Range:	Luxury/Medium	Gift Wrapping Option?	No
Delivery Area:	UK	Returns Procedure:	Down to you

www.vipkids.co.uk

VIP Kids specialises in the design, manufacture and import of high-quality imaginative children's beds, chairs, bedroom furniture, toys, nursery furniture and accessories. You'll find collections featuring the 1930s' reproduction Ferrari F2 Retro Racers, fantastic children's room lighting, handcrafted upholstered loose-cover armchairs, fun light switch covers and wooden mobiles. Children's beds range from toddler beds to mid-sleeper and four-poster styles.

Site Usability:	★★★★★	Based:	UK
Product Range:	★★★★★	Express Delivery Option? (UK)	No
Price Range:	Luxury/Medium	Gift Wrapping Option?	No
Delivery Area:	UK	Returns Procedure:	Down to you

www.vivababy.com

Themes here go under headings such as Summer House, Nautilus, Roses, Tom's Cabin, Flower Power, Sleeping Beauty and Football – does that give you some kind of idea of what to expect? Beware letting your child choose from this website – you may well end up with a Kontiki bunk bed instead of the traditional style you were aiming for, or the amazing Nautilus bed/play area. There's a lot of fun to be had with this delightful range, which offers bed linen and accessories to match.

Site Usability:	★★★★★	Based:	UK
Product Range:	★★★★★	Express Delivery Option? (UK)	No
Price Range:	Luxury/Medium	Gift Wrapping Option?	No
Delivery Area:	Worldwide	Returns Procedure:	They will collect

Chapter 25

Advice Websites, New Parent Guides and Baby Services

Most of the advice websites here want to tell you all you could possibly need to know and more; and it's up to you whether you use them at all or read everything. I'm sure that will depend very much on how much support you have from friends and family who have had children relatively recently, particularly if this is your first. Having said that, sometimes it's hard to know who to listen to.

Information about pregnancy care, birth, feeding, the first few months, the toddler years and how to deal with tantrums is here aplenty and one thing you may well find is that you're over advised. My advice for what it's worth: find one knowledgeable person you trust, listen to her and take the rest as it comes. If you can find a great NCT midwife from your classes whom you're able to speak to when you have a question, you'll be really lucky. You can also use www.midwivesonline.com if you have questions, but it's not the same thing as having someone you know whom you can call.

I have two acknowledgements here: Carol and Gilly, wherever you are, thank you so much - I owe you both more than I can say.

Sites to Visit

www.askbaby.com

AskBaby is one of the best pregnancy and baby care resources available on the internet. Here on this easy-to-use website you can find medical information and advice, facts, opinions and comments on a wide range of pregnancy and baby issues, as well as advice and reviews on buying every type of pregnancy and baby product. To get the most from AskBaby, become a member.

www.babycentre.co.uk

BabyCentre is a comprehensive online destination for pregnancy and baby information. By entering your baby's due date or birthday, you can personalise the site to get information geared to your particular stage in pregnancy or parenting. You can use the search engine as a one-stop research tool to find out whatever you need to know about pre-conception, pregnancy, birth or care of your baby – simply type in a keyword and you'll find a list of articles to help answer your questions.

www.baby-chaos.co.uk

Here's a clearly laid out baby advice and information website, where you can read guides on all the stages of pregnancy, giving birth and afterwards, as well as use the product directory if you're looking for something specific. One of the best things here is that it isn't one of the huge, busy baby advice and information websites. The menus are excellent and you can quickly reach the section you're looking for.

www.babyconcierge.co.uk

This service will be an absolute boon for anyone who's had a baby (or is about to have a baby) and needs their time back urgently. Baby Concierge offers a full baby consultation and shopping service, then does all the work for you. You consult them (by phone or in person) about all your forthcoming needs – nursery, travel products, etc., which they'll help you select according to your lifestyle. Then they'll arrange for them to be delivered when you want them. There is a consultation fee (of course), but otherwise products will be at the RRP.

www.babyhedgehog.co.uk

This is an extremely busy baby website where you can not only shop for baby gifts and equipment and set up your online photo album, but also use the parenting and baby resources. You'll find advice about which books to buy for specific areas and you can join FitBug to help you get back into shape.

Site Usability:	★★★★	Based:	UK
Product Range:	★★★★	Express Delivery Option? (UK)	No
Price Range:	Medium	Gift Wrapping Option?	No
Delivery Area:	UK	Returns Procedure:	Down to you

www.babyworld.co.uk

Clear and easy to use, Baby World offers lots to expecting and new mothers, from advice on trying for a baby, pregnancy and birth through to new parent guides and reviews on products such as slings and carriers, car seats and buggies. You can sign up for the newsletter, join the discussion forums and then pay a visit to the BabyWorld shop, where there's a wide range of recommended items, including premium brands such as Britax, Starchild and Kaloo.

Site Usability:	★★★★★	Based:	UK
Product Range:	★★★★★	Express Delivery Option? (UK)	No
Price Range:	Medium	Gift Wrapping Option?	No
Delivery Area:	Worldwide, but ask for a delivery quote	Returns Procedure:	Down to you

www.chatdanger.com

The minute your children are even hinting that they want access to a computer, you need this website. Chatdanger has been created to inform young people (and parents) about the potential dangers and ways of keeping safe in interactive areas online, such as chatrooms, instant messenger, online games and email, as well as mobile phones. All parents need to read this. You should also go through the seminar at www.kidsmart.org.uk. Believe me, whatever you say to them, your child will inevitably try to do something online you won't be happy with. You need to be prepared.

www.juniormagazine.co.uk

This is almost certainly the most stylish, modern magazine for parents around, offering a fresh and vibrant perspective on parenting and childhood issues. Click through to the website to find balanced and informative features on all aspects of child development, including health, education, fashion and child-friendly travel. It offers insight, suggestions and topical features from a parent's viewpoint, written in an engaging style and presented beautifully. Definitely worth a read.

www.kidsmart.org.uk

This is an essential website for parents whose kids are about to start using a computer and going online. There are a number of resources, including Childnet's parents' seminar, a special interactive presentation for parents online. You'll find advice about filters, plus help and information about interactive services on the internet such as games, chat, peer to peer (that's file-sharing websites where they download music) and Instant Messenger (MSN). Many parents have no idea how these services work or what children are up to when using them. If your child is at that age, you need to know everything possible.

www.midwivesonline.com

Midwives Online has been set up to give you lots of advice and information on pregnancy, birth and breastfeeding in particular. As I've said above, it's not the same as having an actual person to talk to, but if your question is answered here you may well find it helpful. It's clear and well laid out and there's also the Ask a Midwife service where, for a small fee, you can ask your own questions. Don't do this if you need help urgently – they don't guarantee a quick response.

www.motherandbabymagazine.com

Read this magazine on or offline, the choice is yours. There's plenty of information on every aspect of being a mother, plus product reviews on all types of equipment, feeding, sleeping, baby care and playtime. There's also a direct link through to Babies R Us, where you'll find a huge choice of baby products and essentials at very good prices.

Site Usability:	★★★★★	Based:	UK
Product Range:	★★★★★ (Babies R Us)	Express Delivery Option? (UK).	No
Price Range:	Very Good Value	Gift Wrapping Option?	No
Delivery Area:	UK	Returns Procedure:	Down to you

www.nct.org.uk

The NCT (National Childbirth Trust) is the leading charity for pregnancy, birth and parenting in the UK and has over 60,000 members. Use its website to find the local NCT resource near you. It offers Early Days courses (which you need to sign up for) to help you get ready for being a parent, Breastfeeding Support, with a number you can call for advice, and local ante- and postnatal courses. There is also a shop for parents and babies, where all the profits go to the NCT.

www.organised-mum.co.uk

This may not be a baby advice website, or an online baby magazine, but it's somewhere I definitely recommend you take a look if you need help to stay organised (and who doesn't with children?). At Organised Mum you can buy diaries, wall charts, calendars, stickers and the wonderful 'Family Organiser', which I would definitely buy if I thought for a moment my family would help me use it properly by providing the necessary information. Standard delivery is free on orders over £5.

Site Usability:	★★★★	Based	UK
Product Range:	★★★	Express Delivery Option? (UK)	Yes
Price Range:	Very Good Value	Gift Wrapping Option?	No
Delivery Area:	Worldwide	Returns Procedure:	Down to you

www.parentcentre.gov.uk

Parent Centre is an official Department for Education and Skills (DfES) website for parents and carers. It aims to act as a reference book about the education system and a provider of information about the many issues relevant to you and your child. It also directs parents and carers to other sources of information and advice, such as working when pregnant, child benefit and giving money to your children.

www.raisingkids.co.uk

I love what they say here: 'We've … tried to take a sideways view of family life. Kids can make you cry, scream, and tear your hair but they can make you laugh a lot too. Don't keep it to yourself – come and share the joke at raisingkids.co.uk.' So this is not just a baby website, although it covers everything from babies to teens and beyond (so maybe I need this one), but a place where you can 'ask the experts', talk to other parents, read the latest news and features for parents and find out about developments in education.

www.smartneurons.com

Smart Neurons is a children's educational software company whose aim is to help pre-schoolers develop critical thinking, imagination and leadership skills through simple, fun and creative software. You may not want to introduce your child to a computer quite so soon, but if you're happy to do so, this could be a good way. A great deal of thought has obviously gone into these products. The company is based in Texas, USA and you can email with any queries and view the product demos before you buy.

www.special-needs-kids.co.uk

This is an information directory and shopping site to help parents and carers of children with special needs. There's information on products and services, events and campaigns, disability issues, support groups, respite care, clothing, equipment (and safety advice), toys, leisure activities and days out, holidays, where to go for help and advice, and much more. You can buy products directly through the website from other retailers.

Section 3
Everything for Kids

No doubt, having called this 'Everything for Kids', some bright spark is going to let me know about the hugely important item I've missed out. A whole chapter, perhaps, on something that just completely slipped my mind. Well go on, tell me – I'll put it in the next edition.

This section covers clothing, including nightwear and sportswear, footwear of all types from sports shoes to party pumps, activity toys, the huge ranges from the general toy stores, and lots of hobby, model-making and building set retailers. Then there are sites for jigsaw puzzles (13,000 pieces! Daft, don't you think?), games, dressing-up outfitters and magic trick shops and everything for parties.

Let's not forget that this book is about shopping, so if you're thinking that I should be telling you where to take your kids for a day out, how to find help and how to entertain them at home, please stop there. Isn't shopping enough? It's what I'm good at, after all.

Chapter 26

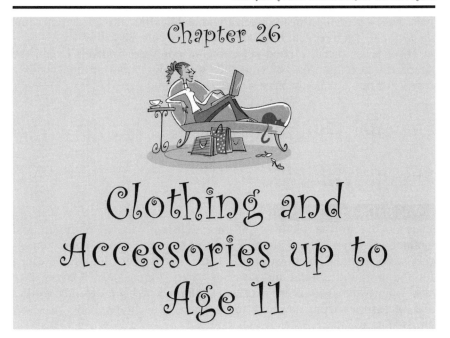

Clothing and Accessories up to Age 11

This chapter is another that I've split into sections. First there's wonderful designer childrenswear where if you buy lots you may find you can't have that vital new season's Marc Jacobs handbag, so think very carefully before you buy. That's not to say don't buy – the clothes are gorgeous and you may like to have your little ones dressed in designer clothes from dawn to dusk – I'm just saying that if you're anything like me, you could get extremely carried away.

Then you can move on to accessibly priced children's clothes, with an excellent choice of everything for everyone, whether your kids are sporty or like to look smart all the time. Are there any of those out there? They definitely weren't mine. The range of prices is huge and you'll find some unique things such as hand knits at quite unexpected value. It's certainly a great place to browse.

As well as the above there's pretty (and usually reasonably priced) nightwear from a range of online retailers, from embroidered nightdresses trimmed with ribbon and lace to grown-up-looking boys' pyjamas – not just those covered with aeroplanes and teddies but the kind that come in navy and white check and look irresistibly cute on a tiny.

There is, as usual, a good selection, so don't tire yourself out in the shops the next time one of your kids suddenly shoots up and needs a new wardrobe – you can have a really good time here.

Designer Childrenswear

Sites to Visit

www.balloonsweb.co.uk

Just looking at the pictures on this website – in the Catimini and Pampolina sections particularly – makes you want to buy something as they're enchanting. Balloonsweb specialises in designer children's clothing for the aforesaid brands and also Miss Sixty, Chipie, Jean Bourget, Ikks and Timberland. This is an excellent children's website offering clothes and accessories from newborn to 14 years, plus pretty baby gifts and christening wear.

Site Usability:	★★★★★	Based:	UK
Product Range:	★★★★★	Express Delivery Option? (UK)	No
Price Range:	Luxury/Medium	Gift Wrapping Option?	No
Delivery Area:	Worldwide	Returns Procedure:	Down to you

www.brora.co.uk

Brora was established in 1992 with the aim of offering classic fine-quality Scottish cashmere with a contemporary twist, at prices that offer real value for money. Although it's not the cheapest, it offers some of the best quality available and in designs and a selection of colours that you won't find anywhere else. The children's and babies' ranges are beautiful, fun and colourful and would make lovely presents.

Site Usability:	★★★★★	Based:	UK
Product Range:	★★★★	Express Delivery Option? (UK)	Yes
Price Range:	Luxury/Medium	Gift Wrapping Option?	Yes
Delivery Area:	Worldwide	Returns Procedure:	Down to you

www.bugalugsuk.co.uk

Ok, I'm going to have a moan. Firstly let me tell you that there's a lovely amount of choice here, with Oilili, Pampolina, Miniman and Ikks just some of the brands on offer. It's an excellent collection and you can get 10% off if you join the mailing list – but please, please tell them to tone down the font and take the pictures on a white background. The site would look so – as in soooooooooooooo – much better. You'll probably buy there, anyway.

Site Usability: ★★★	Based:	UK
Product Range: ★★★★	Express Delivery Option? (UK)	No
Price Range: Luxury/Medium	Gift Wrapping Option?	No
Delivery Area: UK	Returns Procedure:	Down to you

www.childrenssalon.co.uk

This is a family-run business operating out of a shop in Kent and offering designer children's clothes from 0-12 years. Labels include Oilily, Bengh Par Principesse, Oxbow, Gabrielle, Elle, Cacharel, Kenzo, Dior and loads more (and I mean loads). There is also the Petit Bateau range of underwear for boys and girls, nightwear and dressing-up clothes. The company specialises in a gorgeous range of christening gowns and accessories.

Site Usability: ★★★★★	Based:	UK
Product Range: ★★★★	Express Delivery Option? (UK)	Yes
Price Range: Luxury/Medium	Gift Wrapping Option?	No
Delivery Area: Worldwide	Returns Procedure:	Down to you

www.daddyslittlestar.com

Labels stocked here include Mim-pi, Ciao Bimbi, Portofino, Beetlejuice and Salty Dog, with brands being added and changed all the time. Don't expect a hugely sophisticated website from this retailer, based at a shop in North Lincs, but the photographs are clear, there's free delivery on all UK orders and if you see the same item somewhere else at a lower price they'll beat it.

Site Usability: ★★★	Based:	UK
Product Range: ★★★★	Express Delivery Option? (UK)	No
Price Range: Luxury/Medium	Gift Wrapping Option?	No
Delivery Area: Worldwide	Returns Procedure:	Down to you

www.elizabethhurley.com

You may well have read in the press about the Elizabeth Hurley Beach range and here it is online. There's wonderful, sexy, stylish swimwear, chic kaftans, dresses and tops and a choice of knitwear and t-shirts. Then there's a gorgeous range for kids, which includes pretty swimsuits, hooded dresses and kaftans, plus mini beach bags and flip-flops.

Site Usability:	★★★★	Based:	UK
Product Range:	★★★	Express Delivery Option? (UK)	No
Price Range:	Luxury/Medium	Gift Wrapping Option?	No
Delivery Area:	Worldwide	Returns Procedure:	Down to you

www.kidscavern.co.uk

Kids Cavern is one of the top children's designer stores in the North West of England. Its website covers childrenswear over three departments, from newborn to 3 years, 4-10 years and 11-16 years. Designers offered include Timberland, Moschino, DKNY, Burberry, Armani, Miniman, Dior and many more. They'll ship worldwide, although outside the UK and USA you need to email them to find out how much your postage will cost.

Site Usability:	★★★	Based:	UK
Product Range:	★★★★	Express Delivery Option? (UK)	Yes
Price Range:	Luxury/Medium	Gift Wrapping Option?	No
Delivery Area:	Worldwide	Returns Procedure:	Down to you

www.mischiefkids.co.uk

At Mischief Kids you can find a great selection of designer clothing for kids, from labels such as Emile et Rose, Ikks, Mim-Pi, Marese, Trois Pommes and Quiksilver. Click on the brand you're interested in and you can immediately see everything on offer, plus what's available right now (although this could be simplified). This is an excellent website for children's clothing and one that your kids will enjoy looking through too, for its fun and quirky design.

Site Usability:	★★★★	Based:	UK
Product Range:	★★★★★	Express Delivery Option? (UK)	Yes
Price Range:	Luxury/Medium	Gift Wrapping Option?	No
Delivery Area:	Worldwide	Returns Procedure:	Down to you

www.pleasemum.co.uk

This is a company that was established in London in 1971, aiming to provide fashionable, unique and high-quality children's clothing. It now offers its excellent own-brand collections online for children up to age 12/13 and there are some gorgeous outfits here, particularly for girls. There is also designer childrenswear by Moschino, D&G, Armani, Versace and Roberto Cavalli. Do not expect to save money when you visit this website, it's not cheap.

Site Usability:	★★★★	Based:	UK
Product Range:	★★★★	Express Delivery Option? (UK)	No
Price Range:	Luxury/Medium	Gift Wrapping Option?	No
Delivery Area:	Worldwide	Returns Procedure:	Down to you

www.poppy-children.co.uk

At Poppy you'll find a small, pretty range of town and country clothes for children aged one to six years, based on its own unique fabrics and borders. This is a perfect collection of dresses for little 'girly' girls rather than the tomboy variety. It is based on pretty pastels and eye-catching designs for summer and deeper colours for autumn. Then there are padded jackets and cardis to complete the look and you can order fabrics and borders as well.

Site Usability:	★★★★	Based:	UK
Product Range:	★★★★	Express Delivery Option? (UK)	No
Price Range:	Medium	Gift Wrapping Option?	No
Delivery Area:	Worldwide	Returns Procedure:	Down to you

www.shoptommy.co.uk

Yes, US brand Tommy Hilfiger is now online and it's an excellent place for cool kids to shop as the styles are great and it's not overpriced. There's a good selection of modern daywear, from casual shirts and baby cord skirts to colourful knits, jackets and accessories. There's also a gift section and the option of gift boxing for all items offered. This is an easy website to shop from and you'll no doubt find something for yourself there as well. Sizing goes up from age three.

Site Usability:	★★★★★	Based:	UK
Product Range:	★★★★	Express Delivery Option? (UK)	No
Price Range:	Medium	Gift Wrapping Option?	Yes
Delivery Area:	Worldwide	Returns Procedure:	Down to you

www.skuffsandskruffs.co.uk

There's a huge range of labels available here, with DKNY, Confetti, Cati-mini, Jean Bourget, Juicy Couture and Replay just a small example. The web background is very pink, which doesn't help you to see the clothes, but when you click on 'more details' for each product you can see them more easily. The site also offers a lot of great shoe brands, such as Lelli Kelli, O'Neill and Pom D'Api, and they'll deliver worldwide.

Site Usability:	★★★	Based:	UK
Product Range:	★★★★★	Express Delivery Option? (UK)	No
Price Range:	Luxury/Medium	Gift Wrapping Option?	No
Delivery Area:	Worldwide	Returns Procedure:	Down to you

www.teddywear.com

Teddywear is a small internet boutique selling high-quality children's clothes, including brands such as Balu, Catimini, Marese, Miniman, Little Darlings, SULK, Chipie, Lili Gaufrette, Babar, Timberland, DKNY, Diesel, Confetti and Pampolina. You can search by age or brand and as the site updates its stock regularly, keep coming back to see what's available. There's a good selection up to age 9/10 as well as a baby section.

Site Usability:	★★★★	Based:	UK
Product Range:	★★★★	Express Delivery Option? (UK)	No
Price Range:	Luxury/Medium	Gift Wrapping Option?	No
Delivery Area:	Worldwide	Returns Procedure:	Down to you

www.wildchildfashions.com

With labels such as Lacoste, Paul Smith, Ted Baker, Hackett, Timberland, Diesel, DKNY, Nike and Guess, you'll probably have to fight to keep your children off this website and warn your bank manager if you fail. Wildchild is a fairly new childrenswear company aiming to appeal to both children and parents (is such a thing possible?) and has ranges for girls and boys up to mid teens.

Site Usability:	★★★★★	Based:	UK
Product Range:	★★★★	Express Delivery Option? (UK)	Yes
Price Range:	Luxury/Medium	Gift Wrapping Option?	No
Delivery Area:	Worldwide	Returns Procedure:	Down to you

Childrenswear Boutiques

Sites to Visit

www.accessorize.co.uk

Just about as well known on the high street as its sister shop Monsoon, Accessorize is the essential destination if you're looking for a stylish fashion gift for an older child or if your early teen and upwards needs (as in I NEED) a new pair of earrings, flip-flops, party slip-on shoes, scarf or bag. Not only are the prices extremely reasonable but the products are fun and modern. The stores themselves are usually heaving, so take advantage of the fact that you (or they) can now shop online.

Site Usability:	★★★★★	Based:	UK
Product Range:	★★★★	Express Delivery Option? (UK)	No
Price Range:	Very Good Value	Gift Wrapping Option?	No
Delivery Area:	UK	Returns Procedure:	Down to you

www.boden.co.uk

When you're looking for fun, well-priced kids' clothing, don't forget about Boden (or Mini Boden, I should say). This is one of the best collections to choose from, with pretty skirts and tops, fine and chunky knitwear and colourful outerwear, all from 2 to 12 and vying for your attention with cute shoes and boots and enchanting nightwear. The site also offers socks and tights in a wide range of colours.

Site Usability:	★★★★★	Based:	UK
Product Range:	★★★★	Express Delivery Option? (UK)	Yes
Price Range:	Medium/Very Good Value	Gift Wrapping Option?	No
Delivery Area:	Worldwide	Returns Procedure:	Down to you

www.budishh.co.uk

Budishh offers a collection of individually designed and handmade special occasion and partywear for girls between 3 and 10. The pretty styles incorporate beautiful traditional fabrics such as velvet and tweed, taffeta and silk, plus some washable fabrics. Recently it has established a more casual line which includes things like chambray jeans and pretty camisoles, but the overall look is very girly. Couple all this with reasonable prices and you're sure to find your daughter's next party dress here.

Site Usability:	★★★★	Based:	UK
Product Range:	★★★★	Express Delivery Option? (UK)	No
Price Range:	Medium/Very Good Value	Gift Wrapping Option?	No
Delivery Area:	Worldwide	Returns Procedure:	Down to you

www.caramel-shop.co.uk

If you're looking for attractive childrenswear you must pay a visit here, as Caramel has one of the most attractive websites and best collections around. The clothes are designed for babies and children aged 2 to 12 and you can also buy shoes, boots and socks. Each part of the range is divided into themes so you can clearly see what works together and you never feel swamped by the amount of choice.

Site Usability:	★★★★★	Based:	UK
Product Range:	★★★★★	Express Delivery Option? (UK)	Yes
Price Range:	Luxury/Medium	Gift Wrapping Option?	Yes
Delivery Area:	Worldwide	Returns Procedure:	Down to you

www.clothes4boys.co.uk

Here you'll find, yes you guessed it, clothes just for boys, from 2 to 14 years old. Designers include Ripcurl, Salty Dog, Eager Beaver, Regatta and Flyers. There is a great choice, with casual clothes from t-shirts to boarding trousers and football trousers, plus an excellent sale shop and some fun and funky swimwear. You can select to view the range by age or by designer.

Site Usability:	★★★★★	Based:	UK
Product Range:	★★★★	Express Delivery Option? (UK)	No
Price Range:	Medium	Gift Wrapping Option?	No
Delivery Area:	Worldwide	Returns Procedure:	Down to you

www.cosyposy.co.uk

This well-thought-out childrenswear website has gone straight into my list of favourites, as it's attractive to look at, easy to navigate and offers an original and reasonably priced range for boys and girls from 2 to 6, plus a separate babies' collection. Brands include Inch Blue, Cacharel, Elizabeth James and Butterscotch. There are also some very good gift ideas for new babies and children, including gift sets and toys, and you can buy gift vouchers which can be sent out on your behalf.

Site Usability:	★★★★★	Based:	UK
Product Range:	★★★★★	Express Delivery Option? (UK)	Yes
Price Range:	Medium	Gift Wrapping Option?	Yes
Delivery Area:	Worldwide	Returns Procedure:	Down to you

www.littlefolk.co.uk

It was difficult to know where to put this website as these are really gifts for children, but as just about everything in the kids' section would make a great present and the site has some lovely, well-priced t-shirts, I thought I'd drop them in here. These are personalised t-shirts, aged from 3 to 14, with the Little Folk (Twirl the Little Ballerina, Fizzy the Little Fairy and Squirt the Little Elephant are just a few), plus the alphabet letter and name of your choice. There are also personalised bags, bedding, place settings and pictures.

Site Usability:	★★★★★	Based:	UK
Product Range:	★★★	Express Delivery Option? (UK)	Yes for some items
Price Range:	Medium	Gift Wrapping Option?	No
Delivery Area:	UK	Returns Procedure:	Down to you

www.mittyjames.com

Mitty James offers luxuriously soft towelling beach robes and holidaywear for babies, kids, children and teenagers, along with traditional cotton swimwear and classic daywear. Once you're on this website it's difficult to leave without buying something, particularly if you're just off on holiday, as the pictures are filled with prettily coloured childrenswear perfect for holiday and beach. Call for express delivery.

Site Usability:	★★★★★	Based:	UK
Product Range:	★★★	Express Delivery Option? (UK)	Yes if you call them
Price Range:	Medium	Gift Wrapping Option?	No
Delivery Area:	Worldwide, but call them outside the UK	Returns Procedure:	Down to you

www.monsoon.co.uk

With its presence on the high street, almost everyone has heard of Monsoon, offering attractive, not inexpensive but still good-value clothing for everyone, with gorgeous ideas for children. The collection goes from babies up to ten years and always includes pretty colours, particularly gorgeous skirts and dresses and the prettiest partywear.

Site Usability:	★★★★★	Based:	UK
Product Range:	★★★★	Express Delivery Option? (UK)	No
Price Range:	Medium/Very Good Value	Gift Wrapping Option?	No
Delivery Area:	UK	Returns Procedure:	Down to you

www.petitpatapon.com

I'm sure that my kids were never as well behaved as the ones in the pictures here, where delightful girls and boys in gorgeous clothes are happily playing and laughing and modelling. The range goes from newborn layettes to babies and then toddler boys and girls up to age five. Finally there's a girls' range up to age 14 and all the prices are reasonable. Remember to click on your currency first.

Site Usability:	★★★★★	Based:	France/USA
Product Range:	★★★★★	Express Delivery Option? (UK)	No
Price Range:	Medium/Very Good Value	Gift Wrapping Option?	No
Delivery Area:	Worldwide	Returns Procedure:	Down to you

www.purecollection.com

There's pretty cashmere for children here in a choice of attractive colours and including styles such as ballet wraps, cable crew neck and v-neck sweaters. For babies there are bonnets and cot blankets. The delivery and service are excellent and the prices are very good too. If you want something particular in a hurry, call to make sure it's in stock and you can have it the next day.

Site Usability:	★★★★★	Based:	UK
Product Range:	★★★★	Express Delivery Option? (UK)	Yes
Price Range:	Luxury/Medium	Gift Wrapping Option?	Yes
Delivery Area:	Worldwide	Returns Procedure:	Free

www.roseandrobin.com

Rose and Robin is a Danish web shop that offers high-quality children's clothes from a variety of Danish designers such as Fablefant, Mini A Ture, Phister and Philina and Slike and Suus. I have to confess none of these is known to me. However, some of the clothes are very pretty, different from what you'll find in the UK and reasonably priced. When you click on a garment you get several views, plus an enlarged picture where you can see all the detail.

Site Usability:	★★★★★	Based:	Denmark
Product Range:	★★★★★	Express Delivery Option? (UK)	No
Price Range:	Medium	Gift Wrapping Option?	No
Delivery Area:	Worldwide	Returns Procedure:	Down to you

www.tansen.co.uk

This is an eclectic, pretty and different range of clothes and accessories for women, girls and boys inspired by the East. Designs follow the traditions and beauty of Nepal, India and Japan, incorporating embroidery and vibrant colours, fabrics such as silk saris, chiffon, cord and cotton, hand knit and crochet and prints embellished with sequins, beads and jewels. There are some gorgeous things here, particularly for little girls, which would make lovely gifts.

Site Usability: ★★★★		Based:	UK
Product Range: ★★★★		Express Delivery Option? (UK)	Yes
Price Range: Medium		Gift Wrapping Option?	No
Delivery Area: Worldwide		Returns Procedure:	Down to you

www.theirnibs.com

The approach at Their Nibs is to offer a truly distinctive children's clothing collection to fill the gap between the national chains and independent retailers which stock all the usual brands. The collection, which includes lots of prints, is continually updated and inspiration comes from a variety of sources including an in-house 'vintage' collection. There are some pretty clothes for children aged 0-8, including perfect dresses for little flowergirls.

Site Usability: ★★★★★		Based:	UK
Product Range: ★★★★		Express Delivery Option? (UK)	No
Price Range: Medium		Gift Wrapping Option?	No
Delivery Area: Worldwide		Returns Procedure:	Down to you

www.trotters.co.uk

The first Trotters opened its doors in October 1990 at 34 Kings Road, Chelsea, London, catering for children from 0-11 years from top to toe and offering a fantastic range of clothes, shoes, books and toys. New ranges are introduced all the time as Trotters sources from all over the world. The full range isn't offered online, but you'll find everything from babies' romper suits to kids' duffles, wellies, rainmacs and swimwear.

Site Usability: ★★★		Based:	UK
Product Range: ★★★★		Express Delivery Option? (UK)	No
Price Range: Medium		Gift Wrapping Option?	Yes
Delivery Area: Worldwide		Returns Procedure:	Down to you

www.vertbaudet.co.uk

For an excellent range of well-priced, modern, French-designed childrenswear and accessories (and babies things as well), look no further. Choose from babywear including organic baby clothes, girls and boyswear at wonderful value and in natural fabrics, good maternity clothing and enchanting partywear for tiny tots. And that's all just for starters – you have to have a browse here.

Site Usability:	★★★★★	Based:	UK
Product Range:	★★★★★	Express Delivery Option? (UK)	No
Price Range:	Very Good Value	Gift Wrapping Option?	No
Delivery Area:	UK	Returns Procedure:	Free if you register for an account

Children's Nightwear

Sites to Visit

www.adventino.co.uk

Although they do offer other children's clothes here, I have to confess that I was so taken with the nightwear that I thought this was the right place for you to read about this website. It offers pink spotty and wonderfully stripy brushed cotton pjs, traditional soft, white cotton nightdresses and Amish-style dark blue and white check dressing gowns. Some items go up to age ten, others stop at about four.

Site Usability:	★★★★	Based:	UK
Product Range:	★★★	Express Delivery Option? (UK)	No
Price Range:	Very Good Value	Gift Wrapping Option?	No
Delivery Area:	UK	Returns Procedure:	Down to you

www.astonsoflondon.co.uk

Aston's doesn't offer a wide range, but the boys' pyjamas in dark blue with satin piping and embroidered with knights and the girls' Chinese-style pjs and those embroidered with ballet slippers are really attractive. There are excellent kids' bathrobes and embroidered (or personalised) towels here as well.

Site Usability:	★★★★	Based:	UK
Product Range:	★★★	Express Delivery Option? (UK)	Yes
Price Range:	Medium/Very Good Value	Gift Wrapping Option?	No
Delivery Area:	Worldwide	Returns Procedure:	Down to you

www.bonne-nuit.co.uk

I have no idea which of these websites came first (this or the website below), but there are some great things here as well, from 12 months to 10 years, including brushed cotton, striped pyjamas, pretty lace-trimmed and embroidered nightdresses, children's bathrobes and baby hooded towels and baby gift ideas. There's a gift wrap service and delivery (at time of writing) is £3 to anywhere in the world.

Site Usability:	★★★★	Based:	UK
Product Range:	★★★	Express Delivery Option? (UK)	No
Price Range:	Medium	Gift Wrapping Option?	Yes
Delivery Area:	Worldwide	Returns Procedure:	Down to you

www.bon-nuit.com

At Bon Nuit you'll find beautifully made children's clothing and nightwear made from high-quality Swiss cotton. The designs are really pretty – think traditional nightdresses embroidered with pansies, lilies and butterflies, floral jacquard and silk appliquéd pyjamas, soft terry embroidered bathrobes and towels and cute t-shirts and shorts. They'll ship worldwide and at time of writing delivery is free if you spend over £75.

Site Usability:	★★★★	Based:	UK
Product Range:	★★★	Express Delivery Option? (UK)	No
Price Range:	Medium	Gift Wrapping Option?	No
Delivery Area:	Worldwide	Returns Procedure:	Down to you

www.handmadelacecompany.co.uk

Butterfly and floral embroidered pyjamas, nightdresses with seed pearls, pintucks, ribbon and embroidered fairies are just some of the lovely things you'll find here, and they are quite unexpectedly well priced as well. Everything is made in 100% cotton and despatched in a presentation bag, so you'll find some good gift ideas too.

Site Usability:	★★★★	Based:	UK
Product Range:	★★★	Express Delivery Option? (UK)	No
Price Range:	Medium/Very Good Value	Gift Wrapping Option?	No
Delivery Area:	Worldwide	Returns Procedure:	Down to you

www.kidspyjamas.co.uk

This is a small range of pretty and fun printed pyjamas for girls and boys up to age ten. Designs range from robots, cowboys and fire engines for boys to nursery rhymes, cherries and Scottie dogs for girls. There are summer pjs with shorts and simply styled children's kaftans here too. Everything is very well priced and they offer a gift wrap service.

Site Usability:	★★★★	Based:	UK
Product Range:	★★★	Express Delivery Option? (UK)	No
Price Range:	Very Good Value	Gift Wrapping Option?	Yes
Delivery Area:	Worldwide	Returns Procedure:	Down to you

www.littlelazy.com

You know those old-fashioned pjs with personalised embroidery on the pocket? Well, this is where you can buy them for kids, so choose from plain Oxford blue, stripe, pink bubble or plain pink. Then just tell them the name you'd like embroidered and they'll do it for you. Sizes go from real tinies up to 11 years. The site also offers cushions, blankets, duvet covers, hot water bottle covers and more (and you can have personalised too).

Site Usability:	★★★★	Based:	UK
Product Range:	★★★★	Express Delivery Option? (UK)	Yes
Price Range:	Medium/Very Good Value	Gift Wrapping Option?	No
Delivery Area:	Worldwide	Returns Procedure:	Down to you

www.sleepyheadsmailorder.co.uk

Sleepyheads offers seven themes in its 100% cotton range: Ballerinas, Flowers, Sea, Space, Zoo, Racecars and Cowboys. They all come as pyjamas, sleepsuits and nightdresses, plus bedding, chairs, floor cushions, curtains, stickers and lots of other ideas depending on the print. You can order handcrafted children's bedroom furniture here too and check back for the launch of the new daywear range.

Site Usability:	★★★★	Based:	UK
Product Range:	★★★★	Express Delivery Option? (UK)	Yes
Price Range:	Medium	Gift Wrapping Option?	Yes
Delivery Area:	UK, but you can contact them for an overseas quotation	Returns Procedure:	Down to you

www.towels.co.uk

Click through to this website and then to Children's Bathrobes to find a small but attractive and well-priced range in cotton velour, cotton towelling and organic cotton velour. Just about anything you order here (and there are some great towels and adults' bathrobes as well) can be personalised with an embroidered name, initials or message of up to 20 characters.

Site Usability:	★★★★★	Based:	UK
Product Range:	★★★★	Express Delivery Option? (UK)	No
Price Range:	Medium	Gift Wrapping Option?	No
Delivery Area:	EU	Returns Procedure:	Down to you

Chapter 27

Children's Sport and Skiwear

It really isn't so very long ago that I was looking for skiwear for my kids (offline, actually) and the choice was, well, positively meagre. Now, with the most distant of Scottish skiwear shops being able to show their wares to you wherever you are in the world, the ranges have mushroomed – and not just for skiwear but for every type of sport you can think of.

So you can find kids' cricket kit, rugby and football gear, climbing and camping waterproofs and high-tech jackets, golf clothing, kids' trainers by premium brands such as Nike and Adidas and an excellent selection for the junior rider. No doubt I've missed out someone's favourite sport (and no doubt they'll tell me). Having said that, the more popular sports listed here are in alphabetical order, so you shouldn't have much trouble finding what you're looking for.

Sites to Visit

Cricket

www.owzat-cricket.co.uk

Bats by Gunn & Moore, Kookaburra and Gray-Nicolls, plus loads of other brands are available here, together with gloves, pads, kitbags, body protection, accessories and balls. This is a website obviously designed for real cricketers and it's proud of the fact that it has sold to some of the world's top players. You'll definitely find something for the junior cricketer here as the range is excellent.

Site Usability:	★★★★★	Based:	UK
Product Range:	★★★	Express Delivery Option? (UK)	Yes
Price Range:	Luxury/Medium	Gift Wrapping Option?	No
Delivery Area:	EU	Returns Procedure:	Down to you

General Sports Clothing and Footwear

www.adidas-shop.co.uk

Up until now you've had to go to a general sports store to find Adidas footwear and clothing. Now, with this great, modern-designed website you can look at everything in one place. But much better than that, you can also read up on all the latest sports innovations from this famous brand. You'll find sports clothing and footwear for men, women and kids, a small infants' range and Adidas by Stella McCartney.

Site Usability:	★★★★★	Based:	UK
Product Range:	★★★★	Express Delivery Option? (UK)	Yes
Price Range:	Medium	Gift Wrapping Option?	No
Delivery Area:	UK	Returns Procedure:	Down to you

www.jdsports.co.uk

JD Sports has extended its range to encompass Youth and Infant shoes and clothing. The range of brands includes Ben Sherman, Carbrini and Majestic, with trainers and casual sports shoes by Adidas, Lacoste, K-Swiss, Nike and Timberland for the larger sizes (and you can see immediately what's in stock), plus a surprisingly large range from those brands for infants as well.

Site Usability:	★★★★★	Based:	UK
Product Range:	★★★★★	Express Delivery Option? (UK)	No
Price Range:	Medium	Gift Wrapping Option?	No
Delivery Area:	UK	Returns Procedure:	Down to you

www.sport-e.com

Part of Littlewoods Online, this is the place to find discounted sports shoes by Nike, Puma, Reebok, Converse and Lacoste, plus the new season's ranges. There's also a wide range of sportswear for adults and kids, plus sports equipment. The selection is very good. Delivery is free if you spend over £100 and returns are free as well. It's an excellent website and the product list is growing all the time.

Site Usability:	★★★★★	Based:	UK
Product Range:	★★★★	Express Delivery Option? (UK)	No
Price Range:	Medium/Very Good Value	Gift Wrapping Option?	No
Delivery Area:	UK	Returns Procedure:	Free of charge

General Outdoors

www.blacks.co.uk

If you or any member of your family have ever done any camping, walking or hiking (or climbing), you'll probably already have visited Blacks, where you'll find a well-priced (rather than 'designer') range of clothing and accessories and good-value skiwear in season. The Kids' Gear section includes the Peter Storm range of jackets, fleece and waterproofs for infants and kids aged up to 12.

Site Usability:	★★★★★	Based:	UK
Product Range:	★★★★★	Express Delivery Option? (UK)	No
Price Range:	Medium/Very Good Value	Gift Wrapping Option?	No
Delivery Area:	UK	Returns Procedure:	Down to you

www.completeoutdoors.co.uk

Everything for walking, trekking, rambling, camping, climbing and many other activities is available here for men, women and kids, including fleece, jackets, hats and gloves, thermals and waterproof jackets. Sizes for kids start at infants (with a very small range) and the main kids' range at eight. There are lots of accessories here as well.

Site Usability:	★★★★	Based:	UK
Product Range:	★★★★★	Express Delivery Option? (UK)	No
Price Range:	Medium	Gift Wrapping Option?	No
Delivery Area:	UK	Returns Procedure:	Down to you

www.raindrops.co.uk

At Raindrops there's a range of Scandinavian-designed rainwear for children up to about age nine, including well-priced fleece-lined rain jackets, dungarees in a wide choice of colours and waterproof all-in-ones. There's also a good choice of high-quality more general outerwear, from a country that's well known for its love of the outdoors and wet-weather gear.

Site Usability:	★★★★	Based:	UK
Product Range:	★★★	Express Delivery Option? (UK)	Yes
Price Range:	Very Good Value	Gift Wrapping Option?	Yes
Delivery Area:	Worldwide	Returns Procedure:	Down to you

www.samandsid.co.uk

Here you can find stylish children's sun protective swimwear, designed and made in the UK and featuring soft cotton-mix fabrics that provide 50+ UPF protection. This is a very small range but perfect if you're taking your young kids somewhere hot and want a bit more peace of mind than the daily struggle to cover them in sun lotion, although you can buy that, and sunglasses, here as well, and the swimsuits don't replace sunscreen.

Site Usability:	★★★★	Based:	UK
Product Range: ★★★		Express Delivery Option? (UK)	No
Price Range:	Very Good Value	Gift Wrapping Option?	No
Delivery Area:	Worldwide	Returns Procedure:	Down to you

www.sportswearhouse.co.uk

Here's well-priced sportswear by brands such as Fruit of the Loom, Zerzees and Result Kids for a variety of sports such as football and rugby and for general outdoor activities and fitness. Many of the items are offered in a wide range of colours and you can use the personalisation service for names, clubs and schools. There's lots of good adults' general sportswear here as well.

Site Usability:	★★★★	Based:	UK
Product Range: ★★★		Express Delivery Option? (UK)	No
Price Range:	Very Good Value	Gift Wrapping Option?	No
Delivery Area:	Worldwide	Returns Procedure:	Down to you

www.waterproofworld.co.uk

You can find all types of waterproofs and outdoor wear for active kids and toddlers here. There are rain suits and dungarees from Scandinavia, fun raincoats and jackets, Togz all-in-one suits, excellent skiwear from Trespass and Dare2Be and even wetsuits and UV wear for beach and pool from Konfidence and TWF. Finally, there is the ultimate in puddle proofing – the toddler and child waders, which go from shoe size 22 to 38. First-class delivery is included free.

Site Usability:	★★★★	Based:	UK
Product Range: ★★★★		Express Delivery Option? (UK)	Yes if you call them
Price Range:	Medium	Gift Wrapping Option?	No
Delivery Area:	EU	Returns Procedure:	Down to you

Golf

www.118golf.co.uk

With its excellent delivery service and diverse range of products for the golfer, this is an excellent website. The Junior Golf range includes clubs by Nike, Nitro and Ram, junior golf shoes and gloves, plus kids' golf bags and trolleys. This would also be a great place for gifts for the junior golfer as there are lots of gadgets, books and DVDs.

Site Usability:	★★★★★	Based:	UK
Product Range:	★★★★★	Express Delivery Option? (UK)	Yes
Price Range:	Luxury/Medium	Gift Wrapping Option?	No
Delivery Area:	Worldwide	Returns Procedure:	Down to you

www.onlinegolf.co.uk

On this excellent golf website you can find junior golf enthusiasts' clubs and accessories by Wilson Staff, Longridge, US Kids and Nike, with the largest range definitely by US Kids. Then there are shoes, bags and trolleys, and clothing by Ashworth, Nike and Sunderland. The ranges change from season to season and there are good special offers during sale times which are worth taking a look at.

Site Usability:	★★★★★	Based:	UK
Product Range:	★★★★	Express Delivery Option? (UK)	Yes
Price Range:	Medium	Gift Wrapping Option?	No
Delivery Area:	EU	Returns Procedure:	Down to you

www.planetgolfuk.co.uk

At Planet Golf and alongside all the adult clubs, accessories and clothing there's a very good Junior range, which not only includes Hippo, US Kids and Hawk junior club sets but also clothing by Demon (polo shirts, fleece-lined sweaters and t-shirts), shoes, brollies and other accessories. There are kids' waterproofs and wind vests here as well.

Site Usability:	★★★★★	Based:	UK
Product Range:	★★★★★	Express Delivery Option? (UK)	No
Price Range:	Medium	Gift Wrapping Option?	No
Delivery Area:	Worldwide	Returns Procedure:	Down to you

Junior Ski

www.edge2edge.co.uk

The next time you're planning a skiing or snowboarding trip, you should take a look round this website, where you'll find an excellent list of brands. There are junior collections such as Surfanic, Tog 24, Columbia, Dakine, Burton and Peak Performance. You'll also find some excellent discounts, plus rental packages at good prices.

Site Usability:	★★★★	Based:	UK
Product Range:	★★★★	Express Delivery Option? (UK)	No
Price Range:	Medium	Gift Wrapping Option?	No
Delivery Area:	UK	Returns Procedure:	Down to you

www.ellis-brigham.com

This is a wonderful, clearly photographed website for grown-up and junior skiers, offering brands such as The North Face, Helly Hansen and Roxy. Every possible type of clothing and equipment is available, with skis, boots, poles, helmets and goggles just some of the equipment, together with a full range of ski clothing (including colourful, fun ski socks and beanies).

Site Usability:	★★★★★	Based:	UK
Product Range:	★★★★★	Express Delivery Option? (UK)	No
Price Range:	Luxury/Medium	Gift Wrapping Option?	No
Delivery Area:	Worldwide	Returns Procedure:	Down to you

www.littlesky.co.uk

Little Sky specialises in children's branded surf, ski and fashion wear, plus footwear and accessories for kids aged 0–16 years. On this website there's a good range of functional, fashionable and technical wear from brands such as Quiksilver, Roxy, Billabong, O'Neill, Animal, Oxbow, Timberland, Kookai, Elle, Reef, Columbia, Trespass and Brugi. In the summer you can find all you need for your holiday in the sun, from bikinis, boardshorts and funky shirts to UV suits and footwear, while in winter the site focuses on skiwear and accessories.

Site Usability:	★★★★★	Based:	UK
Product Range:	★★★★	Express Delivery Option? (UK)	Yes
Price Range:	Medium	Gift Wrapping Option?	No
Delivery Area:	EU	Returns Procedure:	Down to you

www.littletrekkers.co.uk

It's almost certainly easier to find a good selection of skiwear for adults than it is for kids, but this website makes it simple, offering all-in-one ski suits, salopettes and jackets for children from 6–9 months up to 12 years. There are also accessories such as helmets, neckwarmers, goggles and dark glasses, thermals, hats and gloves.

Site Usability:	★★★★	Based:	UK
Product Range:	★★★	Express Delivery Option? (UK)	Yes
Price Range:	Medium	Gift Wrapping Option?	No
Delivery Area:	EU	Returns Procedure:	Down to you

www.oggie.com

There's a very good selection of junior skiwear here, where you can buy girls' and boys' jackets and skisuits by Dare2be, Helly Hansen and Five Seasons and toddler skisuits by Bush Baby, Columbia and Regatta. A wide range of children's helmets, junior snowboards and a fantastic choice of gloves and headgear are available as well.

Site Usability:	★★★★	Based:	UK
Product Range:	★★★★	Express Delivery Option? (UK)	Yes
Price Range:	Medium	Gift Wrapping Option?	No
Delivery Area:	Worldwide	Returns Procedure:	Down to you

www.patagonia.com

As the sports that Patagonia specialises in are Alpine skiing, rock climbing, Nordic climbing and fly fishing, you won't be surprised that this is a collection of high-tech/highly insulated products. What is surprising (to me, at least) is that it has produced an excellent range for infants and children too, with jackets, vests, fleece, base layers, all-in-ones and gloves for ages from 3 months to 14 years. Nothing is inexpensive, but you can be sure you're buying the best.

Site Usability:	★★★★★	Based:	UK
Product Range:	★★★★★	Express Delivery Option? (UK)	Yes
Price Range:	Luxury	Gift Wrapping Option?	No
Delivery Area:	Worldwide	Returns Procedure:	Down to you

www.simplypiste.com

This is one of a rapidly growing chain of online sporting retailers that includes simplyscuba and simplybeach. At simplypiste there's an excellent, well-laid out collection for men, women and children (and you can actually click straight through to the children's skiwear section, which makes a change). Find ski suits, jackets, salopettes, ski pants, base layer and baby skiwear there, plus lots of accessories such as gloves and goggles, which you have to look for in their separate sections.

Site Usability:	★★★★★	Based:	UK
Product Range:	★★★★	Express Delivery Option? (UK)	Yes
Price Range:	Medium	Gift Wrapping Option?	No
Delivery Area:	Worldwide	Returns Procedure:	Down to you

www.snowandrock.com

Snow and Rock is a well-known retailer for skiers, snowboarders and rock climbers. It offers a full range of equipment, clothing and accessories by brands such as Animal, Billabong, Ski Jacket, Helly Hanson, O'Neill, Quiksilver, Salomon and Oakley. There's also lots of advice on what to buy and advice on fit. The junior section is comprehensive and you'll find everything you could possibly need, from all-in-ones and padded jackets to hats, socks and thermals.

Site Usability:	★★★★★	Based:	UK
Product Range:	★★★★★	Express Delivery Option? (UK)	Yes
Price Range:	Luxury/Medium/Very Good Value	Gift Wrapping Option?	No
Delivery Area:	Worldwide	Returns Procedure:	Down to you

Riding

www.dragonflysaddlery.co.uk

Here you can choose from army camouflage jods (!), Buddies jods and Saddlehuggers in loads of different colours, from pink and blue to the more traditional. Then there are long and short junior jodhpur boots, body protectors, wellies and muck boots and rainproof jackets. In some cases you're offered the children's range right at the start, in others it's right in the category sizing, which makes life a little confusing. There's a good choice though, so it's worth a look.

Site Usability:	★★★	Based:	UK
Product Range:	★★★★	Express Delivery Option? (UK)	No
Price Range:	Medium	Gift Wrapping Option?	No
Delivery Area:	Worldwide	Returns Procedure:	Down to you

www.mad4ponies.com

This is a great site for pony-mad children, as unlike lots of other equestrian websites aimed at riders of all ages, this website is just for kids (girls really) aged 5–16 who love to ride. It has funky pink or purple nubuck jodhpur boots, glitter whips, vibrant grooming kits, sparkly diamante hat covers, colourful jodhpurs and bright and brilliant products for your favourite pony. There's also pony-themed gear for school bags, bedrooms, the bathroom and casual wear.

Site Usability:	★★★★	Based:	UK
Product Range:	★★★	Express Delivery Option? (UK)	Yes
Price Range:	Medium	Gift Wrapping Option?	No
Delivery Area:	Worldwide, but email for a delivery quote for overseas	Returns Procedure:	Down to you

www.saddler.co.uk

At Saddler, you have to click through to the main range first because there isn't a special children's section. However, there's a good choice of junior Barbour jackets, from the standard waxed jacket to the essential padded, cord-collar jacket in lots of colours from burnt orange to apple green. There are also kids' show jackets by Just Togs, hats by FBI Champion and Just Togs, jods by Gorringe in some great colours, plus long and short boots, jackets and body protectors.

Site Usability:	★★★★	Based:	UK
Product Range:	★★★★	Express Delivery Option? (UK)	No
Price Range:	Medium	Gift Wrapping Option?	No
Delivery Area:	Worldwide	Returns Procedure:	Down to you

Rugby and Football

www.newitts.co.uk

Aerobics, archery, athletics, badminton, baseball, basketball, bikes and billiards are the first eight items on the sports menu here, where there's almost everything for every sport you can think of. OK, trampolining, tennis, swimming, rugby and football are just a few more. In the Back to School section you can buy mouthguards, football shirts, rugby shorts, gloves and boots, headguards and kit bags.

Site Usability:	★★★★	Based:	UK
Product Range:	★★★★★	Express Delivery Option? (UK)	Yes
Price Range:	Medium	Gift Wrapping Option?	No
Delivery Area:	Worldwide	Returns Procedure:	Down to you

www.rugbystore.co.uk

This one's strictly for the boys (I hope) and there's a tremendous range, so if you have a young rugby enthusiast in the family you'll not only find some great kit here but some excellent gift ideas as well. The site stocks Kooga, Armourfit and Canterbury (CCC) in the general range, plus junior rugby shirts for most of the teams. Needless to say, there's all the adult rugby gear here too.

Site Usability:	★★★★★	Based:	UK
Product Range:	★★★★★	Express Delivery Option? (UK)	No
Price Range:	Medium/Very Good Value	Gift Wrapping Option?	No
Delivery Area:	Worldwide	Returns Procedure:	Down to you

Sport/Casual Wear

www.extremepie.com

There are enough sportswear brands here to sink a ship, including famous brands such as O'Neill, Quiksilver, Animal, Vans, Billabong, RipCurl, Addict, Extreme and Reef. However, sizes for kids really start at age eight and the range is nothing like as large as it is for adults. This is a good site for anyone who's addicted to sport, or just likes that sporty, casual look.

Site Usability:	★★★★	Based:	UK
Product Range:	★★★★	Express Delivery Option? (UK)	Yes
Price Range:	Medium	Gift Wrapping Option?	No
Delivery Area:	Worldwide	Returns Procedure:	Down to you

www.fatface.co.uk

When you first take a look at the fatface.co.uk website you may be a little disconcerted. It's certainly not like most others, with pictures and type all being used to reinforce Fatface's idiosyncratic 'cool', active style. But it works together. You'll find a wide selection of tops and t-shirts, jackets and fleece, denim and sweats, all in unique fabrics and style and, more often than not, a muted colour palette. Sizes for kids start at age 2-3.

Site Usability:	★★★★	Based:	UK
Product Range:	★★★★	Express Delivery Option? (UK)	Yes
Price Range:	Medium	Gift Wrapping Option?	No
Delivery Area:	Worldwide	Returns Procedure:	Down to you

www.hackett.co.uk

Famous for using Jonny Wilkinson as its model as well as for great quality clothing, you can now buy from Hackett's excellent selection of stylish kids' sportswear, which includes warm jackets, checked shirts, rugby shirts, polo shirts, knitwear, trousers and accessories such as hats and scarves, all in the signature style.

Site Usability:	★★★★	Based:	UK
Product Range:	★★★	Express Delivery Option? (UK)	No
Price Range:	Medium	Gift Wrapping Option?	No
Delivery Area:	UK	Returns Procedure:	Down to you/complicated

www.joulesclothing.com

Joules is a clothing website with a difference. Beautifully photographed and well laid out, there are some excellent fun sporty separates for just about everyone, provided you like stripes and colours (although lots of items are available in black/jet as well). It's mainly aimed at the riding fraternity, although many of the clothes, particularly the jackets and fleece, would have a much wider appeal. For express delivery call them.

Site Usability:	★★★★	Based:	UK
Product Range:	★★★★	Express Delivery Option? (UK)	Yes
Price Range:	Medium	Gift Wrapping Option?	No
Delivery Area:	Worldwide	Returns Procedure:	Down to you

173

Chapter 28

Footwear Shop

You're probably going to say something along the lines of grand-mothers and eggs here (and no, I'm not a grandmother, thanks), but I have to say this: don't even think of buying shoes for your child online - or anywhere for that matter - until he or she has been properly measured and don't expect anything you buy here to last for very long fit wise. I can't begin to tell you how many times my children's feet changed size, from what I can remember it was several times a year, but then I had three close together, so I'm probably not thinking straight (I hope not anyway, no wonder I can't have that handbag).

There are some excellent shoe websites, but the problem with kids, or one of the many, is that if they like something a lot they'll pretend that it fits, that it's not just a tiny bit tight, that they're absolutely fine (as in FINE!!). So be careful buying from here. Just make sure you really know their size and don't say I didn't warn you.

Sites to Visit

www.bigfootlittlefoot.com

Some websites just have great names and this is one of them. (And others don't - I have a personal aversion to the r us and 4u type of name.) It stocks baby and infant shoes by Adidas and Reebok, children and toddler

Adidas, Puma, Reebok and Nike, plus all of those in adult sizes, with Asics and Wilson as well and Animal flip-flops for all.

Site Usability:	★★★★★	Based:	UK
Product Range:	★★★★	Express Delivery Option? (UK)	No
Price Range:	Medium	Gift Wrapping Option?	No
Delivery Area:	Worldwide	Returns Procedure:	Down to you

www.celtic-sheepskin.co.uk

There are some excellent washable (yes, really) sheepskin boots with heavy soles here for kids in colours such as peony, turquoise and lilac as well as the more standard colours. You can also buy cute booties, Aqualamb weatherproof boots, Mongolian boots with outrageously fluffy and colourful yet stylish tops and luxurious Toscana shearling cuffed boots. Don't let them look, they'll probably want them all.

Site Usability:	★★★★★	Based:	UK
Product Range:	★★★	Express Delivery Option? (UK)	No
Price Range:	Luxury/Medium	Gift Wrapping Option?	No
Delivery Area:	UK	Returns Procedure:	Down to you

www.chatham-marine.co.uk

There are just two styles of children's deck shoes here: the classic laced Anchor shoe, which comes in navy or tan, and the Skipper, which has a leather Velcro fastening. Sizing ranges from 1-13 and you can see immediately what is in stock. There are excellent adult deck shoes here as well.

Site Usability:	★★★★★	Based:	UK
Product Range:	★★★	Express Delivery Option? (UK)	No
Price Range:	Medium	Gift Wrapping Option?	No
Delivery Area:	EU	Returns Procedure:	Down to you

www.cloggs.co.uk

This is a great website for kids' sporty shoes as it offers brand names Converse, Doc Martens, Rockport, Vans, Kickers, Uggs and Skechers, plus several more. There's a huge range of shoes for grown-ups as well and it offers a worldwide express delivery service. If you're looking for casual shoes, this website is a must.

Site Usability:	★★★★	Based:	UK
Product Range:	★★★	Express Delivery Option? (UK)	Yes
Price Range:	Medium	Gift Wrapping Option?	No
Delivery Area:	Worldwide	Returns Procedure:	Down to you

www.espadrillesetc.com

Here are gorgeous espadrilles for kids (and you as well, of course) and whether or not you're an espadrilles fan, if you're going on holiday you really should take a look at this summer shoe website. The kids' range includes red and white polka dot, embroidered flowers, funky stripes and pretty gingham, while for adults there's just about every colour, fabric and style you can think of.

Site Usability:	★★★★	Based:	Spain
Product Range:	★★★	Express Delivery Option? (UK)	No
Price Range:	Medium/Very Good Value	Gift Wrapping Option?	No
Delivery Area:	Worldwide	Returns Procedure:	Down to you

www.jdsports.co.uk

JD Sports has extended its range to include Youth and Infant shoes and clothing. The range of trainers and casual sports shoes includes Adidas, Lacoste, K-Swiss, Nike and Timberland for the larger sizes (where you can see immediately what's in stock) and a surprisingly large range from those brands for infants as well. The youth clothing includes Adidas, Ben Sherman, Carbrini and Majestic and is well worth taking a look at.

Site Usability:	★★★★★	Based:	UK
Product Range:	★★★★★	Express Delivery Option? (UK)	No
Price Range:	Medium	Gift Wrapping Option?	No
Delivery Area:	UK	Returns Procedure:	Down to you

www.justconverse.co.uk

I'm not sure I really need to say anything here – you're either a Converse fan or you're not. If you are you'll be in Converse heaven. The site shows you immediately which sizes are in stock – if yours isn't there I suggest that you give them a call and ask when it will be in. Choose from the classic High and Low Top, One Star plimsolls and lots of special designs each season.

Site Usability:	★★★★	Based:	UK
Product Range:	★★★★★	Express Delivery Option? (UK)	Yes
Price Range:	Medium	Gift Wrapping Option?	No
Delivery Area:	UK	Returns Procedure:	Down to you

www.mischiefkids.co.uk

This is a busy, fun, brightly coloured website offering a great range of designer shoes for children, from labels such as Doc Martens, Naturino, Moschino, Lelli Kelly and Oilili. Click on the brand you're interested in and you can immediately see everything they're offering, plus what's available right now (although this could be simplified).

Site Usability:	★★★★	Based:	UK
Product Range:	★★★★★	Express Delivery Option? (UK)	Yes
Price Range:	Medium	Gift Wrapping Option?	No
Delivery Area:	Worldwide	Returns Procedure:	Down to you

www.nhmshop.co.uk

And now for something totally different (I have to say that in every book, sorry). This is the shopping site for the Natural History Museum and you can, for your dinosaur enthusiast, pick up a pair of Dinosoles Stegasaurus or T-rex children's trainers or dinosaur wellies, not to mention a glow-in-the-dark bat t-shirt or ladybird umbrella. Even I'm tempted.

Site Usability:	★★★★	Based:	UK
Product Range:	★★★	Express Delivery Option? (UK)	No
Price Range:	Medium	Gift Wrapping Option?	No
Delivery Area:	Worldwide	Returns Procedure:	Down to you

www.ravel.co.uk

Famous high-street brand Ravel is now offering kids' shoes online. The boys' range includes some good school-style Velcro-fastened shoes, plus hard-wearing boots. For girls there are ballet flats and dancing shoes (no, they're not the same thing) and modern black pumps. The prices are all reasonable and there's helpful sizing information to get you on your way.

Site Usability: ★★★★	Based:	UK
Product Range: ★★★	Express Delivery Option? (UK)	No
Price Range: Very Good Value	Gift Wrapping Option?	No
Delivery Area: UK	Returns Procedure:	Down to you

www.rockpoolkids.co.uk

Rockpoolkids offers deck shoes made from quality nubuck and full-grain leather, lined with pigskin and with a stitched and glued non-slip rubber sole. There are three styles: one with a Velcro strap in sizes 24-32, a classic lace-up in sizes 33-40 and a navy deck shoe with Velcro fastening from size 24-40. All shoes are made in a medium width fitting and are unisex, although some boys might object to the pink! There's also a small, well-priced and sporty range of clothing.

Site Usability: ★★★★	Based:	UK
Product Range: ★★★	Express Delivery Option? (UK)	No
Price Range: Medium	Gift Wrapping Option?	No
Delivery Area: UK	Returns Procedure:	Down to you

www.sheepskin-slippers.co.uk

When you want your feet (or your children's feet) to be as warm and cosy as possible you should buy some slippers from this very simple website. Children's sizes go from 9-2 and you can buy half-collared or plain moccasin styles – there are more styles for adults. For what these are the prices are extremely reasonable and although if you're reading this in the summer you probably won't want to buy right now, you should remember this site for later in the year.

Site Usability: ★★★	Based:	UK
Product Range: ★★★	Express Delivery Option? (UK)	No
Price Range: Medium/Very Good Value	Gift Wrapping Option?	No
Delivery Area: Worldwide	Returns Procedure:	Down to you

www.slipperstore.co.uk

Yes, this really is a slipper store, where everything is reasonably priced and there's a good range for kids. You know that moment when slippers have been the last thing you're thinking of and your little one says 'I have no slippers, we need to go out and get some' (usually at your busiest moment)? Well, this store solves that problem straight away – there are loads of styles in a wide range of sizes for everyone.

Site Usability:	★★★★★	Based:	UK
Product Range:	★★★	Express Delivery Option? (UK)	No
Price Range:	Medium/Very Good Value	Gift Wrapping Option?	No
Delivery Area:	UK	Returns Procedure:	Down to you

www.stewardsons.co.uk

If your family is of the hiking/walking/camping variety, you'll need to do some shopping here. The range of outdoor kids' shoes includes Regatta, Hi-tec and Merell and it also offers Brasher and Fellwalker walking socks, essential for these types of shoes/boots. There's lots of information on all the styles and of course you'll find the adult versions here as well.

Site Usability:	★★★★	Based:	UK
Product Range:	★★★	Express Delivery Option? (UK)	Yes for most places in the UK
Price Range:	Medium	Gift Wrapping Option?	No
Delivery Area:	Worldwide	Returns Procedure:	Down to you

www.tigerfeetshoes.co.uk

Tiger Feet is a specialist children's shoe retailer based in Cheshire. It provides one of the widest choices of children's shoes in the country, with an emphasis on design, quality and fit. Brands on offer include Kickers, Moschino, Rondinella, Geox and Oilili. There is also a wide range of good-quality school shoes up to size 9 (43), including Startrite, Rhino and Ecco, together with sports shoes including Geox and Skechers.

Site Usability:	★★★★★	Based:	UK
Product Range:	★★★★★	Express Delivery Option? (UK)	No
Price Range:	Luxury/Medium	Gift Wrapping Option?	No
Delivery Area:	UK	Returns Procedure:	Down to you

www.vincentshoestore.co.uk

Scandinavian brand Vincent Shoe Store offers practical and fun designs for infants, toddlers, pre-schoolers and children up to shoe size 35 (UK size 3). I'm sure you won't be surprised to learn that top of the list here are kids' snow boots (in season), which are available in lots of colours, plus 'frog' wellies with clever pull-on handles. The range covers everything from sports shoes to party shoes, so it's well worth a look.

Site Usability:	★★★★	Based:	UK
Product Range:	★★★	Express Delivery Option? (UK)	No
Price Range:	Medium	Gift Wrapping Option?	No
Delivery Area:	UK	Returns Procedure:	Down to you

www.wellie-web.co.uk

Here's a website with a name that you won't forget quickly, but if you're someone who spends a lot of time outdoors, particularly in wet weather, and likes your children to come along, you'll find it indispensable. Although the majority of the boots here are for adults (or size 4 plus), it also offers high-quality Aigle and Hunter boots for children, which go from size 8 to size 2, are very reasonably priced and come in lots of colours.

Site Usability:	★★★★	Based:	UK
Product Range:	★★★★	Express Delivery Option? (UK)	No
Price Range:	Luxury/Medium	Gift Wrapping Option?	No
Delivery Area:	UK	Returns Procedure:	Down to you

Chapter 29

Schoolwear and Accessories

So no more of that dreadful queuing at the John Lewis counter next time you need some school uniform – now John Lewis, along with other retailers, offers all the basics online. And if your particular school uniform comes from there, you can always phone them.

Buying school uniform online, whether for a specific school or when you just want some essentials, is fine, provided, of course, you know your child's size. That may sound obvious, but with normal, fast-growing children I've always found it a problem to keep up (and sometimes haven't).

Some of the websites here offer uniforms for specific schools, others just well-priced generic uniform, and they're all equally easy to shop from. Then there are the essential accessories – name tapes (how I hated those), backpacks, pens, pencils and all the other paraphernalia that your kids (if they're anything like mine) will discover they're desperately in need of the day before they go back.

Sites to Visit

www.aitken-niven.co.uk

Aitken & Niven is based in Edinburgh and specialises in school uniforms for Scottish schools such as Auchterarder, Edinburgh Academy and Glenalmond. So if that's where you're based you can order it all from here. In the sport section you can buy (non-school specific) Canterbury training kit, Gilbert rugby balls and rugby boots, plus hockey and cricket bats.

Site Usability:	★★★★	Based:	UK
Product Range:	★★★★	Express Delivery Option? (UK)	No
Price Range:	Medium	Gift Wrapping Option?	No
Delivery Area:	UK	Returns Procedure:	Down to you

www.anythingleft-handed.co.uk

Here there's absolutely anything, from reverse-blade scissors and left-handed nib fountain pens by Pelikano, Cambridge and Inoxcrom to rulers, sharpeners and calligraphy sets. The site has put together some excellent packs of left-handed essentials and advises you which to buy by age and ability. You can also buy left-handed guitars here (think about it).

Site Usability:	★★★★	Based:	UK
Product Range:	★★★★	Express Delivery Option? (UK)	Yes
Price Range:	Medium	Gift Wrapping Option?	No
Delivery Area:	UK	Returns Procedure:	Down to you

www.harrods.com

Click through here to Children/Fashion/School Uniform and if it supplies your school you can order everything online. If in doubt and you need something in a hurry, you should call them, as not everything is always in stock, in which case the delay can be for weeks. In the boyswear collection there's also a high-quality navy blazer and trousers and blue and white shirts.

Site Usability:	★★★★	Based:	UK
Product Range:	★★★★	Express Delivery Option? (UK)	No
Price Range:	Luxury/Medium	Gift Wrapping Option?	No
Delivery Area:	Worldwide	Returns Procedure:	Down to you

www.johnlewis.com

So, as I said above, no more queuing the week before school goes back for John Lewis's excellent range of uniforms. Here you can choose from the carefully edited range of blazers, shirts and blouses, skirts, trousers, socks and tights. The site shows you straight away how many of anything is in stock and offers an express delivery within the UK. The size guide and uniform checklists are well worth using.

Site Usability:	★★★★★	Based:	UK
Product Range:	★★★★	Express Delivery Option? (UK)	Yes
Price Range:	Medium	Gift Wrapping Option?	No
Delivery Area:	UK	Returns Procedure:	Return to store or free

www.marksandspencer.com

You may well already know that you can buy schoolwear from M&S, but did you also know that you can order it online? Everything is well priced and one of the main advantages here is that you'll find garments that are cotton and wool rich, which certainly makes a change from most of the uniforms in man-made fibres (although there's that here too). There's a pretty ballet range as well.

Site Usability:	★★★★★	Based:	UK
Product Range:	★★★	Express Delivery Option? (UK)	Depends on where you live
Price Range:	Medium/Very Good Value	Gift Wrapping Option?	No
Delivery Area:	UK	Returns Procedure:	Free — return by post or to store

www.schofieldandsims.co.uk

Schofield and Sims publishes a wide selection of dictionaries, posters, homework books, school books, educational workbooks and textbooks for schools and for home education that you can buy online. There are dictionaries and workbooks from early years up to Key Stage 2, pre-school reading books and lots of educational, fun and well-illustrated posters. Delivery is free in the UK.

Site Usability:	★★★★	Based:	UK
Product Range:	★★★★	Express Delivery Option? (UK)	No
Price Range:	Medium/Very Good Value	Gift Wrapping Option?	No
Delivery Area:	Worldwide	Returns Procedure:	Down to you

www.schooluniformshop.co.uk

This retailer offers a wide range of schoolwear, from basic essentials such as blazers and rainproof jackets, long- and short-sleeve shirts and different types of trouser to polo shirts and knitwear in a wide range of colours. The prices here are very good and if you spend over £100, UK delivery is free. The site supplies specific schools' uniforms as well, for which you need the reference code, and it aims to stock everything it shows on the website.

Site Usability:	★★★★★	Based:	UK
Product Range:	★★★	Express Delivery Option? (UK)	No
Price Range:	Very Good Value	Gift Wrapping Option?	No
Delivery Area:	UK	Returns Procedure:	Down to you

www.skoolzone.co.uk

Here's an unsophisticated but well-stocked website full of revision guides and books for the learner, some of which start at 6–7 years and others which go right up to A Level. There are books for Key Stage One, Sats and 11+, together with early verbal reasoning, posters and learning magnets and a good range of school bags as well.

Site Usability:	★★★	Based:	UK
Product Range:	★★★	Express Delivery Option? (UK)	No
Price Range:	Medium/Very Good Value	Gift Wrapping Option?	No
Delivery Area:	Worldwide	Returns Procedure:	Down to you

www.staples.co.uk

If you get yourself organised in time and get that essential list from your kids, this is one trip you won't have to make before they go back to school. Here you can find everything from files and pens and rulers to glue sticks. You will, as I know well, also save yourself a huge (and I mean huge) amount of money as they – yes, they – won't be able to go round with that shopping basket and add in all those little extras which cost a fortune. Definitely try to buy it all here, it makes life so much easier.

Site Usability:	★★★★★	Based:	UK
Product Range:	★★★★★	Express Delivery Option? (UK)	Yes
Price Range:	Medium/Very Good Value	Gift Wrapping Option?	No
Delivery Area:	UK	Returns Procedure:	Down to you

www.whsmith.co.uk

On WHSmith's easy-on-the-eye website there's a smaller range than at Staples of back-to-school essentials such as calculators, pens, folders and binders. But you should find just about everything you need (and the range is growing all the time). As this is not quite such a busy, office-based website, you may also find it easier to use.

Site Usability:	★★★★★	Based:	UK
Product Range:	★★★	Express Delivery Option? (UK)	No
Price Range:	Medium	Gift Wrapping Option?	No
Delivery Area:	UK	Returns Procedure:	Down to you

www.wovenlabelsuk.com

Although you can order labels from some of the other school uniform retailers listed here, if that's all you're after, come straight to this well-designed website. It offers iron-on labels with or without telephone numbers, shoe and property labels and the woven variety. You can also order personalised ribbon and luggage straps.

Site Usability:	★★★★★	Based:	UK
Product Range:	★★★	Express Delivery Option? (UK)	Yes
Price Range:	Medium	Gift Wrapping Option?	No
Delivery Area:	UK	Returns Procedure:	Down to you

www.yourschooluniform.com

This is a very well-laid out school uniform website offering free delivery and pretty much anything you might need for schoolwear. There is a wide choice of trousers, skirts, fleece tops, waterproofs, sportswear, tracksuits, t-shirts, polo shirts and other uniform basics. Then there are colourful nylon bags and backpacks, swimming bags, painting aprons, ID watches, goggles, sports bottles, name labels and more.

Site Usability:	★★★★★	Based:	UK
Product Range:	★★★	Express Delivery Option? (UK)	No
Price Range:	Medium	Gift Wrapping Option?	No
Delivery Area:	UK	Returns Procedure:	Down to you

Chapter 30

Dance, Music, Art and Crafts

Here are the websites for your would-be ballerina, artist or musician, where you can buy everything from leotards, pointe shoes and tutus to clarinets and trombones (warn the neighbours first, I suggest). If you check the prices of musical instruments online with your local music store you may well have a surprise, as you can often find good discounts on the exact same item.

The artists' websites here sell the full ranges, from watercolours to oil paints and canvas, plus lots of ideas for crafts, so they can be great for gifts as well.

Sites to Visit

www.artist-supplies.co.uk

Staedtler, Derwent, Sennelier and Windsor & Newton are just a few of the brands on this website, offering a full range of materials for artists and would-be artists. There are easels, paints (oil, acrylic or watercolour), paper and board, canvasses, brushes and folios. It also has a well-stocked crafts section, with calligraphy, candle making, glass painting, needlecraft and stencilling, so there's something for everyone, plus some good gift ideas.

Site Usability:	★★★	Based:	UK
Product Range:	★★★★★	Express Delivery Option? (UK)	Yes
Price Range:	Medium	Gift Wrapping Option?	No
Delivery Area:	Worldwide	Returns Procedure:	Down to you

www.dancedepot.co.uk

This is a great place for dancewear, where you'll find brands such as Pineapple, Capezio and Bloch and everything from RAD-approved examination leotards and skirts, jazz shoes, boots and warm-up clothes to stage and character shoes, a range of costumes and Snazaroo and Charles Fox make-up. There are also enchanting tutus for tinies for those mini wannabe ballet girls.

Site Usability:	★★★★★	Based:	UK
Product Range:	★★★★	Express Delivery Option? (UK)	No
Price Range:	Medium	Gift Wrapping Option?	No
Delivery Area:	UK	Returns Procedure:	Down to you

www.dancedirectworld.com

For anyone who's into (or just starting) ballet or jazz, this is a lovely, essential website. The pictures of the dancing girls on the front lead you straight into a wonderful selection of leotards, skirts and tutus, tights, leggings and warm-up gear, plus tops and pants for jazz, soft and pointe ballet shoes and a selection of sneakers.

Site Usability:	★★★★	Based:	UK
Product Range:	★★★★	Express Delivery Option? (UK)	No
Price Range:	Medium	Gift Wrapping Option?	No
Delivery Area:	Worldwide	Returns Procedure:	Down to you

www.johnsoncrafts.co.uk

Cross stitch, knitting and crochet, tapestry and decoupage are just some of the crafts you'll find here. There's a wide range of kits, including Brambly Hedge, Farm Animals and Charlie 'n Friends (cross stitch), simple and quite complicated tapestry sets, knitting and crochet, threads and accessories and everything you need to get going. Call them if you have any queries - it would be helpful if the site had a rating for how complicated each item is, but it doesn't (yet).

Site Usability:	★★★★	Based:	UK
Product Range:	★★★★★	Express Delivery Option? (UK)	No
Price Range:	Medium	Gift Wrapping Option?	No
Delivery Area:	Worldwide	Returns Procedure:	Down to you

www.musicroom.com

Established in 1995, Musicroom is a global retailer, shipping products out to over 100 countries and offering one of the largest selections of sheet music, song books, books about music and tutor methods in the world. At Christmas time it has a gift selection, including Christmas music, learning guides for different instruments, CDs and instrument accessories. It is an excellent website, so if you have a young musician in the family, do stop off here.

Site Usability:	★★★★	Based:	UK
Product Range:	★★★★★	Express Delivery Option? (UK)	No
Price Range:	Medium	Gift Wrapping Option?	No
Delivery Area:	Worldwide	Returns Procedure:	Down to you

www.signetmusic.com

This is quite a confusing site to look at, probably because the range is so big, but if you're in the market for a new or secondhand musical instrument, you must have a browse as the prices can be very good. The range is amazing and it's helpful that there is a clear manufacturer index offering almost 100 brands, so you can go straight to the product you're looking for. The site also offers online live support (which you may well need) and worldwide delivery for just about everything.

Site Usability:	★★★★	Based:	UK
Product Range:	★★★★★	Express Delivery Option? (UK)	No
Price Range:	Medium	Gift Wrapping Option?	No
Delivery Area:	Worldwide	Returns Procedure:	Down to you

www.themusiccellar.co.uk

This is a clear and easy-to-navigate website, where you can choose from a fantastic selection of musical instruments, from clarinets to grand pianos, acoustic and electric guitars, together with sheet music and a repair service. The instruments are discounted (check the price with your local supplier and/or a price comparison website to make sure), but some of the prices look excellent. Prices for UK shipping are supplied online, but you need to call them for overseas deliveries.

Site Usability:	★★★★★	Based:	UK
Product Range:	★★★★★	Express Delivery Option? (UK)	No
Price Range:	Medium	Gift Wrapping Option?	No
Delivery Area:	Worldwide	Returns Procedure:	Down to you

www.yorkshireartstore.co.uk

Discover a wonderful treasure trove of artists' and craft supplies, from paints, pencils, brushes and inks to clay, craft paper and adhesives, plus fabric art and needlecraft equipment. There are accessories including frames, tapestry wools, stranded cotton and fantasy threads. This is not one of the most highly sophisticated websites, but it's easy to use and quick to order from. Expect a high level of service and speedy delivery and call them if you need advice.

Site Usability:	★★★★	Based:	UK
Product Range:	★★★★	Express Delivery Option? (UK)	No
Price Range:	Medium	Gift Wrapping Option?	No
Delivery Area:	UK	Returns Procedure:	Down to you

Chapter 31

Activity Toys and Outdoor Equipment

I ncluding the word 'toys' here may be a bit misleading as although there are lots of play things here, there are also a number that are definitely not toys, such as trampolines, climbing frames, swings and slides, netball sets, play forts and outdoor games.

Having had a son who broke his arm on a friend's trampoline, I would suggest paying a great deal of attention to the safety products available here. A big trampoline is great for older children but can be dangerous for tinies. The same goes for anything climbable and swingable on, unless you're there all the time. Having said that, it's almost impossible to stop kids from doing daft things. You just have to try.

Sites to Visit

www.activekid.co.uk

Active Kid offers pretty well the full range of TP Toys' climbing frames, sandpits, slides, swings, trampolines (including nets and accessories and wooden playsets). These are all large items which it's so much better to order online (how did you do it before?) as not only do they get delivered – hopefully to your garden – but you can easily access all the information you need without having to wait for a shop assistant to come and help you.

Site Usability:	★★★★★	Based:	UK
Product Range:	★★★★★	Express Delivery Option? (UK)	No
Price Range:	Medium	Gift Wrapping Option?	No
Delivery Area:	UK	Returns Procedure:	Down to you

www.activitytoysdirect.co.uk

This is an unsophisticated but extremely easy-to-use website where you'll find (you probably guessed) activity toys, including lots of ideas for garden fun. There are netball sets, fun rides and aqua slides, swing and slide combinations, foldaway trampolines with net protection for very young children, plus the full-size versions, table tennis tables and climbing frames.

Site Usability:	★★★★	Based:	UK
Product Range:	★★★	Express Delivery Option? (UK)	Yes
Price Range:	Medium/Very Good Value	Gift Wrapping Option?	No
Delivery Area:	UK	Returns Procedure:	Down to you

www.adventuretoys.co.uk

Here you'll find a good range of climbing frames, trampolines and swing sets, and also lots of ride-on tractors and cars, sand and water tables, mini picnic tables, basketball sets, play houses, netball goals, practice tennis nets and trikes. Phew. Brands the site carries include Brio, Little Tikes, TP Toys, Supertramp and Winther. This website is well worth having a good look round.

Site Usability:	★★★★★	Based:	UK
Product Range:	★★★★★	Express Delivery Option? (UK)	Yes
Price Range:	Medium	Gift Wrapping Option?	No
Delivery Area:	UK	Returns Procedure:	Down to you

www.eastermeadactivity.co.uk

Here you can really go for broke and simply add to your basket the superb wooden play fort at over £1000. You'll no doubt be glad to know that there are some other excellent activity 'toys' here as well, such as garden football goals, outdoor chess sets and fabulous Sherwood wooden climbing frames. There isn't a large range, but some of the products are quite unusual, so it's a good place to have a look.

Site Usability: ★★★	Based:	UK
Product Range: ★★★	Express Delivery Option? (UK)	No
Price Range: Luxury/Medium	Gift Wrapping Option?	No
Delivery Area: UK	Returns Procedure:	Down to you

www.enchanted-wood.co.uk

At Enchanted Wood you can order the very good range of Kettler pedal go-karts and trikes, plus Kingswood and Sherwood wooden play systems and accessories. Then for rainy days there's lots of Lego to choose from, from introduction Lego Duplo to Mega Vehicle sets for ages 8+, together with everything Playmobile from Construction and Everyday Living to Playmobile for tinies.

Site Usability: ★★★★	Based:	UK
Product Range: ★★★★	Express Delivery Option? (UK)	No
Price Range: Medium	Gift Wrapping Option?	No
Delivery Area: UK	Returns Procedure:	Down to you

www.gardenadventure.co.uk

This is the serious end of the activity 'toy' online retailers, where you can not only buy a fantastic range of Dino go-karts up to the top-of-the-range Black Magic BF5 at just under £900, plus the Dino pedal-powered train and tender, but also use the services to build (and buy from them) a wide range of log cabins, wooden play houses and adventure climbing frames. If you want something really special, this would be a good place to look.

Site Usability: ★★★★	Based:	UK
Product Range: ★★★★★	Express Delivery Option? (UK)	No
Price Range: Luxury/Medium	Gift Wrapping Option?	No
Delivery Area: UK	Returns Procedure:	Down to you in agreement with them

www.gardengames.co.uk

Whether you're looking for trampolines, climbing frames, swings and slides, junior and full-sized croquet sets, snooker and pool tables, table tennis tables, aqua slides or an old-fashioned wooden sledge, you'll find everything on this friendly website. All the items are well photographed, they offer speedy UK delivery and will also ship to the USA, Canada and Spain.

Site Usability:	★★★★★	Based:	UK
Product Range:	★★★★	Express Delivery Option? (UK)	Yes
Price Range:	Medium	Gift Wrapping Option?	No
Delivery Area:	UK, USA, Canada and Spain	Returns Procedure:	Down to you

www.greatoutdoortoys.co.uk

Alongside the usual outdoor activity kit such as climbing frames and trampolines, here you can buy go-karts by Puky (I know) and In Car, both made in Germany. The ranges go from the entry versions at about £200 to the top-of-the-range In Car Centurian or Puky Panther at just below £500. You can also buy accessories such as extra seats, flashing lights and trailers.

Site Usability:	★★★★★	Based:	UK
Product Range:	★★★★	Express Delivery Option? (UK)	No
Price Range:	Luxury/Medium	Gift Wrapping Option?	No
Delivery Area:	UK	Returns Procedure:	Down to you

www.mastersgames.com

At Masters Traditional Games you'll find a wide range of traditional indoor and outdoor games made in high-quality materials. There is Chinese Checkers with a solid teak board and handcrafted bagatelle boards. You'll also find outdoor draughts, table football, table tennis, roulette, croquet, rounders and bar games such as skittles, Aunt Sally and bar billiards.

Site Usability:	★★★★	Based:	UK
Product Range:	★★★★	Express Delivery Option? (UK)	Yes, if you contact them
Price Range:	Medium	Gift Wrapping Option?	No
Delivery Area:	Worldwide	Returns Procedure:	Down to you

www.outdoortoystore.co.uk

If your tiny has been begging you to get her the Double Seat Ride On Pink Princess Jeep or a Bounce House Castle and Slide, then you've come to the right place. Although you'll find an excellent range of trampolines and nets, swings and slides here, there are also some very different products you won't find everywhere. For outdoor activity toys this is a great place to start.

Site Usability:	★★★★★	Based:	UK
Product Range:	★★★★★	Express Delivery Option? (UK)	No
Price Range:	Luxury/Medium	Gift Wrapping Option?	No
Delivery Area:	UK	Returns Procedure:	Down to you

www.rainbowplay.co.uk

Top-level wooden play systems and climbing frames are the speciality here, although the site offers trampolines, swings and slides as well for kids from twos to teens. Take a look at the King Kong Clubhouse Big Enchilada with its double-level playhouse, three pairs of swing hangers, spiral tubes slide, ship's wheels and even binoculars – it's a real marvel. Be careful before showing your kids this site, they won't want to settle for anything less.

Site Usability:	★★★★★	Express Delivery Option? (UK)	No, but call them to ask for next day if
Product Range:	★★★★★		item's in stock
Price Range:	Luxury	Gift Wrapping Option?	No
Delivery Area:	UK	Returns Procedure:	Down to you
Based:	UK		

www.towerstoys.co.uk

If the bright orangeness (is there such a word?) of this website doesn't stop you in your tracks, take a good look round. There's an amazing range of toys, from sandpits, goalposts and ride-on tractors to Jacques croquet sets, rounders kits, sandpit excavators and pedal go-karts. Then there are snow toys from simple sledges to the Berg steerable, Snowxpress Max. Ask for a delivery quote outside UK mainland.

Site Usability:	★★★★	Based:	UK
Product Range:	★★★★	Express Delivery Option? (UK)	No
Price Range:	Luxury/Medium	Gift Wrapping Option?	No
Delivery Area:	UK	Returns Procedure:	Down to you

www.tptoysdirect.co.uk

When you click through to this website your first thought is that here is yet another website offering the full TP range, but you'd be wrong. Here is where you can buy ends of lines and seconds direct from the factory shop, so think climbing frames, swing sets, multi-product and wooden playsets and water slides for less. All products have TP Toys' standard guarantee. Go shop.

Site Usability:	★★★★★	Based:	UK
Product Range:	★★★★	Express Delivery Option? (UK)	No
Price Range:	Medium/Very Good Value	Gift Wrapping Option?	No
Delivery Area:	UK	Returns Procedure:	Down to you

www.trampledunderfoot.co.uk

These are real trampoline experts offering Jumpking Trampolines and Bazoongi, plus a full range of accessories such as safety nets, covers and ladders. The site also sells mini trampolines, bounce boards, bouncy castles, trampoline parts and replacement pads and springs. There's an excellent buying guide which will help you decide which trampoline will be right for you and how to make it as safe as possible.

Site Usability:	★★★★★	Based:	UK
Product Range:	★★★★	Express Delivery Option? (UK)	Yes
Price Range:	Luxury/Medium	Gift Wrapping Option?	No
Delivery Area:	Worldwide	Returns Procedure:	Down to you

Chapter 32

Children's Bookstores

Some of the bookstores you'll find here are the same places you buy your books, music and DVDs, where they have (usually) vast ranges of children's books for all ages and it really helps if you know what you're looking for. You'll almost always find that the price is less online than offline as the competition to sell books to you over the web is fierce.

But there are also the dedicated children's bookshops where it's fun to have a browse, find out about and choose new books you may not have heard of before. Most of them are colourful and easy to use, so if your child is becoming computer friendly, you can let them have a look around too. At least here the final choice is definitely yours and the kicking and screaming days of 'mummy I really, really want that' in the shop are over (and yes, we went through that as well).

Sites to Visit

www.amazon.co.uk

Of course this is Amazon, so you'll expect to find a huge choice, from books for tinies, toddlers, teenagers and everything in between (including the latest Harry Potter, Ark Angel and Princess Diaries). Having been a huge fan of Amazon for just about as long as it's been in existence, I have to say that it's getting better all the time, with an expanding product range and increasingly good service. The only thing I would say is that there's so much choice it's a little bewildering at times. Take your time, though, and you're bound to find what you're looking for.

Site Usability:	★★★★★	Based:	UK
Product Range:	★★★★★	Express Delivery Option? (UK)	Yes
Price Range:	Medium/Very Good Value	Gift Wrapping Option?	Yes
Delivery Area:	Worldwide	Returns Procedure:	Down to you

www.bookgiant.co.uk

Next time you're looking for a new book, take a quick look at BookGiant. It doesn't have anything like the range of Amazon, but what it does have are very good special offers, with special edition (usually small hardback) copies of brand new children's titles at up to 60% off the normal price. Postage and packing are free if you order three items or more, otherwise it's very reasonable. You need to register to order (so they can send you regular updates and keep your details to make your next order even quicker).

Site Usability:	★★★★★	Based:	UK
Product Range:	★★★	Express Delivery Option? (UK)	No
Price Range:	Very Good Value	Gift Wrapping Option?	No
Delivery Area:	UK	Returns Procedure:	Down to you

www.booksforchildren.co.uk

I'll tell you straight away that this is a book club and that by joining you accept that you'll take a certain number of books within the first year. After that you can cancel. Having said that, it looks to be an excellent service, with in-house reviews of all the books for children up to 12, a monthly magazine telling you what's going on and lots of special offers. Take a look round and decide.

Site Usability:	★★★★	Based:	UK
Product Range:	★★★★	Express Delivery Option? (UK)	No
Price Range:	Very Good Value	Gift Wrapping Option?	No
Delivery Area:	UK	Returns Procedure:	Down to you

www.childrensbookshop.com

The Children's Bookshop specialises in secondhand books (with its main area being 20th-century fiction). It really helps if you know what you're looking for as the site is not that easy to use. If you visit online and you know what to put in the search box, you may well find what you're looking for, so this is an excellent place not just for children's secondhand books but also for gifts and for collectors of specific editions. They're happy to ship worldwide.

Site Usability:	★★★	Based:	UK
Product Range:	★★★★	Express Delivery Option? (UK)	No
Price Range:	Luxury/Medium	Gift Wrapping Option?	No
Delivery Area:	Worldwide	Returns Procedure:	Down to you

www.jonkers.co.uk

At Jonkers you can find modern first editions, fine illustrated books, classic children's fiction and 19th-century literature. So if you have a goddaughter who might appreciate a first edition of Michael Bond's *Paddington Goes to Town*, you'll find it here, plus AA Milne, Enid Blyton, Lewis Carroll and many more. Because some of these books are expensive and precious (up into the £1000s), you can't order online but need to phone using the Freephone number.

Site Usability:	★★★★	Based:	UK
Product Range:	★★★	Express Delivery Option? (UK)	No
Price Range:	Luxury	Gift Wrapping Option?	No
Delivery Area:	Worldwide	Returns Procedure:	Down to you

www.littlebookworms.co.uk

Little Bookworms is a family business offering books, software and activity packs for ages 0–11. Each area is broken down into sections, so you can choose quickly by age and then by type of book, theme or author, and every book's information includes an in-depth editorial review. If you register with the site, you (or your child) can click through to the 'Fun Zone', where there's free access to a library of downloadable activity ideas and printable items suitable for children.

Site Usability:	★★★★★	Based:	UK
Product Range:	★★★★★	Express Delivery Option? (UK)	No
Price Range:	Medium	Gift Wrapping Option?	Yes
Delivery Area:	UK	Returns Procedure:	Down to you

www.play.com

Music, movies and games at very good prices with delivery included are on offer from this Channel Islands-based website. It offers a huge range of films for all ages on DVD, CDs and games for most systems, plus special offers, such as two DVDs for £12, 30% off specific boxed sets and 40% off a wide choice of current releases. Because delivery is included you can order individual disks as often as you want to rather than having to group orders together to save on postage. Service is excellent.

Site Usability:	★★★★★	Based:	Channel Islands
Product Range:	★★★★★	Express Delivery Option? (UK)	No
Price Range:	Medium/Very Good Value	Gift Wrapping Option?	No
Delivery Area:	Worldwide	Returns Procedure:	Down to you

www.redhouse.co.uk

Red House specialises in children's books for all ages, from babies to young adults. It produces a catalogue each month, featuring an introduction from a leading author, and the bright and colourful website carries a wide selection of handpicked books which is updated regularly. There's even a safe, fun online community for children, including competitions, things to do and a moderated message board. Every book is discounted and P&P is free when you buy four or more books.

Site Usability:	★★★★	Based:	UK
Product Range:	★★★★	Express Delivery Option? (UK)	Yes
Price Range:	Medium/Very Good Value	Gift Wrapping Option?	No
Delivery Area:	UK	Returns Procedure:	Down to you

www.thebookplace.com

If you want a new bookshop to look at, you could have a browse on this very clear site, which offers a wide range and shows availability as soon as you search for your book. It also has a good selection of signed copies

199

(not always children's books) which would make excellent gifts and you can read the weekly press reviews on the latest releases. Postage is £2.75 per single book order, plus 50p for each additional book. They also offer worldwide shipping and express delivery.

Site Usability:	★★★★	Based:	UK
Product Range:	★★★★	Express Delivery Option? (UK)	Yes
Price Range:	Medium	Gift Wrapping Option?	Yes
Delivery Area:	Worldwide	Returns Procedure:	Down to you

www.waterstones.co.uk

Waterstones' website is extremely clear and easy to use and a lot less cluttered than many of the online bookstores. You can browse categories from the Children's Book Page menu, which includes areas such as Character Books, Fiction (by age), Early Years, Picture Books, Activity Books and Leisure Interests, Hobbies and Sports. Delivery is free on orders over £15 within the UK and they offer surface or courier services for international orders.

Site Usability:	★★★★★	Based:	UK
Product Range:	★★★★★	Express Delivery Option? (UK)	Yes
Price Range:	Medium	Gift Wrapping Option?	Yes
Delivery Area:	Worldwide	Returns Procedure:	Down to you

www.whsmith.co.uk

Click through to Books/Children's and School on WHSmith's easy-on-the-eye website and you'll find a wealth of choice, from adventure and animal stories, fairy tales, magical tales and fantasy to historical fiction, myth and legend. There's also an excellent selection of early learning books, including *Learn to Write, What's My Colour?* and *Maisy's Amazing Word Book*. With over 4000 titles in this area alone, there's a great deal to choose from, so take your time.

Site Usability:	★★★★★	Based:	UK
Product Range:	★★★★★	Express Delivery Option? (UK)	No
Price Range:	Medium	Gift Wrapping Option?	No
Delivery Area:	UK	Returns Procedure:	Down to you

Chapter 33

General Toy Shops

These are the places you can find just about everything, whether you're looking for a specific type of toy or you just want to browse for some new ideas. Sometimes the Home Pages are so busy you really don't know where to start, but take a moment, look for the menu and get going.

I find it much easier to shop here than in a toy store and although you may well say that's because I've had lots of practice - and I have - it's more because I hate crowded shops filled with lots of yelling kids, at times when I'm desperately looking for something to buy quickly because I just want to get out of there as fast as I can. So no longer do I go out searching for that elusive shop assistant - I can find everything I need and all I need to know - right here.

Sites to Visit

www.amazon.co.uk

If you still think of Amazon as a bookshop, it's time to think again. Just click through to Toys and Kids and you'll find every toy and game you can think of. No, it's not all just sitting in a large warehouse - in a lot of cases Amazon acts as the conduit through which other toy shops can sell their products. What it means is that you get a fantastic choice and no fuss ordering through a retailer you know and trust.

Site Usability:	★★★★★	Based:	UK
Product Range:	★★★★★	Express Delivery Option? (UK)	Yes
Price Range:	Luxury/Medium/Very Good Value	Gift Wrapping Option?	Yes
Delivery Area:	Worldwide	Returns Procedure:	Down to you

www.brainydays.co.uk

To be quite honest, although this is a good, fun children's toy and gift website, I'm not sure why it's aimed at the 'brainy' ones. There's a wide selection of items such as Pocoyo bean bag toys, Corolle of France dolls, gorgeous Lilliputian interactive soft toys from Belgium, Cambridge electronic kits (ok, so these are quite clever) and the bestselling Golden Coin Maker Kit. There's a lot to choose from, so have a browse.

Site Usability:	★★★★	Based:	UK
Product Range:	★★★★★	Express Delivery Option? (UK)	No
Price Range:	Medium	Gift Wrapping Option?	No
Delivery Area:	Worldwide, but outside Europe postage is very high	Returns Procedure:	Down to you

www.dollshouse.com

Whether you're new to the world of dolls' houses or a dedicated miniaturist, the Dolls' House Emporium should fill you with inspiration. The site features fully decorated dolls' houses and thousands of miniatures in colour-co-ordinated room sets, plus carpets and flooring, lighting and wallpapers. You can also see a selection of 1:12-scale dolls' houses shown open and fully furnished to give you ideas.

Site Usability:	★★★★★	Based:	UK
Product Range:	★★★★	Express Delivery Option? (UK)	No
Price Range:	Luxury/Medium	Gift Wrapping Option?	No
Delivery Area:	Worldwide	Returns Procedure:	Down to you

www.gamleys.co.uk

Action Man, Bratz Dolls, Dora the Explorer (love that one), Little Tikes, My Little Pony, Peppa Pig, Pixel Chix (!?), Pocoyo, Polly Pocket and Power

Rangers are just some of the brands on offer here. Then for tinies there are pre-school toys by Fisher Price, Mega Bloks, Teletubbies and Tomy. Provided you stick to the clear menus of categories and brands, you shouldn't get lost; go off on a tangent and you almost certainly will be.

Site Usability:	★★★★★	Based:	UK
Product Range:	★★★★★	Express Delivery Option? (UK)	No
Price Range:	Medium	Gift Wrapping Option?	No
Delivery Area:	UK	Returns Procedure:	Down to you

www.hamleys.co.uk

If you've ever visited this world-famous Regent Street toy emporium (I hate the word but it's the only way to describe this store), you'll know that there's a huge range of gadgets, games, soft toys, puzzles, stocking fillers and every toy you can think of at all price levels and for all ages. In fact, it's a disastrous place to take more than one child at a time as there's so much to see. There's a highly edited range here on the website, although the list of products on offer is growing all the time.

Site Usability:	★★★★★	Based:	UK
Product Range:	★★★★	Express Delivery Option? (UK)	No
Price Range:	Luxury/Medium	Gift Wrapping Option?	No
Delivery Area:	Worldwide	Returns Procedure:	Down to you

www.lambstoys.co.uk

This is another of those toy websites that offers so many brands it's hard to know where to start. To help you I'll tell you that it has an excellent range of Meccano, Hornby and Scalextric, Lego, Schleich Models, Flashing Storm scooters and Power Rangers. Then for little girls there's Zapf Baby Annabel, Chou Chou and Colette, plus Miss Milly and My Model makeup and hairstyling sets (and lots more). Phew.

Site Usability:	★★★★★	Based:	UK
Product Range:	★★★★★	Express Delivery Option? (UK)	Yes
Price Range:	Medium	Gift Wrapping Option?	No
Delivery Area:	Worldwide	Returns Procedure:	Down to you

www.lilyandagathe.com

Based in the Catalan region of France bordering on Spain, Lily and Agathe is a small English/French-speaking company with a love of all things beautiful, charming and vintage. Here you'll discover exceptional and timeless gifts and toys with a lean towards nostalgia. Many of the items here are one-offs, so if you see something you like, buy it quick. And if you like the overall idea, keep checking back.

Site Usability:	★★★★	Based:	UK
Product Range:	★★★★	Express Delivery Option? (UK)	No
Price Range:	Medium	Gift Wrapping Option?	Yes
Delivery Area:	Worldwide	Returns Procedure:	Down to you

www.mailorderexpress.com

Mail Order Express claims to be the largest toy website in Europe and who am I to argue? It's a hugely busy site with loads of offers and pre-order invitations on the Home Page but where, thankfully, you can shop by brand or by categories such as Music, Gadgets, Party, Science, Toy Vehicle, Dolls and Accessories. Take a look for yourself.

Site Usability:	★★★★	Based:	UK
Product Range:	★★★★★	Express Delivery Option? (UK)	Yes
Price Range:	Medium/Very Good Value	Gift Wrapping Option?	No
Delivery Area:	Worldwide	Returns Procedure:	Down to you

www.sayitwithbears.co.uk

This is one of those websites that obviously started off doing one thing and then branched out, because you can find not only bears here but elephants, rabbits, cats, Labradors and dalmations, plus lots of other dogs. So if you know someone who collects soft toys or needs a feel-good gift, you should take a look here. Oh yes, and you can buy Lovvie Bears, Thank you Bears and Anniversary Bears here as well.

Site Usability:	★★★★	Based:	UK
Product Range:	★★★★★	Express Delivery Option? (UK)	Yes
Price Range:	Medium	Gift Wrapping Option?	Yes
Delivery Area:	Worldwide	Returns Procedure:	Down to you

www.theentertainer.com

This is one of the largest independent toy retailers in the UK, with a huge range and an excellent, easy-to-navigate website, with 'More Toys, More Value and More Fun' as its motto. Here you can search by brand, type of toy, age group or price and you can choose from so many, including Baby Annabel, Dr Who, Hornby, Mattel, Nintendogs and Playmobil. Find something you like and you'll be offered lots more like it, helping you to narrow down your choice quickly.

Site Usability:	★★★★★	Based:	UK
Product Range:	★★★★★	Express Delivery Option? (UK)	Yes
Price Range:	Luxury/Medium	Gift Wrapping Option?	No
Delivery Area:	Worldwide	Returns Procedure:	Down to you

www.toysbymailorder.co.uk

Toys by Mail Order specialises in toys, gifts, nursery items and jigsaw puzzles for children of all ages. The menus are easy to use as, once you've clicked on Online Shop, you can see all the brands and all the different types of toy, such as baby toys, puzzles, soft toys and arts and crafts. There's also a selection of games, ranging from Early Learning Games to Murder Mystery. They offer fast delivery, a gift wrapping service and personalised messages for special occasions.

Site Usability:	★★★★	Based:	UK
Product Range:	★★★★★	Express Delivery Option? (UK)	Yes, two-day service
Price Range:	Medium	Gift Wrapping Option?	Yes
Delivery Area:	Worldwide	Returns Procedure:	Down to you

www.toysdirecttoyourdoor.co.uk

Some general toy websites make you (me in any case) want to run away, they're so busy on the Home Page. On this website you're immediately drawn in, from the train running across the top of the screen to the clear menu, information and special offer details. It sells Playmobil, Thomas trains, Sylvanian Families, Lego and Duplo, Brio, Schleich animals and much more.

Site Usability:	★★★★★	Based:	UK
Product Range:	★★★★★	Express Delivery Option? (UK)	No
Price Range:	Medium	Gift Wrapping Option?	No
Delivery Area:	Worldwide	Returns Procedure:	Down to you

www.toysrus.co.uk

This one you'll definitely have heard of (or seen no doubt) as the UK branch of the US toy megastore. Personally, I think the shops are just too huge to cope with, so it's great that they're online, although this website is one of the busiest around. There's a fantastic range of well-priced toys and equipment for children of all ages, including multi-media PCs, games, bikes and outdoor fun products. You can also click through to Babiesrus, with its selection for the younger members of the family.

Site Usability:	★★★★	Express Delivery Option? (UK)	No
Product Range:	★★★★★	Gift Wrapping Option?	No
Price Range:	Medium/Very Good Value	Returns Procedure:	Free by Freepost or collection
Delivery Area:	UK, but there are separate Canada and US websites		

Chapter 34

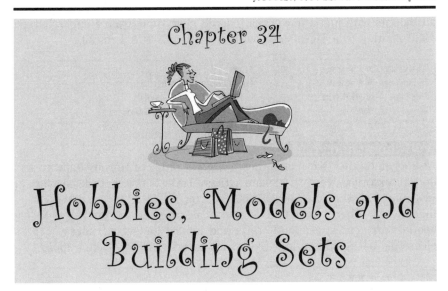

Hobbies, Models and Building Sets

Having had two boys (sorry, do I keep going on about that?), I know only too well that this is a fantastic area to buy from for rainy days. We had countless holidays when, if they couldn't go outside and weren't allowed to watch endless TV, all they complained about was being bored. A visit down to the model shop always solved that one.

As good model shops are few and far between, your time may well be short and that rainy day is frequently unexpected, my advice is to always have something up your sleeve for those occasions. Have a look round here and if yours are anything like my children, make sure you spend the same on both.

Sites to Visit

www.airfix.com

Just about every boy has at some time made an Airfix model (or usually part made and left). The joy of opening all those tiny tins of paint and spending hours making a mess and sticking all those bits together seems irresistible. Well, here it all is online, on a simple site where you can order all the kits with just a few clicks. There's everything from a supercharged 1930 Bentley to a Tiger Moth, with clear details for them all.

Site Usability: ★★★★★	Based:	UK
Product Range: ★★★★★	Express Delivery Option? (UK)	No
Price Range: Luxury/Medium	Gift Wrapping Option?	No
Delivery Area: Worldwide	Returns Procedure:	Down to you

www.boogaloo.co.uk

At Boogaloo (love that name) there's a good range of Hornby Railway sets and accessories, from the Steam Driven Train Set with teak coaches at just under £500 to the Local Freight Starter Set at £39.99 and everything in between. Then you'll find Digital Scalextric, jigsaw puzzles and essential carry cases, arts and crafts and lots of gadget gift ideas such as electronic backgammon and crossword puzzle solvers. Take a look.

Site Usability: ★★★★★	Based:	UK
Product Range: ★★★★★	Express Delivery Option? (UK)	Yes
Price Range: Luxury/Medium	Gift Wrapping Option?	Yes
Delivery Area: Worldwide for most items excluding US	Returns Procedure:	Down to you

www.lego.com

Lego kits seem to have become more and more complicated – you practically need an engineering degree to build some of them (well, I never was very good at that sort of thing). Let your son on this website if you dare. Everything is brilliantly shown, including Star Wars, Lego Sports, building sets, Robotics and the very latest editions. You can take the Club tour, order the magazine or click on to the Games Page.

Site Usability: ★★★★★	Based:	UK
Product Range: ★★★★★	Express Delivery Option? (UK)	Yes
Price Range: Medium	Gift Wrapping Option?	No
Delivery Area: Worldwide	Returns Procedure:	Down to you

www.modelhobbies.co.uk

Model Hobbies is the perfect place for the model enthusiast. It has an extremely well-laid out website and offers models by over 50 different manufacturers, plus all the paints, tools and brushes you could possibly need. There are miniature soldiers here as well. The site cleverly highlights the newest kits to hit the market so that you keep coming back for more. You can buy gift vouchers too.

Site Usability:	★★★★★	Based:	UK
Product Range:	★★★★★	Express Delivery Option? (UK)	No
Price Range:	Luxury/Medium	Gift Wrapping Option?	No
Delivery Area:	Worldwide	Returns Procedure:	Down to you

www.modelrockets.co.uk

You can buy model cars, tanks and planes from several different websites, but there are very few specialising in rockets. By rockets I mean real enthusiasts' stuff, from starter sets and ready-to-fly kits to competition-standard models. Don't be fooled into thinking that the rockets themselves are inexpensive – by the time you've invested in the engine and all the bits and pieces you can spend a small fortune. They can give hours of fun however, until they blow themselves to bits or land on the back of a lorry, never to be seen again (yes, that one happened to us).

Site Usability:	★★★★	Based:	UK
Product Range:	★★★★	Express Delivery Option? (UK)	No
Price Range:	Luxury/Medium	Gift Wrapping Option?	No
Delivery Area:	Worldwide	Returns Procedure:	Down to you

www.otherlandtoys.co.uk

Otherland Toys offers a wide selection and this website is particularly good for boys. I suggest when you're looking round that you click on 'only show items in stock' as there's so much to choose from anyway and at least you won't be looking at what they don't have. There are remote-control cars at all levels, excellent gadgets, Meccano Magic and lots of outdoor ideas. Make sure you have your cup of coffee with you when you start – you'll need it.

Site Usability:	★★★★★	Based:	UK
Product Range:	★★★★★	Express Delivery Option? (UK)	Yes, Fedex worldwide
Price Range:	Luxury/Medium/Very Good Value	Gift Wrapping Option?	Yes
Delivery Area:	Worldwide	Returns Procedure:	Down to you

www.slotcity.co.uk

Slot City is one of the largest independent retailers of slot cars in the UK and Europe and you can only buy online. The site offers the full range of Scalextric, plus other brands such as Carrera from Germany and SCX from Spain - household names in their own countries but almost impossible to find here until now. You'll also find Hornby and Carrera model kits. Everything is ready for immediate delivery unless you're told otherwise on the website.

Site Usability:	★★★★	Based:	UK
Product Range:	★★★★★	Express Delivery Option? (UK)	No
Price Range:	Luxury/Medium	Gift Wrapping Option?	No
Delivery Area:	All EU countries and the USA	Returns Procedure:	Down to you

Chapter 35

Puzzles and Games

I'll have to come clean here and admit that I've never had the patience for jigsaw puzzles – writing books, yes, but fiddling around with all those tiny pieces? Definitely not for me.

However, as we have close friends whom we visit frequently who always have something huge and complicated on the go (and kept beautifully neat on a movable board), I know that jigsaws are a wonderful hobby if you're that way inclined and here you'll find a lot to choose from, including some which have thousands of pieces.

Games are a different matter, with chess, backgammon and draughts having played great importance in my family from time to time, usually until we have to admit that that essential piece really is lost and we have to give up. Below you'll find retailers offering everything from basic, well-priced versions to some beautiful sets which would make excellent gifts.

Sites to Visit

www.barneys-newsbox.co.uk

Many of the online retailers offering jigsaw puzzles are based in the Lake District – why? Well, I would have thought it's obvious – if you're into jigsaws, they're the perfect answer to a rainy day, for sure. Anyway, here you'll find mainly fairly large to extremely large puzzles, starting at 500 pieces and going up to 1500. The Bright Ideas animal puzzles are so lovely it's tempting even for me to give it a go.

Site Usability:	★★★★★	Based:	UK
Product Range:	★★★★★	Express Delivery Option? (UK)	No
Price Range:	Luxury/Medium	Gift Wrapping Option?	No
Delivery Area:	Worldwide	Returns Procedure:	Down to you

www.chessbaron.co.uk

If you know someone who's a chess enthusiast, you'll almost certainly find something for them from this retailer based in Taunton, Somerset. It offers only artisan-made chess boards and pieces, so if you're looking for any other type of game you'll need to go somewhere else. There are over 100 sets on offer, from well-priced travel sets retailing for under £50 to exquisitely made rosewood or ebony sets at about £300.

Site Usability:	★★★★★	Based:	UK
Product Range:	★★★★	Express Delivery Option? (UK)	No
Price Range:	Luxury/Medium	Gift Wrapping Option?	No
Delivery Area:	Worldwide	Returns Procedure:	Down to you

www.farscapegames.co.uk

You may be looking for a complete travel games compendium or just a new reasonably priced backgammon set, your favourite game may be Mah Jong, dominoes, monopoly or bridge, but whatever you're looking for, you're sure to find it here. This without having to go to your local store and decide whether you should be in the children's section or somewhere else, then finding that, after all, there are only a couple of options for your chosen game.

Site Usability:	★★★★★	Based:	UK
Product Range:	★★★★	Express Delivery Option? (UK)	Yes
Price Range:	Medium	Gift Wrapping Option?	No
Delivery Area:	Worldwide	Returns Procedure:	Down to you

www.jigsaw-puzzles-online.co.uk

I've never had the patience to tackle mega jigsaw puzzles, but I know that there are those who do and who keep them out year round for rainy-day entertainment. This site is aimed at puzzle enthusiasts of all ages as it caters for everyone, with 60-piece puzzles for children and going right up to the (horrendous to me) 13,000-piece puzzle by Clementoni – I wouldn't know where to start, would you?

Site Usability:	★★★★★	Based:	UK
Product Range:	★★★★★	Express Delivery Option? (UK)	Yes
Price Range:	Luxury/Medium	Gift Wrapping Option?	No
Delivery Area:	Worldwide	Returns Procedure:	Down to you

www.lingardsgames.co.uk

This website is definitely not just for children, it's for anyone who likes games, including jigsaw puzzles (think double-sided and 1000-piece puzzles). There are family games such as Monopoly, Labyrinth, World of Warcraft, Robo Rally, Murder Mystery and Casino Games, plus for small ones Ludo, Junior Scrabble and Halli Galli. Don't think that because I haven't mentioned something it's not available here, it almost certainly will be.

Site Usability:	★★★★	Based:	UK
Product Range:	★★★★★	Express Delivery Option? (UK)	No
Price Range:	Medium	Gift Wrapping Option?	No
Delivery Area:	Worldwide	Returns Procedure:	Down to you

www.puzzleplaza.co.uk

At Puzzle Plaza you can find a range of Disney jigsaw puzzles for children, 3D jigsaw puzzles, high-quality Whimsy wooden jigsaw puzzles, heart-, round- and panorama-shaped puzzles and 500–1500 piece puzzles with attractive scenes and world maps. There are travel games such as dominoes, snakes and ladders and Memo Kid, plus metal puzzle brainteasers.

Site Usability:	★★★★★	Based:	UK
Product Range:	★★★★	Express Delivery Option? (UK)	No
Price Range:	Medium	Gift Wrapping Option?	No
Delivery Area:	Worldwide	Returns Procedure:	Down to you

www.shopping-emporium-uk.com

This is a brightly coloured, unsophisticated website offering Italian-made sets for backgammon, dominoes and solitaire, bridge, roulette, poker and other games at a wide range of price levels. Then there are darts boards, billiard tables, mini football tables and a great deal more. Expect to spend a lot of time here as there's so much to see and choose from.

Site Usability:	★★★★	Based:	UK
Product Range:	★★★	Express Delivery Option? (UK)	No
Price Range:	Luxury/Medium	Gift Wrapping Option?	No
Delivery Area:	Worldwide	Returns Procedure:	Down to you

Chapter 36

Dressing Up and Magic Tricks

When I was a child (yes, me, this time) my parents had a friend who was a member of the Magic Circle, the most prestigious society of magicians. I'll never forget the wonder and fascination of some of the things he could do and, needless to say, he never got away with coming to visit without putting on a performance, however small.

I'm not suggesting that your children should aspire to the same levels, but I'm sure that it's much easier for them to read about and learn magic tricks today than it was then – there's so much information available and so many trick sets to buy. Just take a look below and you'll see what I mean.

Regarding choice and information, the same applies to dressing up as you can order from an amazing array of costumes for kids of all ages, from enchanting fairies and ballerinas to the more grown-up Superman or Cleopatra. There's a good range of prices here, so have a look at as many of the sites as you can before choosing and then don't forget to buy that essential dressing-up box to keep it all in.

Sites to Visit

www.a2z-kids.co.uk

Choose from Historical Costumes, Girls' Party Costumes, Books, Rhymes and Fairytales, Christmas and Nativity, Animals and Creatures such as Scooby Doo and Dinosaur, Superman Returns, Disney, and toddler and infant costumes. The menus here are particularly good and although you can find the same types of costumes elsewhere, you can narrow down your search on this website very fast.

Site Usability:	★★★★★	Based:	UK
Product Range:	★★★★	Express Delivery Option? (UK)	Yes
Price Range:	Medium	Gift Wrapping Option?	No
Delivery Area:	Worldwide	Returns Procedure:	Down to you

www.charliecrow.com

This is a fun website for kids' dressing-up costumes of all kinds and there are some great extras here as well, including party games with instructions, recipes for nibbles like Cheesy Straws, Self Portrait Pizzas and (!) Swamp Jelly, some daft stories and a really helpful party planner to try to keep you sane.

Site Usability:	★★★★★	Based:	UK
Product Range:	★★★★★	Express Delivery Option? (UK)	Yes
Price Range:	Medium	Gift Wrapping Option?	No
Delivery Area:	Worldwide	Returns Procedure:	Down to you

www.costumecrazy.co.uk

If your child fancies himself in a Zoot Suit or as a Clone Trooper at the next fancy dress party he goes to, then this is the place. For girls there are the Country and Western or Spiderella outfits and needless to say there are simply loads more to choose from. There are angel and fairy wings, wands and halos, witches' broomsticks, devil horns and Cleopatra's snake. There'll definitely be a problem here when it's 'make your mind up time'.

Site Usability:	★★★★★	Based:	UK
Product Range:	★★★★★	Express Delivery Option? (UK)	Yes
Price Range:	Medium	Gift Wrapping Option?	No
Delivery Area:	Worldwide	Returns Procedure:	Down to you

www.dudethatscoolmagic.co.uk

You'll probably have to keep this book close to hand to be able to re-member the name of this website (well, I certainly would) and this online store is worth remembering as it's bursting with magic tricks, card tricks, street magic, close-up magic tricks, props and magic illusions for both the beginner and the more experienced 'magician'. It's a colourful website and includes an excellent section on Children's Magic Shows.

Site Usability:	★★★★★	Based:	UK
Product Range:	★★★★★	Express Delivery Option? (UK)	Yes
Price Range:	Medium	Gift Wrapping Option?	No
Delivery Area:	Worldwide	Returns Procedure:	Down to you

www.hopscotchdressingup.co.uk

Hopscotch has got the children's dressing-up market sewn up with its lovely, bright website full of dressing-up box clothes for children, from angels and fairies to witches and wizards, cowboys and Indians to kings and queens and everything in between. There's no question that if your child has been asked to a fancy dress party and is determined to really look the part, you absolutely have to visit here.

Site Usability:	★★★★★	Based:	UK
Product Range:	★★★★★	Express Delivery Option? (UK)	Yes
Price Range:	Medium/Very Good Value	Gift Wrapping Option?	No
Delivery Area:	Worldwide	Returns Procedure:	Down to you

www.magicalkingdom.co.uk

I love this website, dedicated to free printable art and including magic tricks for tinies, clip art, stories, games, invitations (and envelopes) and greetings cards. You just have to let your would-be magician loose on your computer so he or she can read up about the tricks and follow the stories, then you can print off invitations and greetings cards and choose from the envelope designs. Take a look.

Site Usability:	★★★★	Delivery Area:	Worldwide
Product Range:	★★★	Based:	UK
Price Range:	Free		

www.magicbox.uk.com

This is one of the UK's largest magic dealers. If your would-be magician is really a beginner, you can start off with children's tricks and cabaret or beginners' magic, plus there are plenty of books for beginners as well. This is a real 'magic shop', so be careful what you choose and call the sales team if you have any queries.

Site Usability:	★★★★	Based:	UK
Product Range:	★★★	Express Delivery Option? (UK)	Yes
Price Range:	Medium	Gift Wrapping Option?	No
Delivery Area:	Worldwide	Returns Procedure:	Down to you

www.magichat.co.uk

To get the best out of this website you need to register in order to be able to take advantage of the huge number of free tricks designed for beginners and experienced magicians alike. Once you've registered you can access the tricks, sign up for the monthly newsletter, create a personal area for storing your favourites and personalise your trick recommendations. You could get sidetracked on to lots of the other website recommendations, but I'd take a while to browse here first.

Site Usability:	★★★★★	Based:	UK
Product Range:	★★★★★	Express Delivery Option? (UK)	Yes
Price Range:	Medium	Gift Wrapping Option?	No
Delivery Area:	Worldwide	Returns Procedure:	Down to you

www.magicshop.co.uk

MagicShop.co.uk is the online face of The Merchant of Magic, a team of dedicated magicians which aims to combine the best selection of high-quality magic, fast delivery and expert friendly advice. The site holds a range of over 4000 magic tricks permanently in stock and you can expect to receive your order 'magically' fast (all orders over £50 get free over-night delivery). This website is dedicated to the real enthusiast, although there's a range for beginners and children's magic shows here as well.

Site Usability:	★★★★★	Based:	UK
Product Range:	★★★★★	Express Delivery Option? (UK)	Yes
Price Range:	Medium	Gift Wrapping Option?	No
Delivery Area:	Worldwide	Returns Procedure:	Down to you

www.magictricks.co.uk

You'll find some wonderful ideas for gifts here, from the Cyclopedia of Magic, Wizard School Video and DVD, card magic sets, pub tricks (??) and the Ultimate Magic Trick Set – a compilation of some of the greatest close-up magic tricks ever invented – and this is just a small selection of what's on offer. You can also buy gift vouchers and lots of the own-brand products at all price levels.

Site Usability:	★★★★	Based:	UK
Product Range:	★★★★	Express Delivery Option? (UK)	No
Price Range:	Medium	Gift Wrapping Option?	No
Delivery Area:	Worldwide	Returns Procedure:	Down to you

www.ollipops.com

I suppose that puppets aren't strictly dressing up, but rather than put them in toys and gifts I thought this was where they belonged. At Olli-pops there's a lovely range of glove puppets, from animals such as squir-rel, toad and white rabbit, all beautifully dressed, the fabulous dragon puppet, finger puppets, long-sleeved puppets and much, much more, including the bestselling Rabbit in a Lettuce. Take a look.

Site Usability:	★★★★	Based:	UK
Product Range:	★★★★★	Express Delivery Option? (UK)	No, but delivery is free for most items
Price Range:	Medium	Gift Wrapping Option?	No
Delivery Area:	Worldwide	Returns Procedure:	Down to you

www.partydomain.co.uk

Party Domain supplies really well-priced dressing-up costumes with lots at below £10. There are costumes for grown-ups here as well, so make sure that you click through to the right place, unless you're all going to the same party, of course. The site also sells all sorts of fun and themed hats, balloons, masks and (if they want to go that far) wigs.

Site Usability:	★★★★★	Based:	UK
Product Range:	★★★★★	Express Delivery Option? (UK)	Yes
Price Range:	Medium/Very Good Value	Gift Wrapping Option?	No
Delivery Area:	Worldwide	Returns Procedure:	Down to you

www.themagicgadget.co.uk

Here you can buy books on magic, close-up magic tricks, kids' magic tricks, Fire, Flash and Smoke tricks, trick accessories and lots of demo DVDs. It's a busy but well-laid out website and there's almost certainly something for everyone, from complete beginners to real enthusiasts. There are also lots (and I mean lots) of special offers that are well worth looking through.

Site Usability:	★★★★	Based:	UK
Product Range:	★★★★	Express Delivery Option? (UK)	Yes
Price Range:	Medium	Gift Wrapping Option?	No
Delivery Area:	UK	Returns Procedure:	Down to you

www.toytidy.co.uk

You're going to love this website, believe me, as along with all the different storage ideas for children you can find some excellent toy boxes which would be perfect for dressing-up paraphernalia. There are solid wood and fabric-covered boxes plus, and most specially, beautiful, handpainted, personalised boxes covered with fairies, teddies or trains. Expensive, I know, but absolutely gorgeous.

Site Usability:	★★★★	Based:	UK
Product Range:	★★★★	Express Delivery Option? (UK)	No
Price Range:	Luxury/Medium	Gift Wrapping Option?	No
Delivery Area:	UK	Returns Procedure:	Down to you

Chapter 37

Party Accessories and Birthday Cakes

This area will be close to the heart of anyone trying to organise a child's birthday party and there's now no excuse for not being totally ahead of the pack. The first thing to do is to sit down with your child and agree the type of theme he or she would like. Then - preferably on your own or you'll find yourself ordering absolutely everything - you can choose the tableware, party bags, decorations and accessories.

Provided you allow enough time for delivery, this will surely take away so much of the effort of finding the small but very special and important extras that go into making your party an exceptional one. There's everything here apart from the entertainer - that one's down to you, of course.

Sites to Visit

www.bestbirthdays.co.uk

I really like this website, not just because it has a good choice of themes (because most of the party websites do that) but because it's dedicated to children and more simply designed than most. You always have to pick your theme first and here is no exception, so whether you want Spiderman or My Little Pony, you all need to agree on that, then click through to buy tableware, balloons and decorations, bags, presents and accessories.

Site Usability:	★★★★	Based:	UK
Product Range:	★★★★	Express Delivery Option? (UK)	Yes
Price Range:	Medium	Gift Wrapping Option?	No
Delivery Area:	Worldwide	Returns Procedure:	Down to you

www.caketoppers.co.uk

On this website you can order a birthday cake for next-day delivery (just in case you've forgotten to get one ready in time), order a celebration cake to be sent anywhere in mainland UK and choose from traditional sponge and iced fruit cakes to arrive on the date of your choosing. The site's novel speciality is edible pictures – so send them your photo, drawing or any image and they'll return it as an edible decoration on a cake. They also offer mini decorated cupcakes and shortbread with your choice of photo.

Site Usability:	★★★★	Based:	UK
Product Range:	★★★	Express Delivery Option? (UK)	Yes
Price Range:	Medium/Very Good Value	Gift Wrapping Option?	No
Delivery Area:	UK	Returns Procedure:	Down to you

www.cheesecake.co.uk

Let me get the cheesecake bit over with first (not strictly birthday, I know, unless you have an addict in the house). There's everything here from Chocolate Toffee Walnut Smash and Raspberry Split to Charlie's Original New York New York double baked, so order one for the adults now. Then you can go and order your sponge birthday cake from somewhere else. Just thought there should be something here for you too.

Site Usability:	★★★★	Based:	UK
Product Range:	★★★	Express Delivery Option? (UK)	Yes
Price Range:	Medium	Gift Wrapping Option?	No
Delivery Area:	UK	Returns Procedure:	Down to you

www.fabulousfirst.co.uk

This is another website from Party Ark (see below), but as I thought that website was so good I wanted you to be able to go directly to this one as

---

well (but only, obviously, if it's a first birthday you're planning). Choose from Hugs and Stitches, One Special Girl (or Boy), Old MacDonald or Party Jungle and then click through and you'll find all you need as individual items or pre-prepared party packs to make life simple. There are toys, gifts and birthday cards here too.

Site Usability:	★★★★★	Based:	UK
Product Range:	★★★★★	Express Delivery Option? (UK)	Yes
Price Range:	Medium	Gift Wrapping Option?	No
Delivery Area:	Worldwide	Returns Procedure:	Down to you

www.greatlittleparties.co.uk

They've definitely made an effort here to get away from totally theme-driven party supplies (although ultimately it's best to do that here as well and yes, there are lots to choose from, from Peter Pan and Noddy to Thomas the Tank Engine and Fifi and the Flowerpots). Alongside these you can order party music CDs, party games, books (party food recipes and planning a party), birthday cake candles and gift wrap. So this is definitely a one-stop shop. There are christening party supplies here as well.

Site Usability:	★★★★★	Based:	UK
Product Range:	★★★★★	Express Delivery Option? (UK)	Yes
Price Range:	Medium	Gift Wrapping Option?	No
Delivery Area:	EU	Returns Procedure:	Down to you

www.jane-asher.co.uk

I'm sure you've heard of Jane Asher, actress, film star, writer, lifestyle expert and cake designer extraordinaire, but did you know that you can buy some of her marvellous cakes online? Well, now you do. Just click through to her website and her Mail Order cake section and you'll find a choice of about 40 designs for all sorts of occasions. You can choose from three sizes of cake and sponge or fruit filling. UK delivery only and you need to allow up to ten days for your cake to arrive.

Site Usability:	★★★★★	Based:	UK
Product Range:	★★★★	Express Delivery Option? (UK)	No
Price Range:	Luxury	Gift Wrapping Option?	No
Delivery Area:	UK	Returns Procedure:	Down to you

www.londoncakes.com

Although at the moment this website says that it really delivers only to London, if you call them they may well have expanded the delivery area (and yes, I do have inside information on this). All the cakes are hand-made by this family-run bakery. In the Cakes for Children section you'll find traditional cakes which you can customise, plus sporting themes and cakes decorated with butterflies, dinosaurs, teddies and mermaids.

Site Usability:	★★★★	Based:	UK
Product Range:	★★★	Express Delivery Option? (UK)	Yes
Price Range:	Medium	Gift Wrapping Option?	No
Delivery Area:	London and other areas if you call them	Returns Procedure:	Down to you

www.need-a-cake.co.uk

This family-run cake company will send out most of its cakes to you anywhere in the UK. Because it has so many designs you need to call to order and confirm prices. It also offers a good range of cake-making accessories such as cake tins and icing bags if you want to make your own. The company has now launched its Mother Brown's range of muffins and flapjacks so you can order those too.

Site Usability:	★★★	Based:	UK
Product Range:	★★★	Express Delivery Option? (UK)	No
Price Range:	Medium/Very Good Value	Gift Wrapping Option?	No
Delivery Area:	UK	Returns Procedure:	Down to you

www.party2u.co.uk

This website is focused on first birthday parties and although there are lots of ideas for slightly older children, if you're planning his or her first party this is the place to start. The tableware and accessories are delightful and it's easy to make your choice. Buy your wrapping paper and cake candles here too.

Site Usability:	★★★★★	Based:	UK
Product Range:	★★★★★	Express Delivery Option? (UK)	Yes
Price Range:	Medium	Gift Wrapping Option?	No
Delivery Area:	Worldwide	Returns Procedure:	Down to you

www.partyark.co.uk

Let's move for a moment from the online party retailers catering for everyone from 0-80 and settle on this prettily designed website just for tinies. You have the option of choosing each item to go with your theme, be it Dancing Fairies or Knights and Dragons, or you can go straight to Party Packs where they've done it all for you. There are tips and advice, planning help and absolutely everything to make your life easier.

Site Usability:	★★★★★	Based:	UK
Product Range:	★★★★★	Express Delivery Option? (UK)	Yes
Price Range:	Medium	Gift Wrapping Option?	No
Delivery Area:	Worldwide	Returns Procedure:	Down to you

www.partybox.co.uk

At Partybox, although there is a huge amount of choice (the site is for grown-ups as well), it's quite simple to navigate. Choose from the menus on the left for children's parties 0-3 or 3 and up, or click on Party Essentials for invitations, party bags, streamers, decorations, party bag gifts and party games. Then there's Dress Up – yes, there's all of that here too. The best way to get round is to pick your theme first and the rest should be easy.

Site Usability:	★★★★★	Based:	UK
Product Range:	★★★★★	Express Delivery Option? (UK)	Yes
Price Range:	Medium	Gift Wrapping Option?	No
Delivery Area:	UK	Returns Procedure:	Down to you

www.partydelights.co.uk

This is a fun and colourful website and it's well laid out, so although you're bombarded with choice you shouldn't find it too difficult to shop even though it's for adults too. Click to the Party Planner at the foot of the left-hand margin, make your list, then get going. As on most of these websites, the range of themes is astonishing, so you need to know whether you're going for a Fairy Princess, Safari or Happy Feet party. Once you've done that, everything is together in one place and life becomes simple.

Site Usability:	★★★★★	Based:	UK
Product Range:	★★★★★	Express Delivery Option? (UK)	Yes
Price Range:	Medium	Gift Wrapping Option?	No
Delivery Area:	Worldwide	Returns Procedure:	Down to you

www.partypacks.co.uk

This is another place where you pick your theme first, but thankfully it's just for kids. Click through to your choice, then select from Circus, Pirate, Farm Animals, Fairies and others. Once you've done that you can order your tableware, invites and balloons, party bags, gift ideas, costumes and lots of other accessories. They're excellent value if you're entertaining loads of kids as you can place bulk orders.

Site Usability:	★★★★	Based:	UK
Product Range:	★★★★	Express Delivery Option? (UK)	No
Price Range:	Very Good Value	Gift Wrapping Option?	No
Delivery Area:	Worldwide	Returns Procedure:	Down to you

www.partysparkle.co.uk

At the time of writing delivery to the UK is free if you spend over £25, so take a look round here. Make sure you click on Children's Party Supplies on the Home Page first to avoid being caught up in the wedding areas. The themes include Juggles the Clown, Pirates of the Caribbean and Glamour Girl. Alongside the usual tableware and accessories there are small gift ideas and (very inexpensive) pre-filled party bags and packs.

Site Usability:	★★★	Based:	UK
Product Range:	★★★★	Express Delivery Option? (UK)	Yes
Price Range:	Very Good Value	Gift Wrapping Option?	No
Delivery Area:	Worldwide	Returns Procedure:	Down to you

www.thecakestore.com

The Cake Store offers a range of wonderful birthday cakes for children, including enchanting cakes for toddlers – you really need to take a look round to see the designs. At the moment the company delivers only within the M25 area (so if that's not you but you don't live far away, make sure you invite someone who can take delivery and bring your cake for you). Prices include delivery and you need to allow 7–10 days for your order to arrive as every cake is handcrafted specially for you.

Site Usability:	★★★★	Based:	UK
Product Range:	★★★★	Express Delivery Option? (UK)	No
Price Range:	Luxury/Medium	Gift Wrapping Option?	No
Delivery Area:	UK within M25	Returns Procedure:	Down to you

Section 4
Useful Information

Chapter 38

Top Tips for Safe Online Shopping

There are so many websites to choose from, for just about every product you can think of, not just fashion and beauty. Whether you're buying kitchen equipment, a new bed, cashmere knit or lipstick, the basic rules for buying online are the same. Here are the important things you need to know before you buy. Just keep them in mind before you start ordering and you should have no problems. Happy shopping.

- *Secure payment.* Make sure that when you go to put in your payment information, the padlock appears at the foot of the screen and the top line changes from http:// to https://. This means that your information will be transferred in code. To make sure you're clear about this, just go to www.johnlewis.com, put something in your basket, then click on 'Go to Checkout'. You'll immediately see the changes and those are what you're looking for each time. If they don't happen, don't buy.
- *Who are they?* Don't buy from a retailer unless you can access their full contact details. Ideally these will be available from the 'Contact Us' button on the Home Page, but sometimes they are hidden in Terms and Conditions. You should be able to find their email address, plus location address and telephone number. This is so that you can contact them in case of a problem. I get really annoyed by websites

which hide behind their email addresses – they need to be out there saying to you, the prospective customer, 'This is who we are and this is where we are, get in touch if you need us'. Sometimes they don't.

- *Privacy policy*. If it's the first time you're buying from this retailer you should check their privacy clause telling you what they'll be doing with your information. I suggest you never allow them to pass it on to anywhere/anyone else. It's not necessarily what *they* do with it that will cause you a problem.

- *Returns policy*. What happens if you want to return something? Check the retailer's policy before you order so that you're completely informed about how long you have to return goods and what the procedure is. Some retailers want you to give them notice that you're going to be sending something back (usually for more valuable items), others make it quick and simple – they're definitely the best.

- *Keeping track*. Keep a record, preferably printed, of everything you buy online, giving the contact details, product details and order reference so that if you need to you can quickly look them up. I also keep an email folder into which I drag any orders/order confirmations/payment details just in case I forget to print something. Then if you have a problem you can just click on the link to contact them and all the references are there.

- *Statements*. Check your bank statements to make sure that all the transactions appear as you expect. Best of all keep a separate credit card just for online spending which will make it even easier to check.

- *Delivery charges*. Check out the delivery charges. Again, some retailers are excellent and offer free delivery within certain areas while others charge a fortune. Make sure you're completely aware of the total cost before you buy. If you're buying from the US you will have to pay extra shipping and duty, which you'll either have to fork up for on delivery or on receipt of an invoice. My advice is to pay it immediately.

- *Credit card security*. Take advantage of the new MasterCard Secure-Code and Verified by Visa schemes when they're offered to you. Basically they provide you with the extra facility of giving a password when you use your registered cards to buy online from signed-up retailers – a kind of online chip and pin. They're excellent and they're going to grow. For extra security, pay online with a credit rather than a debit or any other type of card as this gives you added security from the credit card companies on goods over £100 in value.

- *Shred the evidence.* Buy a shredder. You may think I'm daft, but most online and offline card fraud is due to someone having got hold of your details offline. So don't let anyone walk off with your card where you can't see it and don't chuck out papers with your information on where they can be easily accessed by someone else. You have been warned.

- *Payment don'ts.* Don't ever pay cash, don't pay by cheque (unless you've got the goods and you're happy with them), don't ever send your credit card details by email and don't give your pin number online to anyone *ever*. I'm amazed at the stories I hear.

- *PC security.* Make sure your computer is protected by the latest anti-virus software and an efficient firewall. Virus scan your system at least once a week so that you not only check for nasties but get rid of any spyware.

- *Auction websites.* Be very careful using an auction website. Make sure that you know absolutely what you're doing and who you're buying from. This is not to say that everyone who sells on auction websites is waiting to get you, but some of them definitely are.

- *Fakes and replicas.* Be wary of anyone selling you 'replica' products – don't go there. If you're tempted to buy from someone selling you something that looks too cheap to be true, it probably is. If you're buying expensive products, always check on the retailer's policy for warranties and guarantees.

- *Additional information.* Don't give any information that isn't neces-sary to the purchase. You're buying a book, for goodness sake. Why do they need to know your age and how many children you have?

- *Take your time.* Don't buy in a hurry. Take the time to check the above before you click on 'Confirm Order'. If in any doubt at all, don't buy.

Have I managed to put you off yet? I assure you that's not my intention, but you really need to be aware of the above. Once you've carried out the checks just a few times you'll do them automatically. The internet is a marvellous place, but it's also a minefield of unscrupulous people waiting to catch you out. Don't let them.

Chapter 39

Deliveries and Returns – What to Look For and How to Make Them Easier

Deliveries

Deliveries from online retailers are getting increasingly better and more efficient. In many cases you can have your order tomorrow. Find a retailer you like who's stating the old 'within 28 days' policy and call them to find out if they're really that daft (being polite here). With most companies offering express delivery, who on earth is willing to wait for 28 days unless something is being specially made for them (in which case it may well take longer but at least you'll be aware before you order)?

Most companies offer the following:

- Standard delivery
- 24-hour delivery (for a small extra charge)
- Saturday delivery (very occasionally)
- EU delivery and sometimes EU Express
- Worldwide delivery and sometimes Worldwide Express.

The problem is that you very often don't find out about all these and the relevant charges until you've put something in your basket (note to online retailers: please make 'Delivery Information' a key button on your home page, it saves so much time). Yes, I have researched this information for you, but sometimes I had to practically place an order to discover a retailer's policies – ridiculous (are you listening out there?).

Returns

This is an area that often puts people off buying online (or from catalogues, for that matter). Well, don't be put off.

You will, of course, have read up on the company's returns policy before you bought, so you know how much time you have, but you might like to know the following:

- You are entitled to a 'cooling off' period (usually seven days), during which you can cancel your order without any reason and receive a full refund.
- You're also entitled to a full refund if the goods or services are not provided by the date you agreed. If you didn't agree a date, you are entitled to a refund if the goods or services are not provided within 28 days.

Having said that, and assuming that once you've started you're going to become a regular online shopper, the following will make your life easier:

- Buy a black marker pen, roll of packing tape and some different-sized jiffy bags (I use D1, H5 and K7, which are good for most things) just in case you want to return only part of an order and the original packing is damaged or too big.

- Keep these where the rest of the family can't get at them. (That tells you something about my family, doesn't it? Why doesn't anyone *ever* put things back?)

- Make sure that you keep the original packaging and any paperwork until you're sure that you're not sending stuff back and keep it somewhere easy to find.

- If you want to be really clever, go to www.vistaprint.co.uk and order some address labels. They're cheap and incredibly useful for returns, Recorded and Special Delivery postings and lots of other things.

- Don't be put off if a premium retailer wants you to call them if you're returning something valuable. It's essential that the item is insured in transit and this is something they usually arrange – for really expensive goods they may well use a courier service to collect from you.

- Rejoice when returns are free. Standard postage and packing is more and more frequently becoming free of charge from large online retailers. We'll be ordering far more when returns are free as well.

Chapter 40

Price Comparison Websites

There are, as I'm sure you've realised by now, hundreds of websites for every product, of which most of the best are listed here. If you're going to invest in something expensive like a high-tech buggy or car seat, you want to know that you're getting the best price (and it almost certainly won't be found on the first website you visit). So where do you go next?

My recommendation is that you first identify the make and model you want to buy and you can do that just by going on to one well-stocked online retailer. Read all the information you want, get an initial price, copy the item code and make (or just the make and model name) and paste it into the search box of one of the price comparison websites listed below. Be aware that on these websites you won't find absolutely every retailer, but there will be quite enough of a choice for you to see a wide range of prices.

Use these websites too for electrical equipment, appliances, computers, cameras and everything photographic. Just remember that you always need to know what you're looking for first.

There are lots of other price comparison websites. The ones here are the ones I always use and find the best, so rather than giving you a huge choice I've just selected a small number to make things easy.

www.uk.shopping.com

This is an excellent price comparison website. If you haven't given them an exact specification of the product you want (and as I've said, it's better if you can), you'll get a list of all the possible options and the relevant websites, plus website reviews. Make your choice and then you can compare prices on the exact item you want. You'll get all the information you need to decide based on price (of course), stock availability, delivery charge and site rating. You then simply click through to buy from the preferred retailer or wherever you choose.

www.kelkoo.co.uk

With Kelkoo you really do need to know the exact specification of what you're looking for to get the best results, as you don't get a defined product list offering you everything containing your initial search criteria but a mixture of relevant products. If you specify exactly what you want you'll get all those products at the top of the page, with prices, site ratings, descriptions and delivery costs.

Chapter 41

Help If Something Goes Wrong

If something goes wrong and you've paid by credit card, you may have a claim not only against the supplier of the goods but also against the credit card issuer. This applies to goods or services (and deposits) costing more than £100 but less than £30,000 and does not apply to debit or charge cards.

Contact the retailer with the problem initially by email and making sure you quote the order number and any other necessary details. If you don't get immediate assistance, ask to speak to the manager. Normally this will end your problem. However, if I tell you that I ordered some expensive goods from a luxury store recently which didn't arrive when I expected them to, was treated rudely by the call centre assistant and then unbelievably rudely by the manager, you'll get the message that this doesn't always work. Ok, it's the company's fault for recruiting these people in the first place and not instilling in them the message that even if the customer isn't always right they should always be treated with the utmost care and politeness. What they're looking for is not your first order, believe me, it's turning you into a loyal repeat customer. Those types of customers are the most valuable of all.

Again it's not things going wrong that cause most of the trouble, it's how the company sorts things out. Do it right, make you feel really important and do that little bit extra and they've got you hooked. Handle things badly and they've not only lost this order but any future orders. Not only that but they've lost your goodwill with regards to recommending them to others. Stupid, stupid, stupid – are you listening out there?

In my case, and probably because I'm pushier than most people and didn't stop at the manager, I got what I wanted. (Note: push hard. Contact the company's owner if you can or press office if need be and tell them what's going on.) And no, I'm not going to tell you who my problem was with, sorry.

If after all of this you do not get a satisfactory result to your complaint, you can contact www.consumerdirect.gov.uk (for the UK) or call on 08454 040506 for what to do next. If your problem is with a retailer based in Australia, Canada, Denmark, Finland, Hungary, Mexico, New Zealand, Norway, South Korea, Sweden, Switzerland or the US, you can click through for help to www.econsumer.gov, a joint project of consumer protection agencies from 20 nations.

If (horror) you find that someone has used your credit card information without your authorisation, contact your card issuer immediately. You can cancel the payment and your card company must arrange for your account to be re-credited in full.

Chapter 42

UK, European and US Clothing Size Conversions

Here's a general guide to the clothing size conversions between the US, Europe and the UK. If you need size conversions for other specific countries, or other types of conversions, go to www.onlineconversion.com/clothing.htm where you'll find them all.

To be as sure as possible that you're ordering the right size, check the actual retailer's size chart against your own measurements and note that a UK 12 is sometimes a US 8 and sometimes a 10, so it really pays to make sure.

Women's shoe size conversions										
UK	3.5	4	4.5	5	5.5	6	6.5	7	7.5	8	8.5
EU	36.5	37	37.5	38	38.5	39	40	41	42	43	43.5
US	6	6.5	7	7.5	8	8.5	9	9.5	10	10.5	11

Men's shoe size conversions

UK	7	7.5	8	8.5	9	9.5	10	10.5	11	11.5	12
EU	40.5	41	42	42.5	43	44	44.5	45	46	46.5	47
US	7.5	8	8.5	9	9.5	10	10.5	11	11.5	12	12.5

Men's clothing size conversions

US	UK	EU
32	32	42
34	34	44
36	36	46
38	38	48
40	40	50
42	42	52
44	44	54
46	46	56
48	48	
58		

Women's clothing size conversions

US	UK	France	Germany	Italy
6	8	36	34	40
8	10	38	36	42
10	12	40	38	44
12	14	42	40	46
14	16	44	42	48
16	18	46	44	50
18	20	50	46	52

Children's Sizing

Babies' and children's sizing is based mostly on age and height and this applies wherever you are. Here are some basic guidelines to both clothing and shoe sizes for the UK, Europe and US. Measurements are never exact and will differ from brand to brand. When in doubt, take a size up.

Age	Height (cm)	Height (in)
6–12m	76	30
12–18m	83	33
18–24m	90	35.5
2–3y	98	38.5
3–4y	104	41
4–5y	110	43.5
5–6y	116	45.5
7–8y	128	50
9–10y	140	55
11–12y	152	60
13–14y	164	64.5

Children's shoe size conversions

UK	5.5	6	6.5	7	7.5	8	8.5	9	9.5	10
EU	23	23.5	24	24.5	25	25.5	26	26.5	27	27.5
US	6.5	7	7.5	8	8.5	9	9.5	10	10.5	11

UK	10.5	11	11.5	12	13	1	1.5	2	3
EU	28	28.5	29	30	31	32.5	33	33.5	34.5
US	11.5	12	12.5	13	1	2	2.5	3	4

Chapter 43

Top 20 Websites for Busy Mums

There's no doubt that the best way to use this book is to take your time and browse through the different categories, using each one as and when you need to. For those times when you're in a rush and need a good choice fast, here are my top 20, which offer a wide range of well-photographed products and excellent service from an easy-to-navigate website. Enjoy.

Sites to Visit

Designer Maternity wear

www.blossommotherandchild.com

Blossom caters for the fashion-conscious expectant mum by combining high-end fashion, comfort and functionality without sacrificing quality or style. You'll also find designer jeans such as James, Rock & Republic and 7 For All Mankind customised with the exclusive Blossom Band. The luxurious collections include ready-to-wear, lingerie, denim, swimwear and organic baby. For AW 2007 the site will offer a collection of ready-to-wear and baby designed by Clements Ribeiro exclusively for Blossom.

Site Usability:	★★★★	Based:	UK
Product Range:	★★★★	Express Delivery Option? (UK)	Yes
Price Range:	Luxury/Medium	Gift Wrapping Option?	No
Delivery Area:	Worldwide	Returns Procedure:	Down to you

Maternity Boutiques

www.bloomingmarvellous.co.uk

There's a wide choice of well-priced but good-quality clothes for expectant mothers and babies on this fun, colourful website. Whether you're looking for casual wear or city clothes, you're sure to find something as the site offers a wide range, from sophisticated skirts and tops to lots of modern, casual options. There's also information on how to dress with a bump and a monthly newsletter to sign up for, so make this one of your first stops for browsing when you're expecting a baby.

Site Usability:	★★★★★	Based:	UK
Product Range:	★★★★★	Express Delivery Option? (UK)	No
Price Range:	Medium/Very Good Value	Gift Wrapping Option?	No
Delivery Area:	Worldwide	Returns Procedure:	Down to you

www.isabellaoliver.com

Isabella Oliver is a maternity wear company for pregnant women who love clothes. The sexy designs in soft jersey fabrics have signature-style details like ruching and wrapping to flatter new curves. Every item comes gift wrapped and the brochure and website include style tips to pick up on the season's trends. You can see each item as a model shot, drawing and also using the clever and innovative catwalk animation. As well as day and evening separates you can buy lingerie, loungewear, sophisticated sleepwear, chic outerwear, sun and swimwear.

Site Usability: ★★★★★	Based:	UK
Product Range: ★★★	Express Delivery Option? (UK)	Yes
Price Range: Luxury/Medium	Gift Wrapping Option?	Yes
Delivery Area: Worldwide	Returns Procedure:	Free

www.jojomamanbebe.co.uk

This is a pretty website offering a good choice for expectant mothers, babies and young children. The drop-down menus on the Home Page take you quickly and clearly to everything you might be looking for, whether it's maternity occasionwear or safety gates for young children. There's a range of underwear and swimwear as well. The site has some good present ideas and offers gift vouchers and boxes as well to make your life easier.

Site Usability: ★★★★★	Based:	UK
Product Range: ★★★★	Express Delivery Option? (UK)	No
Price Range: Medium	Gift Wrapping Option?	No
Delivery Area: Worldwide	Returns Procedure:	Down to you

Lingerie and Swimwear

www.figleaves.com

Thank goodness for Figleaves, where you'll find what is almost certainly the best range of nursing/maternity bras and briefs on the net. There is everything from simple styles to simply glamorous ranges, with as much lace and embroidery as you could possibly want. There's also a good choice of maternity swimwear, although this is nowhere near as stylish as the lingerie. You can be sure when you buy here that you'll receive a speedy, efficient service with free delivery worldwide.

Site Usability: ★★★★★	Based:	UK
Product Range: ★★★★★	Express Delivery Option? (UK)	Yes
Price Range: Luxury/Medium/Very Good Value	Gift Wrapping Option?	Yes
Delivery Area: Worldwide	Returns Procedure:	Free in the UK

Baby Bags

www.twoleftfeet.co.uk

This is a fantastic baby equipment website claiming to offer the largest selection in the UK. In the baby bag and rucksack section you'll find a wide range from Oi Oi, Premaxx, Samsonite, Avent and Little Company in every shape and size you can think of. As this is something you'll use all the time, make sure that the one you buy is large enough, has a changing mat and will take you from short to long-haul journeys.

Site Usability:	★★★★★	Based:	UK
Product Range:	★★★★★	Express Delivery Option? (UK)	Yes
Price Range:	Medium	Gift Wrapping Option?	No
Delivery Area:	UK	Returns Procedure:	Down to you

Gifts for New Mums

www.thewhitecompany.com

This is one place I turn to immediately for gifts for friends who've just had a baby and for babies as well. It's a collection that just seems to get better all the time, with beautiful photography and reasonable prices (not to mention excellent service) combining to make you want to buy much more than you set out to. Take a look at the supersoft towelling robes and pretty toiletry sets or luxurious cushions and throws. For babies there are cashmere shawls, satin-edged polar fleece blankets and pretty gift sets in different prints, plus lots of other ideas.

Site Usability:	★★★★★	Based:	UK
Product Range:	★★★★★	Express Delivery Option? (UK)	Yes
Price Range:	Medium	Gift Wrapping Option?	Yes
Delivery Area:	Worldwide	Returns Procedure:	Down to you

Baby Clothing

www.balloonsweb.co.uk

Just looking at the pictures on this website, in the Catamini and Pamplona sections particularly, makes you want to buy something as they're absolutely enchanting. Balloonsweb specialises in designer children's clothing for the aforesaid brands and also Miss Sixty, Chipie, Jean Bourget, Ikks and Timberland. This is an excellent children's website offering clothes and accessories from newborn to 14 years, plus pretty baby gifts and christening wear.

Site Usability:	★★★★★	Based:	UK
Product Range:	★★★★★	Express Delivery Option? (UK)	No
Price Range:	Luxury/Medium	Gift Wrapping Option?	No
Delivery Area:	Worldwide	Returns Procedure:	Down to you

www.mamasandpapas.co.uk

This company combines great attention to detail, high-quality fabrics and pretty designs in the babywear section. It covers everything from a gorgeous selection for the newborn, called 'welcome to the world', excellent, well-priced basics and exquisite and innovative clothes for girls and boys. This is a beautifully photographed website offering loads of advice on what to buy. They only deliver to the UK but you can click through to the US-based site.

Site Usability:	★★★★★	Based:	UK
Product Range:	★★★★★	Express Delivery Option? (UK)	No
Price Range:	Medium	Gift Wrapping Option?	No
Delivery Area:	UK, but US site available	Returns Procedure:	Down to you

Baby Equipment

www.kiddicare.com

Kiddicare is a large independent retailer of baby and nursery equipment and nursery furniture and claims to keep everything in stock ready to send out to you. You can buy Avent sterilisers and feeding bottles, Grobags, buggies and travel cots, highchairs, rockers and baby swings, plus equipment for the home including playpens, stair gates, cots, changing units and nursery furniture. Delivery is free to most of the UK and takes about four working days.

Site Usability:	★★★★★	Based:	UK
Product Range:	★★★★★	Express Delivery Option? (UK)	No
Price Range:	Medium	Gift Wrapping Option?	No
Delivery Area:	UK	Returns Procedure:	Down to you

Baby and Pre-school Toys

www.beyondtherainbow.co.uk

This is a marvellous website for toys and games for your pre-schooler. Not only is it colourful, fun and well laid out, but there's a wide selection, in sections such as Bashing and Banging (great for small boys), Pull and Push Along Toys and Activity Toys as well as the straightforward learning variety. There are also some great wall charts to help to learn to tell the time and to spell, plus the Maths Bus. Delivery is free on orders over £50.

Site Usability:	★★★★★	Based:	UK
Product Range:	★★★★★	Express Delivery Option? (UK)	Yes
Price Range:	Luxury/Medium	Gift Wrapping Option?	No
Delivery Area:	UK	Returns Procedure:	Down to you

Gifts for Babies

www.babygiftgallery.co.uk

The range of baby gifts on offer here is very wide, so be prepared to take your time. In particular take a look at the christening gifts of sterling silver bangles, Doudou et Compagnie House of Barbotine Gift Boxes, Emile et Rose, keepsake boxes and photo albums. Then you might want to browse through baby gift boxes which you can customise yourself and babywear by Bob and Blossom, Emile et Rose, Inch Blue, Little Blue Dog, Toby Tiger and more. It is a lovely website for baby gifts, so do take a look.

Site Usability:	★★★★★	Based:	UK
Product Range:	★★★★★	Express Delivery Option? (UK)	Yes – call them
Price Range:	Luxury/Medium	Gift Wrapping Option?	Yes
Delivery Area:	Worldwide	Returns Procedure:	Down to you

www.bellini-baby.com

Every time I think 'that's enough, no more baby gift websites' I come across another that you simply have to know about and this is one of those. Perfect for luxury, expensive gifts, Bellini Baby offers you the opportunity of buying beautiful baskets and hampers (most of which include champagne, so they're for you too) with Takinou of France soft toys, Bebe-Jou soft cotton terry baby dressing gowns, pampering essentials and chocolates, all gorgeously wrapped and hand tied with ribbon.

Site Usability:	★★★★★	Based:	UK
Product Range:	★★★★	Express Delivery Option? (UK)	They aim for next day for all UK orders
Price Range:	Luxury	Gift Wrapping Option?	Yes
Delivery Area:	Worldwide	Returns Procedure:	Down to you

Nursery Bedding and Furniture

www.nurserywindow.co.uk

Once you arrive at this website you'll find it very hard to leave. There are some seriously lovely things here for children's rooms, from unusual bedding, Moses baskets and high-quality cots and furniture to gift baskets for new babies and – everything is beautifully photographed. Just click on the area of the online shop you're interested in, enter, and you'll certainly be hooked. You can also buy fabric to match the bedlinen. Nothing is cheap, but it's all beautiful quality.

Site Usability:	★★★★★	Based:	UK
Product Range:	★★★★	Express Delivery Option? (UK)	No
Price Range:	Luxury/Medium	Gift Wrapping Option?	No
Delivery Area:	UK	Returns Procedure:	Down to you

www.thechildrensfurniturecompany.co.uk

It's well worthwhile having a good look round and investing here, as these are not children's things for the short term but pieces of furniture that will last and last, with childish accents that you can remove and change, such as bunks that can be debunked and safety rails that can be removed, engraved panels which can be swapped for plain ones and brightly coloured panels which flip to reveal more muted tones. When you take a good look you'll fully understand why it has been awarded the Guildmark by The Worshipful Company of Furniture Makers.

Site Usability:	★★★★★	Based:	UK
Product Range:	★★★★★	Express Delivery Option? (UK)	No
Price Range:	Luxury/Medium	Gift Wrapping Option?	No
Delivery Area:	UK		

Designer Childrenswear

www.childrenssalon.co.uk

This is a family-run business operating out of a shop in Kent and offering designer children's clothes from 0-12 years. Labels on offer include Oilily, Bench Par Principesse, Oxbow, Gabrielle, Elle, Cacharel, Kenzo, Dior and loads more (and I mean loads). There is also the Petit Bateau range of underwear for boys and girls, nightwear and dressing-up clothes. The company specialises in a gorgeous range of christening gowns and accessories.

Site Usability:	★★★★★	Based:	UK
Product Range:	★★★★	Express Delivery Option? (UK)	Yes
Price Range:	Luxury/Medium	Gift Wrapping Option?	No
Delivery Area:	Worldwide	Returns Procedure:	Down to you

TOP 20 WEBSITES FOR BUSY MUMS

Children's Boutiques

www.caramel-shop.co.uk

If you're looking for attractive childrenswear you must take a look here, as Caramel has one of the most attractive websites and best collections around. The clothes are designed for babies and children aged 2-12 and you can also buy shoes, boots and socks. Each part of the range is divided into themes so you can clearly see what works together and you never feel swamped by the amount of choice.

Site Usability:	★★★★★	Based:	UK
Product Range:	★★★★★	Express Delivery Option? (UK)	Yes
Price Range:	Luxury/Medium	Gift Wrapping Option?	Yes
Delivery Area:	Worldwide	Returns Procedure:	Down to you

www.cosyposy.co.uk

This well-thought out childrenswear website has gone straight into my list of favourites, as it's attractive to look at, easy to navigate and offers an original and reasonably priced range for boys and girls from 2-6, plus a separate babies' collection. Brands include Inch Blue, Cacharel, Elizabeth James and Butterscotch. There are also some good gift ideas for babies and children, including gift sets and toys, and you can buy gift vouchers which can be sent out on your behalf.

Site Usability:	★★★★★	Based:	UK
Product Range:	★★★★★	Express Delivery Option? (UK)	Yes
Price Range:	Medium	Gift Wrapping Option?	Yes
Delivery Area:	Worldwide	Returns Procedure:	Down to you

Children's Books, Toys and Games

www.amazon.co.uk

I doubt that you still think of Amazon as just an amazing place to buy books, but in case you do, you ought to take a look at the baby toy department as well (in Games and Toys). You may be horrified by the fact

249

that the first page shows you only 24 out of almost 3000 items, but my advice is to take a look at the menu on the left and choose the amount you roughly want to spend (unless you know the specific brand, which I never do). There's always going to be almost too much to see at Amazon, but who can complain?

Site Usability:	★★★★★	Based:	UK
Product Range:	★★★★★	Express Delivery Option? (UK)	Yes
Price Range:	Luxury/Medium/Very Good Value	Gift Wrapping Option?	Yes
Delivery Area:	Worldwide	Returns Procedure:	Down to you

Children's Party Accessories

www.partydelights.co.uk

This is a fun and colourful website and it's very well laid out, so although you're bombarded with choice you shouldn't find it too difficult to shop, even though it's for adults too. Click to the Party Planner at the foot of the left-hand margin, make your list, then get going. As on most of these websites, the range of themes is astonishing, so you definitely need to know whether you're going for a Fairy Princess, Safari or Happy Feet party. Once you've done that everything is together in one place and life becomes simple.

Site Usability:	★★★★★	Based:	UK
Product Range:	★★★★★	Express Delivery Option? (UK)	Yes
Price Range:	Medium	Gift Wrapping Option?	No
Delivery Area:	Worldwide	Returns Procedure:	Down to you

Index